x/ CO AMW 486

Duquesne Studies

LANGUAGE AND LITERATURE SERIES

VOLUME EIGHTEEN

General Editor:
Albert C. Labriola

Advisory Editor:
Foster Provost

Editorial Board:
Judith H. Anderson
Donald Cheney
Ann Baynes Coiro
Mary T. Crane
Patrick Cullen
A. C. Hamilton
Margaret P. Hannay
A. Kent Hieatt
William B. Hunter
Michael Lieb
Thomas P. Roche, Jr.
Mary Beth Rose
John M. Steadman
Humphrey Tonkin
Susanne Woods

Jonson's Spenser

Jonson's Spenser

Evidence and Historical Criticism

James A. Riddell & Stanley Stewart

DUQUESNE UNIVERSITY PRESS
Pittsburgh, Pennsylvania

621484

Copyright © 1995 by Duquesne University Press
All Rights Reserved

No part of this book may be used or reproduced, in any manner
whatsoever, without written permission, except in the case of short
quotations for use in critical articles and reviews.

Published in the United States of America by

DUQUESNE UNIVERSITY PRESS
600 Forbes Avenue
Pittsburgh, Pennsylvania 15282-0101

Parts of chapters 2 and 4 previously appeared
in the *Ben Jonson Journal* and *Studies in Philology*,
and are reprinted with permission.

Library of Congress Cataloging in Publication Data

Riddell, James A.
    Jonson's Spenser: evidence and historical criticism / by James A.
Riddell and Stanley Stewart.
    p.   cm. — (Duquesne Studies. Language and literature
series; v. 18)
    Includes bibliographical references and index.
    ISBN 0-8207-0263-3 (alk. paper)
    1. Jonson, Ben, 1573?–1637—Knowledge—Literature. 2. Spenser,
Edmund, 1552?–1599—Influence. 3. Influence (Literary, artistic,
etc.) I. Stewart, Stanley, 1931– . II. Title. III. Series.
PR2642.L5R53   1995
822'.3—dc20   95-11767
                                                        CIP

For Cecilia and Barbara

Contents

ACKNOWLEDGMENTS

In the years that we have been preparing this text, we have received kind assistance, both intellectual and financial, from numerous friends, colleagues and institutions. By offering encouragement and helpful criticism, many colleagues and students have helped us along the way. As the lawyer might say, these include but are not limited to: Jean R. Brink, Joseph Childers, Cyndia Clegg, Scott Crider, Daniel and Elizabeth Story Donno, Richard Harp, S. K. Heninger, Jr., M. Thomas Hester, Bernd Magnus, Jean-Pierre Mileur, Lila Geller, Grace Ioppolo, Jerry Leath Mills, John Mulryan, James Nohrnberg, James Stanger, John M. Steadman, Edward W. Tayler, Paul Voss, H. R. Woudhuysen, and R. V. Young. In addition to anonymous readers for Duquesne University Press and Susan Wadsworth-Booth, senior editor of the Press, Robert C. Evans, Albert C. Labriola, Steven May, David McPherson and Michael Warren read the entire manuscript, and offered helpful criticism.

Over the years we have received the patient and good-humored assistance of members of the staffs of the British Library and the Henry E. Huntington Library, especially, Kelli Bronson, Alan Jutzi, Thomas Lange, Virginia Renner, Frances Rouse, Robert Schlosser and Mary Wright. Academic administrators have been extremely cooperative and supportive, in particular, Brian Copenhaver, dean of the College of Humanities and Social Sciences, and Steven Axelrod, chair of the Department of English, both at the University of California, Riverside; and Agnes Yamada, chair of the Department of English at California State University, Dominguez Hills.

At the very least, our debts are twice as large as that of the author of any individually written study. We have received the unflagging support of our home institutions—the University of California, Riverside, and California State University, Dominguez Hills—in the form of research support for travel, microfilming, photocopying and photography. We know that this study could not have been done without the continued support of the Huntington Library. We are most grateful for this help through the four years of our work on this study in the form of an Andrew Mellon Grant, which provided for two months of uninterrupted study. Above all, we are enormously indebted to Martin Ridge and Robert Ritchie, directors of research for the Henry E. Huntington Library. Without the assistance of several Huntington Library-British Academy Exchanges, for which they nominated us, we would not have been able to spend several months in London, not only working on background material at the British Library (which alone was a major help), but transcribing Jonson's notes from the newly discovered copy of the 1617 Folio of Spenser's *The Faerie Queen: The Shepheards Calendar: Together with Other Works* (1617). Indeed, without that support our work on this volume, copiously annotated by Ben Jonson, would not have been feasible. For the same reason, we want to thank, too, Sasha Ward, of the British Academy, for her gracious assistance while we were in London.

The 1617 Folio was described in a bookseller's catalog in 1884. After that (see introduction) it apparently disappeared until 1986, when it was purchased by J. Paul Getty, KBE. We are fortunate—and very grateful—to be the recipients of Mr. Getty's generosity and forbearance, in that it has taken us much time, and many trips to

London, to complete the task of transcribing, checking and rechecking Jonson's marks and annotations. And we are grateful, too, for the generous assistance of our interlocutor, Mr. Robert Harding of Maggs Brothers—and to Maggs Brothers, Limited, who generously provided us with office space so that we could work with Mr. Getty's copy of the Spenser Folio annotated by Jonson.

James Riddell
California State University, Dominguez Hills

Stanley Stewart
University of California, Riverside

ABBREVIATIONS AND BIBLIOGRAPHICAL NOTE

Unless otherwise indicated, all citations from Spenser in our text are from *The Works of Edmund Spenser: A Variorum Edition* (ed. by Edwin Greenlaw, et al.), hereafter referred to as *Var*; where we cite from Jonson's copy of the 1617 Spenser Folio we retain the spellings of that volume, even when they appear to be eccentric (we specify "Jonson's copy" because we are aware that its spellings are not always consistent with other printings of the 1617 Folio). Citations from Jonson are from *Ben Jonson* (ed. by C. H. Herford and Percy and Evelyn Simpson), hereafter referred to as H&S. For the reader's convenience, we cite references to Spenser and to Jonson in our text, but to avoid distracting parenthetical citations, we have placed all other documentation in the footnotes. Unless otherwise indicated, we have regularized i/j and u/v, expanded contractions, and we have silently ignored obvious printers' errors, meaningless capitals, small capitals, italics and the like. Unless otherwise noted, books published before 1700 bear a London imprint. For Jonson's copy of the 1617 Folio of *The Faerie Queen: The Shepheards Calendar: Together With the Other Works of England's Arch-Poët, Edm[und] Spenser*, see acknowledgments.

Abbreviations

ELR	*English Literary Renaissance*
Epig	*Epigrammes*, H&S, vol. 8
Epith	Spenser's *Epithalamion, Var*
For	*The Forrest*, H&S, vol. 8
FQ	*The Faerie Queene*
H&S	*Ben Jonson*. Ed. by C. H. Herford and Percy and Evelyn Simpson. 11 vols. Oxford: Clarendon Press, 1928–52.
JEGP	*Journal of English and Germanic Philology*
MofQ	*Masque of Queenes*
MLN	*Modern Language Notes*
NLH	*New Literary History*
N&Q	*Notes and Queries*
PLL	*Papers on Language and Literature*
PMLA	*Publications of the Modern Language Association*
PQ	*Philological Quarterly*
RES	*Review of English Studies*
RQ	*Renaissance Quarterly*
SC	*The Shepheardes Calender* (1579), *Var*
SB	*Studies in Bibliography*
SLI	*Studies in the Literary Imagination*
SP	*Studies in Philology*
SQ	*Shakespeare Quarterly*
Und	*The Under-wood*, H&S, vol. 8
UV	*Ungathered Verse*, H&S, vol. 8

Var   *The Works of Edmund Spenser: A Variorum Edition*. Ed. by Edwin Greenlaw et al. 8 vols. and Index. Baltimore: The Johns Hopkins Press, 1932–57.

YSP   *The Yale Edition of the Shorter Poems of Edmund Spenser*. Ed. by William A. Oram, Einar Bjorvand, Ronald Bond, Thomas H. Cain, Alexander Dunlop, and Richard Schell. New Haven and London: Yale Univ. Press, 1989.

Introduction

U nsophisticated observers, many of them students, sometimes say that "literary research" is a contradiction in terms, simply because critical practice does not, strictly speaking, constitute a field of knowledge. Even in those areas where literary criticism might be said to involve or overlap supposed domains of disciplined discourse—enumerative and descriptive bibliography, structural and historical linguistics, historiography and the history of ideas—the state of knowledge remains either static, and so in no need of further inquiry, or extraliterary, in the sense that by treating or arranging only external features of the documentary record, criticism in these modes does not address the "literariness" of literature. Of course, the *sine qua non* of literary value ("interest") may itself be the subject of historical inquiry, but even here the "facts" of social change appear only as entries in the annals of changing tastes.

Such observations are in error, but the error is understandable and even informative. For many unaccustomed to critical practices, "knowledge" is what scientists discover in laboratories or field studies. If the literary scholar knows anything about Shakespeare or Spenser or

Donne or Jonson, it is only what everyone else has learned from centuries of accumulated scholarship, which, now institutionalized, merely requires a quasi-ritualistic handing down of unchanging and unchangeable lore. It is conceivable that something "new" might be turned up in one of our remote archives—the British Library, the Public Record Office, the Huntington Library. As it happens, books that Jonson owned turn up with almost astonishing frequency. Very recently Christopher Martin discovered that a 1581 edition of Petrarch in the Folger Shakespeare Library was in fact at one time Ben Jonson's. That Jonson once owned the volume had been known, but its whereabouts was not. Martin, as he says, found it quite by accident.[1] On the other hand, H. R. Woudhuysen, by diligently searching through libraries in pursuit of books that Jonson might have owned, has been able to record more than threescore of them that were previously unknown.

But the possibility of newly uncovered "lost" material does not inform the attitudes of nonhumanists, and perhaps only a small percentage of practicing critics give it much thought. "Discovery" is not likely, because everything is already "known," everything worth saying has already been said, passed down from our knowledgeable predecessors of the eighteenth and nineteenth centuries.

Probably science doesn't work so neatly as often imagined on the mechanically empirical model. In any case, the literary canon is not in fact static, but always changing, and not only because of the clamor of competing ethnic, gender and economic interests. The body of evidence changes, and it does so at times and in ways that might not at all fit the picture of the one-in-a-century document ferreted out in a research library, a picture that may itself betray a bias toward the otherworldly, antiseptic precincts of "Science." The discovery of Thomas Traherne is largely a twentieth century event, and it began, not at the Bodleian Library, but at a book-barrow near Charing Cross. Only a decade ago, the *Times Literary Supplement* announced discovery of yet another Traherne manuscript, this one rescued, not by a persistent book collector scouring shelves in remote antique shops, but by a man who looked for spare auto parts at a Lancashire dump site.[2] Nor are recent canonical changes limited to what could be called a minor Renaissance poet. Within the last few years, Jeanne Shami has turned up the first autograph copy of a Donne sermon, this at the Folger Library, where it had resided unnoticed for decades, as theories about Donne's method of composing his sermons proceeded apace.[3] Criticism, not only of Donne, but of Jacobean pulpit practice, has this much more evidence, then, with which to work in describing the religious prose of the time.

Evidence changes things, but not everything. We agree with Herford and Simpson, who, in their comments on the books that they list as having been in Ben Jonson's library, wistfully observe: "How priceless a First Folio would be with indications of the thousand lines that Shakespeare should have blotted" (H&S 1:261). But we would add that, given the apposite status of Spenser in the English canon of nondramatic poetry, Jonson's remarks on the "First Folio" of Edmund Spenser's *Works* would be of comparable value.

That Jonson probably owned such a copy of Spenser (actually a second printing of the first folio of the complete poetical works) has long been suspected. Recently, Ann Barton stated that "Jonson's copy of the 1617 edition of Spenser's works, sold at auction in 1884, cannot now be traced."[4] In his catalog of *Ben Jonson's Library and Marginalia*, David McPherson lists the 1617 Folio (*STC* 23085) with this comment: "Jonson's copy: Crossley's sale, Sotheby's 21 July 1884, p. 153. 'Numerous marginal notes, suggested meanings of words etc. in the Poem, and other marks and notes in his handwriting,' says the catalogue."[5] This noncommittal statement of fact allows that the book may have existed in 1884, but little else; McPherson makes no assumption about the book's

authenticity or present existence. Ten years before Mc-
Pherson's *Annotated Catalogue* appeared, in the Arundel
Esdaile Memorial Lecture for 1964, A. N. L. Munby af-
firmed that among the books in Jonson's "by no means
negligible" collection of Renaissance authors was a copy—
"profusely annotated"—of Edmund Spenser's *Works*,
1617."[6] Munby's opinion leads back through that of
Herford and Simpson (they claim that the volume, "with
numerous Ms notes," had appeared in the Crossley's Sale,
July 1884" [H&S 1:264]) to W. C. Hazlitt, who in 1898 included what appears to be the same item in a list of
books that had been owned by Jonson.[7]

After more than a century, this volume has now come
to light, found not in a landfill or on a bookseller's bar-
row, but in a private collection. Thanks to the generosity
of its present owner, J. Paul Getty, KBE, we have been
given access to it, and are able now to give some account
of the volume and its whereabouts for the last hundred
years. On 6 June 1986, Christie's conducted an auction
sale of books from the Edward James Collection at West
Dean Park, West Sussex. Although a part of the James
Collection, Jonson's copy of Spenser did not appear in the
auction, but through Maggs Bros., was acquired by private treaty for Mr. Getty. It seems clear now that, although Herford and Simpson directed attention to
"Crossley's Sale, July 1884," they probably did not look
at the Catalogue itself, for they merely repeat Hazlitt's
description. David McPherson did consult the sale Catalogue, for he quotes directly from it. The book sold in the
fourth day of the Sale, in the session devoted to folios (lot
1529). It was entered with the heading "Jonson" rather
than "Spenser," presumably reflecting an assessment of
where its greatest appeal might lie. The Catalogue description reads:

> JONSON (BEN). Spenser (E.) The Faerie Queen, Shep-
> heards Calendar, with his other Works, *woodcuts, slight-
> ly wormed and stained, old calf* [no period]
>   *H.L. for Mathew Lownes, 1617*

BEN JONSON'S OWN COPY, WITH HIS SIGNATURE ON TITLE, AND NUMEROUS MARGINAL NOTES, suggested meanings of words, etc. in the Poem [sic], and other marks and notes, in his HANDWRITING. A few of the Notes have been slightly cut into by the binder, but they are for the most part entire.

It appears that we owe the preservation of this literary artifact at least partly to William Dodge James, father of the Edward James whose collection was sold. We infer this from Sotheby's copy of the Catalogue in the British Library (shelfmark S.C., Sotheby 91.), which is made up of sheets laid down in an account book, these full of notes of buyers' names and prices realized. According to the annotator of the Catalogue, Jonson's Spenser was bought for ten guineas by one "James," probably William Dodge, father of Edward. Willie James, as he was called, was born 7 December 1854 and died 22 March 1912; he was a famous big-game hunter, and a favorite of the Prince of Wales, who as Prince and later as King Edward VII was entertained by Willie James and his wife at West Dean Park, which James bought in 1891 and left to his only son, Edward.

The volume's importance had been noticed before it entered James Crossley's[8] collection. In July 1865, the auctioneers Puttick and Simpson conducted a sale of "The Fourth and Concluding Portion of the Famous Dering Collection of Deeds and Charters, with other Ancient Manuscripts of the Highest Importance." The third day of the three-day sale, which took place on Saturday, 15 July, was devoted to "Miscellaneous Manuscripts," and included:

754 JONSON (BEN). Spenser (Edm.) The Faerie Queen, The Shepheard's Calendar, and other works.
   folio, by *H. L. for Mathew Lownes*, 1617
BEN JONSON'S COPY, WITH HIS SIGNATURE ON THE TITLE, AND VERY NUMEROUS MANUSCRIPT NOTES. Although these notes extend throughout the volume, they are most numerous in the early part of it. They consist of side notes by way of reference, suggested meanings of words or allusions in

the poem [sic], and other notes and marks which indicate
the most careful and word by word study of the author.
The criticism of one poet upon another is always replete
with interest, and when two such celebrated names as
EDMUND SPENSER and BEN JONSON are thus brought in juxta-
position, as in this volume, nothing remains to bespeak
for it a distinguished place in any cabinet.

A copy of the Catalogue (no doubt the auctioneers') in the
British Library[9] has been taken apart and its leaves alter-
nated with blue account-book leaves on which prices and
purchasers are listed. Lot 754 was bought for £12 by one
Cadby, his only purchase of the day. In all likelihood he
was the bookseller J. H. W. Cadby of 74 New Street, Bir-
mingham,[10] a man more notable for his enterprise than
his literacy, to judge from his improvement in the description that follows. On the front pastedown of the volume we have been discussing, there is a description that
looks to be a nineteenth century bookseller's (Cadby's)
notice in his catalog—which, a comparison will show,
was very much indebted to the Puttick and Simpson description above and which, in turn, seems to have influ-
enced Sotheby's cataloguer:

> IMPORTANT LITERARY DISCOVERY.
> JONSON (BEN).— SPENSER (EDM.) The Faerie Queen,
> the Shepheard's Calendar, and other Works, sm. folio, *old
> calf*, £21.
> > *H. L. for Mathew Lownes, 1617.*
> BEN JONSON'S COPY, WITH HIS SIGNATURE ON THE TITLE,
> AND VERY NUMEROUS MANUSCRIPT NOTES. Although these
> Notes extend throughout the volume, they are most nu-
> merous in the early part of it. They consist of side notes
> by way of reference, suggested meanings of words or illu-
> sions [sic] in the poem [sic], and other notes and marks,
> which indicate the most careful and word-by-word study
> of the author. The criticism of one poet upon another is
> always replete with interest; and, when two such cel-
> obrated names as EDMUND SPENSER and BEN JONSON are
> thus brought in juxta-position, as in this volume, nothing

remains to bespeak for it a distinguished place in any cabinet.

Presumably this description enticed James Crossley to buy the volume—at, as it turns out, double the price it would fetch in the sale of his own library. The rather lavish descriptions by the Puttick and Simpson cataloguer and his successors, as well as the portion of the Dering collection in which the volume was·sold, serve to emphasize that since it first came into the public market its commercial value has been thought to lie in the annotations. Its presence in the auction catalog of the Crossley sale was noticed by Ellis (261).

Since the collations of Spenser folios vary greatly, it might be helpful now to establish the order of the various parts in the copy that Jonson marked, along with some observations on the volume's title page. The full title reads:

> The | Faerie Queen: | The | Shepheards Calendar: | Together | With The Other | Works of England's Arch-Poët, | Edm. Spenser: | ¶ Collected into one Volume, and | carefully corrected. | Printed by H. L[ownes] for Mathew Lownes. | Anno Dom. 1617. (STC 23085)

A full and very useful bibliographical description of the 1611 and 1617 folio editions is that of Francis R. Johnson, *A Critical Bibliography of the Works of Edmund Spenser Printed before 1700.*[11] As Johnson points out, copies of the folio vary considerably, and "it is quite possible that no fixed order was followed in arranging the sections" (45). Nevertheless, he finds that the more than 50 copies he examined could be segregated into four "groups."[12] Jonson's Spenser falls into Group 4 by virtue of its having the 1617 title page and the second printing of both parts of *The Faerie Queene*, "the second printing of the *Colin Clout* and minor poems section" (47). It has also the 1617 *Shepheards Calendar*, as do almost all of the Group 4 copies, and the first (1612–13) printing of *Mother Hubberds Tale*,[13] as do about two-thirds of the copies in Group 4.

The order of the various parts in the present volume is
as follows. The section numbers and the letters identify-
ing printings are taken from Johnson. As can be seen
from the placement of Section 4, the Letter to Raleigh
appears at some remove from The *Faerie Queene*. The
seven parts are:

Section 1 *Title.*
Section 2 *The Faerie Queene*, first part (books 1 to 3).
          B. Second printing (sometime between 1613
          and 1617)
Section 3 *The Faerie Queene*, second part (books 4 to 6
          and the Cantos of Mutabilitie)
          B. Second printing (1612–13)
Section 5 T*he Shepheards Calendar.*
          B. Second printing (1617)
Section 6 *Prosopopoia or Mother Hubberds Tale.*
          A. First printing (1612–13)
Section 4 The letter to Raleigh, the commendatory po-
          ems and dedicatory sonnets.
          B. Second printing (1617)
Section 7 *Colin Clouts come home againe* and the rest
          of the minor poems.
          B. Second printing (1617)

It should be noted that the title page border is that first
used for The *Countesse of Pembrokes Arcadia* (1593),
printed by Thomas Creed for William Ponsonby.[14] It was
subsequently used a number of additional times, but apparently not between 1598 (also for the *Arcadia*) and
1611, when it was first employed on a title page of
Spenser's works. Roderick Eagle is perhaps more mysti-
fied than necessary: "Curiously enough," he observes, "it
was not used on the *Faerie Queene* which Field printed
for Ponsonby in 1596, even though the block was in
Ponsonby's possession until his death in 1604. Nor was it
used on the *Faerie Queene* of 1609, as it was in 1611."[15]
It is easy enough to work out why the block was not used
for the quarto of 1596, why it was not for the 1609 folio
is another matter. The simple answer is that Henry

Lownes probably did not come into possession of it until after 1609. It does not appear in either variant of the Ar*cadia* that Lownes and George Eld printed in 1605 (for Simon Waterson or for Mathew Lownes), and surely it would have been had Lownes access to it. He used it for the 1611 *Faerie Queene*, the 1613 *Arcadia* (unnoticed by McKerrow and Ferguson), and, of course, the 1617 *Faerie Queene*.

Often, especially for those not familiar with Jonson's prodigious markings of his many books, the question of authenticity arises. This copy belonged to Jonson. On the title page (fig. 1), we see Jonson's familiar autograph at the bottom right and fragments of his motto, "*tanquam explorator*," in tailends of a few descenders in the top righthand corner. The rest of the motto was lost to the binder when the volume was rebound, most probably in the eighteenth century. W. W. Greg and Peter Croft have described Jonson's hand and have provided illustrations of it.[16] According to Greg:

> Jonson wrote a characteristic but not particularly tidy hand, rather less humanistic in style than one might have expected. The general impression is Italian, but it is by no means pure. A certain number of letters by him are preserved of which one of the earliest [1605] and probably the latest [1635] are here reproduced. There seems to have been some increase of regularity with age. (23)

Greg's observation that toward the end of his life Jonson's hand became, if anything, not less but more consistent gives support to our argument in chapter 3 that Jonson, at least until a year or two before his death, remained vigorous and active.

Croft discusses a manuscript of about 1609 and gives a detailed analysis of some of the characteristics of Jonson's hand at that time. Although Jonson's notations in his Spenser come some years later and although in the Spenser he is perforce writing in a very limited space, several of Croft's charateristics can be seen in the illustrations accompanying our text. Jonson's hand, says Croft, "is predominantly Italic, but it derives a strong vernacular flavour from the admixture of several distinctive Secretary forms. The 'reversed' Secretary *e*, which Jonson uses interchangeably with the Greek *e*, was ubiquitous at this period and occurs freely in hands which are otherwise pure Italic." In our illustrations both forms of *e* are common. More particularly, "The orthodox 'two stemmed' Secretary *r*" which Croft singles out can be seen in our figure 2 at 2.9.22 "imperfecte," between lines 3 and 4 and "distributed" after line 9. For the "flat-topped Secretary *c*" to which Croft calls attention, see figure 3, the *ch* in *w^{ch}*, line 7 of 2.7.24 (compare this with the not "flat-topped" *c* in *w^{ch}* at line 6 of 2.7.21). Finally, and probably most tellingly, Jonson uses what Croft calls "a hybrid form of *p* . . . in which the head is made in the Secretary manner though the leftward curve, generally extended into a loop, at the base of the descender is Italic in origin (when its descender is looped Jonson's *p* resembles the form commonly assumed by the *per/par* abbreviation in Secretary hands)." For an example of such a *p*, we refer the reader to figure 4, at 1.10.40 "prisoners," after line 4. The Secretary *h*, "with its descending bow," that Croft discusses does not appear often, but it does appear, as at sig. H4^v (fig. 5).

On the other hand, some qualities that Croft notices as being characteristic of Jonson's hand in the examples that he draws upon, particularly a distinctive *a*, are not found in these Jonson notations. This is easily accounted for. In the illustrations provided by both Greg and Croft, Jonson is writing in space that is relatively plentiful. The *a* that Croft describes is a flourish, to be indulged in where space will allow.[17] Similarly, the ampersands found in the Greg and Croft illustrations *are* different from those in Jonson's Spenser, and for the same reason—the restrictions of space in the margins of a book. (Ampersands, by the way, are not discussed by Croft.) Ampersands in Greg and Croft are broad and fluent, those in Jonson's notations are formed quite differently and are compact. The ampersand of Jonson's Spenser does appear elsewhere in his notations to books that he owned, however. It appears a number of times in his notations to *Chorus Poetarum*,[18] for instance at sigs. 2F5[v], 2V7[v], 4D1[v], and 4O5[v]. It also appears in his notations to one of his copies of Vitruvius[19] (see fig. 6).

Jonson's markings are for the most part in ink, although, as we note in chapter 2, there are some in pencil. In Jonson's copy of Stobaeus in the Huntington Library,[20] several pages with Jonson's characteristic flowers and vertical lines are all marked in pencil, and the same is true of the Vitruvius, just noticed. In the Spenser Folio, some passages are marked in both, and where the markings overlap, it appears that ink has been used on top of the pencil. At one or two places (as in "Mother Hubberds Tale") we note that the hand differs from that found almost everywhere else in the book, as the letters are larger and formed in a different manner. Although we are doubtful that this hand is Jonson's, we cannot say with assurance that it is not.

In the following pages, we attempt to elucidate Jonson's markings and annotations to the Spenser Folio. To begin, we contextualize Jonson's annotations by taking a close look at his treatment of Spenser in his published works, paying special attention to traditional views of Jonson's criticism of Spenser's works. In the second chapter, we turn to Jonson's 1617 Folio itself, examining evidence of his reading of the minor poems. Then, in chapter 3, we analyze Jonson's markings to The *Faerie Queene*, the poem so long thought to exhibit an allegorical strategy and a stanzaic pattern that the great poet and critic did not like. We conclude with a chapter dedicated to a quite narrow topic: the famous stanza 22 from canto 9 of book 2 of *The Faerie Queene*. Our focus will be on the relation between Jonson and Sir Kenelm Digby's celebrated analysis of that stanza;[21] we will argue that Jonson has played a far more important role in the development of Spenser criticism than many of us have been taught to believe.

1

Aliquid Aprehendo

Jonson Claims Spenser

This is my own custom; from the many things which I have read, I claim some one part for myself.

Seneca

In 1925, Herford and Simpson stated with their accustomed magisterial poise that Ben Jonson "turned away with indifference, or even dislike" from "much that we count among [the] chief glories" of literary London in his time (H&S 1:10). If critics react to this assertion with a readiness to believe, it is probably because they know that Jonson was a man of strong likes and dislikes, and that he seldom commented on any poetic endeavor without rendering a critical judgment. Dryden seems to be thinking about this strong, opinionated quality in Jonson's poetry and criticism when he observes that "Jonson invades authors like a monarch; and what would be theft in other poets, is only victory in him."[1] Jonson's eulogy of Shakespeare may be the best known case in point. Here, the poet firmly establishes an exclusive right of real poets to praise Shakespeare. If "some infamous Baud, or Whore, / Should praise a Matron," would it help or hurt her reputation? Jonson's point seems to be that criticism emanates from a particular point of view, and the same is true of the value imputed to it. Claiming that for the "Soule of the Age" no praise could be "too much," Jonson puts Shakespeare (his "beloved, The AUTHOR") in a class by himself—above Chaucer, Beaumont, Kyd, Marlowe and Spenser. Alone among English poets, Shakespeare belongs with the famous writers of Greek and Roman antiquity.

If "To the memory of ... William Shakespeare" (H&S 8:390–92) can be taken as evidence of Jonson's judgment of "what [Shakespeare] hath left" behind in the nature of "reputation," then Shakespeare, without contemporary or English equal, is by himself a "Moniment without a tombe" (line 22), an author "for all time" (line 43). And yet in the same poem Jonson could still write that Nature was responsible for only a part of Shakespeare's ability: "Who casts to write a living line, must sweat" (line 59). The assertion is, of course, a statement of principle, and so only incidentally applicable to Shakespeare. The question is: how does the principle express itself in this instance? For some critics, this proverbial declamation cannot be read without irony; Dryden, who thought that there was little in Jonson to "retrench" or "alter," nevertheless famously found that poem "an insolent, sparing, and invidious panegyric."[2] Just how hard did Jonson think the "Sweet Swan of *Avon*" labored to "make those flights upon the bankes of *Thames*" (lines 71, 73)? Many Jonsonians will hear reverberations in this passage from the sharp and frequently quoted remark in *Discoveries*: "*I remember*, the Players have often mentioned it as an honour to *Shakespeare*, that in his writing, (whatsoever he penn'd) hee never blotted out line. My answer hath beene, Would he had blotted a thousand" (H&S 8:583).

It is less often noticed that in this very passage Jonson proceeds to tell why he is not here making "malevolent speech" but only candidly correcting the erroneous judgment of others. The problem, as Jonson sees it, is that ignorant critics praise Shakespeare for one of his most serious faults. And if one praises Shakespeare for a blatant shortcoming, then one will no doubt err in the opposite direction by undervaluing his greatest virtues. Jonson claims that he honored Shakespeare's memory on this side of "Idolatry," and explains why he could go no further:

> Hee was (indeed) honest, and of an open, and free nature: had an excellent *Phantsie*; brave notions, and gentle expressions: wherein hee flow'd with that facility, that sometime it was necessary he should be stop'd: *Sufflaminandus erat*; as *Augustus* said of *Haterius* [he should have been checked]. (H&S 8:584)

Jonson's critical point, which reiterates a theme stated often in *Timber*, is that of excess. Shakespeare flourished in spite of this fault, but he was, nevertheless, at times undisciplined: "His wit was in his owne power; would the rule of it had beene so too" (H&S 8:584). Shakespeare "had an excellent *Phantsie*"; he virtually "flow'd with" it. Jonson's figure of liquidity suggests, more than ease of movement, an inclination toward shapelessness, not a poetic virtue but a vice. Thus, "sometime it was necessary he should be stop'd."

Depending upon the context, Jonson could fault Shakespeare for his laxity or praise him for his rigor. In "To the memory of . . . Shakespeare," Jonson states the general principle, "he, / Who casts to write a living line, must sweat" (lines 58–59), and then acknowledges Shakespeare's devotion to hard work: "a good *Poet's* made, as well as borne. / And such wert thou" (lines 64–65). This line of thought shows how Jonson's judgment of Shakespeare cannot be lifted from any single observation. The performance was, and therefore the judgment must be, complete and complex:

> Many times hee fell into those things, could not escape
> laughter: As when hee said in the person of *Caesar*, one
> speaking to him; *Caesar, thou dost me wrong*. Hee re-
> plyed: *Caesar did never wrong, but with just cause*: and
> such like; which were ridiculous. (H&S 8:584)

We are not in a position to resolve the textual question
raised by Jonson's reference to Caesar's speech in act 3 of
Shakespeare's play.[3] It will suffice for our purpose to recognize the syntactical balance that Jonson imposes between praise and blame, virtue and vice, mastery and
undiscipline. Although Dryden considered Jonson's panegyric on Shakespeare "insolent, sparing, and invidious,"
he understood that because Jonson was "a most severe
judge of himself as well as others," Jonson's admiration
of Shakespeare is about what we should expect. But here
Dryden is himself being too severe. Neither the poem
nor the passage in *Discoveries* is invidious or grudging.
Rather, Jonson offers a balanced judgment. Indeed, with
more effort, Shakespeare could have avoided what Jonson
takes to be unintended lapses. Shakespeare was not seeking laughter in the passage in question from *Julius Caesar*; had he bothered to "blot" the line, he would have
improved the play. But—and this is Jonson's judgment—
Shakespeare "redeemed his vices, with his vertues. There
was ever more in him to be praysed, then to be par-
doned." If Jonson were, as a critic, merely extending pardon, we might concede Dryden's point. But Jonson is saying that the praise Shakespeare deserves, makes pardon
irrelevant. Even without the discipline that Jonson retro-
actively wishes on him, Shakespeare earns a unique
place in Jonson's pantheon of English authors.

This is not, of course, to imply that Herford and
Simpson thought of a Shakespeare play as one of the
"chief glories" of the literary scene from which Jonson
"turned away with indifference, or even dislike." This
honor they accord to Spenser. They suggest—and the

suggestion helped shape two generations of Jonson criticism—that Jonson did not care for Spenser's magnum opus: "The splendid torso of the *Faerie Queene* (1589–96), 'writ in no language' and in Italianate stanzas, can never have been to his mind" (H&S 1:10). The ease with which the phrase from *Timber* slides in with a vague invocation of another phrase from the *Conversations with William Drummond of Hawthornden* marks an emerging consensus in literary studies in the twentieth century, which holds that Jonson did not like Spenser. Nor has the view been much altered during the latter half of the century. For instance, citing Jonson's whimsical treatment of the belief in fairies in *The Alchemist* in support of his judgment, even David Norbrook, who sensibly warns against taking the *Conversations* with too much credulity,[4] insists that "Jonson's skeptical temper found the whole cult of the Faery Queen somewhat absurd."[5]

Yet the way in which a figure functions in one Jonsonian work may not explain how it works in another. For instance, David Riggs discusses the political situation surrounding composition and production of *A Particular Entertainment of the Queene . . . at Althorpe* in 1603.[6] Performed during the progress south of Queen Anne and Prince Henry a month before the coronation, the masque may be slight as a theatrical achievement,[7] but it does show that Jonson had no ideological objection to favorable treatment of fairies in general, or of the Faery Queen in particular. Despite the high jinks that the Satyr blames on her, Queen Mab is also the figure who pays Queen Anne the high tribute of comparison with the original of Spenser's Faery Queen:

> This is shee,
>   This is shee,
> In whose world of grace
> Every season, person, place,
>   That receive her, happy be,
>   For with no lesse,

Then a kingdomes happinesse,
   Doth shee private *Lares* blesse,
     And ours above the rest:
     By how much we deserve it least.
   Long live ORIANA
To exceed (whom shee succeeds) our late DIANA.
                    (H&S 7:124–25)

It could be argued that the Satyr's remarks deprecating Mab merely underscore the contextual nature of Jonson's handling of this or any other theme. For in the context of the occasion, with Queen Anne and Prince Henry on their way to London and the Coronation, the Faery Queen celebrates the continuity of values from Tudor to Stuart reign. Indeed, as Jonson's marginal note implies, Anne's fertility appears in contrast to its opposite in Elizabeth, with an implied judgment about the political difficulties caused by the sovereign's barrenness. Anne brings "with her the Prince, which is the greatest felicitie of kingdomes" (H&S 7:125). The implied contrast touches the way in which ORIANA (Anne) "exceeds" the "late DIANA" (Elizabeth).

We should add, however, that Herford and Simpson—and now Norbrook—are only reiterating a view of Jonson's opinion of Spenser that had already established itself. A dozen years before the Oxford editors had their say on the subject, perhaps with one of the same utterances in mind, William Macneile Dixon made this assertion:

> If one shares Jonson's mind . . . nothing is easier than to prepare a brief for the *Advocatus diaboli*, to charge [Spenser's] poem with utter lack of unity, to complain that neither man nor woman appears in it, that lifeless phantoms flit there through landscapes as unreal as themselves, that the coming and going of the characters is wholly aimless and irrational.[8]

Moreover, Dixon makes this statement despite his opinion that "Jonson is almost singular" in his aversion to Spenser, the "majority" of his contemporaries giving the author of *The Faerie Queene* their "undivided allegiance."[9] Toward the latter half of this century, the notion that Jonson didn't like Spenser has more or less been accorded popular acceptance. For instance, in her recent popular biography of Jonson, Rosalind Miles argues that "Jonson never really liked Spenser's major work, the allegorical *Faerie Queene*, finding it far-fetched and obscure."[10]

It seems that historically critics have not known what to say about Jonson's opinion of Spenser, preferring to exercise either a stoical silence on all but the elliptical remarks in *Timber*, or to exhibit an innocent credulity toward *Ben Jonson's Conversations with William Drummond of Hawthornden*, which R. F. Patterson describes as "the chief and most authentic source for the facts of Jonson's life."[11] Although Drummond's *Conversations* purports to record Jonson's opinions, expressed toward the end of his walking trip to Scotland in 1618–1619, in fact Jonson's comments, even if accurately represented, may not be very helpful in clarifying his reading of Spenser. Not only are specific remarks on Spenser ambiguous, but Jonson's tone is equivocal, and he seems to enjoy contradicting himself without worrying about whether or not Drummond will recognize lapses and reversals. It may be that Jonson even enjoyed the slow, perhaps sober, reactions of his host.

If we take Jonson as Drummond did—at face value—we might easily suppose, as far as Spenser's talents were concerned (the confusion between Cuddie and Colin aside), that Jonson admired only a few lines from the October Eclogue: "he hath by Heart some verses of Spensers Calender about wyne between Coline and percye" (H&S 1:136). But, although ambiguous, some remarks in *Conversations* could reasonably be construed as evidence that Jonson *admired* Spenser's poetry, including *The Faerie Queene*.[12] For instance, the work opens with the news that Jonson planned to write "ane Epick Poeme

intitled Heroologia of the Worthies of his Country"
(1:132). True, Drummond notes that Jonson liked neither
"Spencers stanzaes" (but he proposed to write an epic in
heroic couplets) "nor his matter," and yet Drummond
recalls that Jonson approved the subject of Spenser's "fiction" as the best possible for an English epic: "for a
Heroik poeme he said ther was no such Ground as King
Arthurs fiction and that S. P. Sidney had ane intention to
have transform'd all his Arcadia to the stories of King
Arthure" (H&S 1:136). It could be argued in this connection that Jonson's subsequent remarks on Drayton suggest criticism of Spenser for not transmogrifying material
of England and its civil wars and disruptions. But, again,
this objection presupposes that Jonson did not like *The
Faerie Queene*, did not like "Spencers stanzaes," showed
fondness for only one passage of *The Shepheardes Calender*, and so on. And these assertions, as we shall see,
are not true.

We would do well, then, to remember George Saintsbury's caveat about the *Conversations*:

> Did Jonson really say these things to Drummond? Did he
> say them as they are said? . . . 'How would a fellow like
> Jonson and a fellow like Drummond be likely to feel and
> behave towards each other?' we ask. And then you sud-
> denly remember that your own conception of 'a fellow
> like Jonson' is very largely—more largely than from any-
> thing else—derived from this very document, which oth-
> ers have used, and you probably will then use, as a test of
> itself![13]

The basis, that is, for the current notion that Jonson was
indifferent to Spenser's poetry is a modern assessment of
Jonson, which is itself based on what may be called a
self-validating text. The yield has been largely a psychological reading of Jonson the man, and from this
reading a supposition of *what must have been* his attitude toward Spenser. This was put directly enough, if

somewhat crudely, not long after Herford and Simpson. In 1931, E. K. Broadus offered the following:

> Because [Jonson] was himself a rather hard-headed, sharp-eyed, clear-thinking sort of man, impatient of sentimentality and romantic extravagance, and given to laughing at other people's follies, he turned for his models in logic and satiric poetry to such Latin poets as Horace and Martial.
>
> Thus minded, he did not fall in with the imitators of the dreamy, smooth-flowing, honey-sweet Spenser.[14]

The psychological argument set out by Herford and Simpson and followed by others has been supplanted, or perhaps merely augmented, by the political argument of David Norbrook and other new historicists, who argue that poets were merely the puppets of courtiers. This has led them to assume that there was an alignment of interests, reflected in an alignment of kinds of poetry. That is, Puritans were fond of pastoral poetry, and non-Puritans were fond of the nonpastoral.[15] The political implications of this alignment yield two distinct camps: on the one side, Prince Henry, Lord Zouch, Essex, Ralegh, Spenser, Drayton, Wither, Browne of Tavistock; on the other side, King James, Donne, Corbett and, of course, Ben Jonson. This bifurcation into opposed, if not warring, camps certainly simplifies lives, tastes, and history. It also makes some questions difficult to answer, as, for instance, this one: why did Jonson write commendatory poems for such distinctly pastoral works as *The Faithful Shepherdess*, *Annalia Dubrensia* and *Britannia's Pastorals*? Indeed, Norbrook is led at times to conclusions that need to be corrected:

> Jonson and the Spenserians responded to [the political events of 1613–14] in rather different ways. Jonson does not seem to have shared in the extreme mourning for Henry's death. Though he seems by this time to have returned to the Church of England he did not like the militant apocalyptic fervour that was espressed in so many of the elegies.[16]

"Apocalyptic fervour" may have had something to do with Jonson's not sharing in the "extreme mourning"; but a more compelling reason may be that he was, at the time, out of the country, tending to young Wat Ralegh. But Norbrook continues:

> The years 1613–1614 saw a revival of pastoral poetry; and in adopting the persona of the plain-speaking shepherds the Spenserians were indicating their dissatisfaction with contemporary events. . . . In a commendatory poem Michael Drayton, who was described by a contemporary as 'our still reviving Spencer,' praised Browne for redeeming the world of pastoral[,] which, he said, was 'utterly neglected' today. Neither Donne nor Jonson was fond of the pastoral convention, partly because of its prophetic associations. (207–08)

And elsewhere:

> Jonson's sceptical temper found the whole cult of the Fairy Queen somewhat absurd: in 'The Alchemist' he was to present belief in fairies as the whimsical fantasy of a foolish London clerk.[17]

As he (a bit grudgingly) acknowledges,[18] Norbrook is here following Frances Yates, who asks:

> What is Ben Jonson trying to do in these scenes [of Doll Common as Queen of Faery]? Surely, her royal Grace, the Fairy Queen, had an illustrious original. . . . By fouling the sacred image of the Fairy Queen he would seem to be attempting to break the Elizabeth cult.[19]

In this argument both Yates and Norbrook are heirs to Edmund Wilson, who complained that Jonson's "filthy travesty of Marlowe's *Hero and Leander* [in *Bartholomew Fair*] in terms of bankside muck has an ugliness which makes one suspect that Jonson took an ugly delight in defiling a beautiful poem."[20] These critics alike fail to recognize that what is being parodied is not what is being satirized. Jonson has no interest in attacking Marlowe or Spenser; on the contrary, he is attacking dunces who fail to *understand* the poets.[21]

But we must return to the issue of the historical devel-opment of perceptions on Jonson's judgment of Spenser. Jonson's opinion of *The Faerie Queene*, in particular, has been beclouded by comments on his supposed distaste for the Spenserian stanza, hence, the deprecatory ring of "Italianate stanzas" echoing from the ambiguous (and perhaps apocryphal) remark in Drummond's *Conversa-tions*. This comment requires a close look. Some critics (Herford and Simpson, Rosalind Miles) infer from Drum-mond's recollection of this remark that Jonson objected to "Spenserian stanza," this probably because, in the same sentence, Drummond also infers from Jonson's lan-guage that he also did not like Spenser's "matter" as ex-pressed in that unworthy stanzaic form. So, it follows, disliking both its form and matter, Jonson dismisses *The Faerie Queene*. But, later on, after noting the financial circumstances of Spenser's demise, Drummond records "that in that paper S. W Raughly had of the Allegories of his Fayrie Queen by the Blating beast the Puritans were understood by the false Duessa the Q of Scots" (H&S 1:137). We may see these remarks in one of two ways. Either they present logical difficulties, or they encourage an equivocal reading of Jonson's critical engagement with Drummond. Clearly, the issue here is the "matter," not the metrical system of the poem. But, then too, it is not clear what "paper" Jonson is referring to, or even what form Ralegh is supposed to have "had of the Allegories of his Fayrie Queen." In "A Letter of the Authors expound-ing" ("23. January. 1589"), Spenser purports to elucidate "the general intention, and meaning" of his work. But Drummond records very precise, narrow, topical refer-ences. This particular paper dealt with "the Blating beast" and "the Q of Scots." As R. F. Patterson laconi-cally points out, Drummond's "that paper" does not seem to designate "A Letter of the Authors expounding." Since the "Blating beast" makes no appearance in the 1590 edition, it appears not to be a subject of the Letter to Ralegh. As Patterson deftly understates the case: "A fuller copy of this letter ['To the Right noble, and Valorous Sir Walter Raleigh'], or a different document altogether, is obviously meant here."[22]

This conclusion is so obvious to some critics that they have surmised that Drummond is referring to a document entirely different from Spenser's "Letter of the Authors expounding." We must recall that, although Drummond refers to the document twice, he does not mention a "Letter." In the earlier remark, it is not clear to whom the "he" in "he had not delivered in Papers" refers, and this ambiguity is only increased by this second entry: "in that paper S. W Raughly had of the Allegories." Who "delivered" "that paper" or those "Papers"? Indeed, the problem may be more difficult than even Patterson's skeptical remarks suggest. One could hold, consistent with Drummond's account, that Drummond is referring to a document that Jonson himself "had delivered in Papers to Sir Walter Raughlie."[23] After 1590, Spenser's own "Letter" was in print and did not need to be "delivered" to anybody, certainly not to Ralegh. On the other hand, Jonson and Ralegh belonged to the Society of Antiquaries, which met at the Mermaid Tavern in Bread Street. In 1612, Jonson traveled to Paris with Ralegh's son (in the role of tutor), and Jonson helped Ralegh—while he was in the Tower—with the section on the Punic Wars in his *History of the World*.[24]

Let us, then, review the evidence. "A Letter of the Authors expounding" appears to be a set piece, dated at about the time of Spenser's close relations with Ralegh. In 1589, the two were often in each other's company.[25] But their trip to London together that year marked the end of their close relationship, for after that time their paths moved in quite different directions. Indeed, it is hard to see how Spenser could have delivered "that paper" to him, being for a large part of the time in Ireland, with Ralegh either in the Tower or in disgrace at Sherbourne. On the other hand, Ralegh and Jonson were literary friends whose association in London continued despite Ralegh's personal difficulties.

It appears to us, then, that the "he" in "he had delivered in Papers to Sir Walter Raughlie" is the same person who analyzed portions of the second part of *The Faerie Queene* in a manner more specific and topical than did Spenser in his Letter to Ralegh—a manner much like that imputed to the garrulous Jonson of *Conversations with William Drummond*. By this suggestion, we mean to say no more than that Jonson elaborated his views in an analysis, which he handed to Ralegh, perhaps even while his friend was in the Tower. We do not wish to overlook the circumstances of Jonson's visit, and the vagaries attendant upon Drummond's recollection of the event. Above all, we do not overlook the social and rhetorical aspects of the *Conversations*. Jonson was a houseguest of a poet not known for his quickness of wit. Indeed, no matter what we say about the *Conversations*, it ought to jibe with the asymmetry of the participants in the interchange recorded. Consider, for instance, Drummond's solemn recollection of Jonson's opinion that his host's "verses . . . were all good," except for one flaw: "that they smelled too much of the schooles and were not after the Fancie of the tyme" (H&S 1:135). Drummond allows that Jonson thought his poems read like academic exercises, and showed little awareness of what was going on in the current creative scene.

This account would seem to be straightforward enough, were it not for the fact that Drummond seems to have forgotten Jonson's ostensibly earlier advice on how he might improve his poetry:

> He recommended to my reading Quintilian (who (he said) would tell me the faults of my Verses as if he had Lived with me) and Horace, Plinius 2dus Epistles, Tacitus, Juvenall, Martiall, whose Epigrame Vitam quae faciunt Beatiorem etc: he heth translated. (H&S 1:132)

Thus, Drummond's "verses [are] all good," except for the

writing. The case seems hopeless, but only from an artistic point of view, even though—or especially because—Drummond, earnest Scot that he is, cannot see it. For, if Jonson is right, Drummond has already read too much, imitated too much, been too much the academic.[26] So in order to improve his work Drummond must stop writing and start his studies all over again, with Quintilian and Horace and the best of Tacitus, and so on. And the series trails off into a statement of a hard fact irrelevant to Drummond's development as a poet, namely, Jonson's recent achievement as a translator. In every area of poetic endeavor, Drummond's guest is better than he. Happily, Drummond seems to miss the connection between these remarks, however garbled they might be in the recollection, and Jonson's admonition that Drummond abandon his poetic career: "He dissuaded me from Poetrie, for that she had beggered him, when he might have been a rich lawer, Phystian, a Marchant" (H&S 1:149). To Drummond, related to royalty and living on the inherited estate, poetry was not this sort of serious threat. Jonson is telling Drummond to improve his writing by giving it up; he should write no poetry until he ceases being what he is: a student who did not learn his lessons. But the social and economic lesson is also clear. For Jonson points out, by the implied comparison between himself and his host, that Drummond need not fret about his poor prospects as a poet, for he already has what poetry cannot give Jonson: wealth and social position.

We are suggesting that Jonson's remarks, as recorded by Drummond, must be considered in the context of Jonson's visit to Drummond. And swift changes of perspective may have led Jonson to be amused, but Drummond not to see the point. The suggestion that Jonson did not like the stanzaic form, even if linked to *The Faerie Queene*, must be taken in relation to similar remarks aimed at Campion and Daniel. We are tempted to say that Jonson, who knew he would not last the two weeks at Drummond's estate without imparting some negative opinions of his host's poetry, thought he might get off to a good start with Drummond on one important poetic issue: rhymed couplets. And yet no reader can take seriously Drummond's recording of Jonson's hatred of all other rhyme schemes: "he detesteth all other Rimes" (H&S 1:132). Again, the context with regard to Spenser is telling. Drummond has just begun his account with a discussion of Jonson's' "intention to perfect [complete?] ane Epick Poeme intitled Heroologia of the Worthies of his Country" (H&S 1:132). Like Jonson's special tribute to Spenser in *The Golden Age Restored*, this project, apparently already underway, will compete with Spenser's as a national epic, but it will do so only in its metrical system. For Jonson proposes to imitate Spenser, in almost the same manner as for decades Milton would plan to do, by writing an epic, somewhat like Drayton's ("of all the Worthies"), but unlike *Poly-Olbion* in that it would be "perfected" without Drayton's "Long Verses," which, like "Spencers stanzaes," if we are to believe Drummond, "pleased him not" (H&S 1:132–33).

It is important to see that, again, Jonson singles Spenser out. Had Drayton "performed what he promised," he would have written an "excellent" poem. But he did not follow out his plan "to writte the deads of all the Worthies" (H&S 1:132–33). If we consider all of these remarks in series as an assertion of Jonson's idea of the order of English poets, we are in a position, we think, to understand the place of honor that Jonson allocates to Spenser. Drunk or sober, Jonson is talking about his own "Heroologia," which, it appears, he has begun in (unforced) rhymed couplets. Of Jonson's thoughts on the best subject for such a poem, Drummond writes:

> for a Heroik poeme he said ther was no such Ground as King Arthurs fiction and that S. P. Sidney had ane intention to have transform'd all his Arcadia to the stories of King Arthure. (H&S 1:136)

As we shall see in the next chapter, Jonson seems to have

advanced a picture of a divine trinity of modern English poets: Sidney, Spenser, Jonson. Sidney and Spenser fell without completing the task (but Spenser got at least halfway). Both great English predecessors point toward the one historical narrative. Drayton and Daniel missed the "Ground" of English epic, par excellence, and that is the subject, or at least the proposed subject, of Jonson's epic. Yes, Jonson planned to "overgo" Sidney and Spenser, the former by carrying out an unfulfilled plan, the latter by carrying out the task in a more appropriate, less "forced," metrical system. Jonson will, then, place himself directly in the line of Spenser: by writing a long narrative poem. And (if we may be permitted to speculate), it will treat national heroes, especially King Arthur.[27]

We suggested that much of what we know as Jonson's antipathy for Spenser emanates from the *Conversations with Drummond*; and although we must be grateful for this document, we must also recognize that it provides no direct comment, or any indirect comment, which suggests unambiguously what Jonson thought of Spenser's *Faerie Queene*. But with the discovery of Jonson's own, copiously annotated copy of the 1617 Folio of *The Faerie Queen: The Shepheards Calendar: Together with the other Works of England's Arch-Poët, Edm. Spenser*, we have hard evidence of Jonson's immediate reactions to Spenser's magnum opus, and to many of his minor works as well. This new evidence justifies a careful reexamination of many of our assumptions, for instance, about a split between poets at the turn of the century along Spenserian/Jonsonian lines.

For instance, we must reconsider the impact of Drummond's account of Jonson's views on metrics. We have already recalled Drummond's observation that Jonson did not like the stanzaic pattern of *The Faerie Queene*, "the meaning of which Allegorie he had delivered in Papers to Sir Walter Raughlie" (H&S 1:132). Consistent with that analysis, we would say that Drummond infers that Jonson did not like what came to be known as

"Spenserian stanza." This particular remark seems to resonate with Jonson's previous diatribe "against Campion and Daniel," and more specifically, with the statement that Jonson "detesteth all other Rimes" but couplets. Likewise, Drummond avers, Jonson held tha "crosse Rimes and Stanzaes... beyond 8 lines... were all forced," that is, presumably, contrived and, so, faulty (H&S 1:132).

How seriously, now, are we to take this blanket condemnation of alternating ("crosse") rhyme from the author of "Drink to me only with thine eyes," "Epithalamion" and *The Golden Age Restored*? We do not need to deny that Jonson liked, and had surely mastered, the couplet (and the triplet, for that matter) in order to say that Jonson is probably having a bit of fun at Drummond's expense. He has said that stanzas that go beyond eight lines are "all forced." So, Spenserian stanza, with its interlocking, alternating rhyme scheme also misses out by being one line too long (just as, for instance, the creator of the hexameter misses the mark by obtusely refusing to delete the extra foot).

In fact, Jonson realized that Spenser had composed in a variety of verse forms. "Spencers stanzaes" in *The Faerie Queene* were indeed one line too long, and they employed an artificial, "forced," interlocking rhyme scheme. But the stanzas in "The Teares of the Muses" have only six lines, and, although employing alternating rhyme in the first quatrain, they end in couplets. We know that Jonson paid special attention to "The Teares of the Muses," because in his own copy of the 1617 Folio, on at least two occasions (in pencil and in ink), he marked the text of the poem with underlinings and with his typical florilegia and vertical lines in the margins.[28] Consider these verses from the "Polyhymnia" section:

> Heapes of huge words uphoorded hideously,
> With horrid sound though having little sence,
> They thinke to be chiefe praise of Poetry;

And thereby wanting due intelligence,
Have mard the face of goodly Poësie,
And made a monster of their fantasie.

(lines 553–58)[29]

Here (fig. 7), Jonson placed one of his blossom figures in
the margin. The stem descending from the blossom in-
tersects another line; it appears that Jonson meant to
bracket the entire stanza. This impression fits the fact
that, farther to the right, we see an exclamation mark.
Jonson appears to be struck by the text with which,
through the character of Polyhymnia (the Muse of Rhetoric), Spenser ridicules the literary insensibility of those
who would try to speak in the ancient, grand manner.
Once the promise of royalty, the forms she once spon-
sored have been appropriated by "the base vulgar" (line
567). Jonson's attention is arrested by Spenser's grotesque
description of the literary consequences of this devolution of interest in Polyhymnia's art. Great size and sound
are the perceivable expressions of "little sence"; the
modern practitioner has a quantitative method of measur-
ing quality: volume in expense of time, volume in sound.
Hence, "goodly Poësie" is changed into a "monster."
More is less.

Interestingly, Jonson makes no marks as Polyhymnia
turns her attention to Queen Elizabeth. There are few
exceptions to the devolution of interest in literary skills.
Jonson is interested in Spenser's judgment of those poets
and patrons who have lost their way:

But all the rest as borne of salvage brood,
And having beene with Acornes alwaies fed,
Can no whit savour this celestiall food;
But with base thoughts are into blindnesse led,
And kept from looking on the lightsome day:
For whom I waile and weepe all that I may.

(lines 589–94)

Again (fig. 8), Jonson brackets the stanza with a flower

and stem, and in this case underlines the second and third lines of the stanza. In his reiteration of a favored theme—mistreatment of poets by those who could and should sponsor the art—Spenser attracts Jonson's interest—and, we infer, his consent.

It seems hard to believe that Jonson is put off here by Spenser's alternating rhymes. And it is even less likely that Jonson disapproved of the variation in line lengths and stanzaic pattern in another of Spenser's poems, "Epithalamion." As Alexander Dunlop, one of the editors of the *Yale Shorter Poems*, observes, the stanzas here "vary in length from seventeen to nineteen lines (excluding the seven-line envoy) according to no pattern that has been explained" (*YSP*, 659). Indeed, critics have come to see how deeply Jonson's "Epithalamion" (*Und* 75) is indebted to its great Spenserian predecessor text.[30] Both poems recognize the proximity of the wedding day to the summer solstice, and Jonson's wedding song follows Spenser's in its invocation to the sun: "Though thou hast past thy Summer standing" (the wedding at Roehamptom took place on 25 June 1632). Virginia Tufte[31] notes Spenser's influence in the uneven line lengths and in the closing alexandrine of Jonson's stanzas:

> See, the Procession! what a Holy day
>   (Bearing the promise of some better fate)
> Hath fil<l>ed, with *Caroches*, all the way,
>   From *Greenwich*, hither, to *Row-hampton* gate!
>   When look'd the yeare, at best,
>   So like a feast?
>   Or were Affaires in tune,
> By all the Spheares consent, so in the heart of June?
>   (lines 9–16)

As in *The Golden Age Restored*, so here the stanzaic form, with its alexandrine close, seems to suggest a deference to and elevation of Spenser. And there are other ways in which "this Paire" of poems, like the loving couple themselves, "doth intertexe" (line 60). According

to the OED, the figure comes from weaving: to weave together, to intertwine, to create an intertexture. In both
epithalamia, the bride is designated by exactly the same
figure ("mayden Queene" [Spenser, line 158]; "Maiden
Queene" [Jonson, line 47]). Both poems draw on the
figurative language of the Song of Songs by associating
the bride with lilies and roses (Spenser, line 43; Jonson,
lines 57–58); and, we think, it seems likely that Jonson
even transfigured Spenser's "happy hands" (line 225) to
"happy bands" (line 129), for the context in which the
figures occur is quite similar:

> Behold, whiles she before the altar stands,
> Hearing the holy priest that to her speakes,
> And blesseth her with his two happy hands,
> How the red roses flush up in her cheekes,
> And the pure snowe, with goodly vermill staine,
> Like crimsin dyde in graine:
> That even the Angels, which continually
> About the sacred Altar doe remaine.
> (Spenser, lines 223–30)

> O happy bands! and thou more happy place,
>   Which to this use, wert built and consecrate!
> To have thy God to blesse, thy King to grace,
> And this their chosen Bishop celebrate,
> And knit the Nuptiall knot,
>   Which Time shall not,
>   Or cankere'd Jealousie,
> With all corroding Arts, be able to untie!
> (Jonson, lines 129–36)

Finally, Jonson divides his wedding song into exactly 24
stanzas, like Spenser, with a prayer for the fruit of marriage (continuance "of the large Pedigree" [line 176]) apposite to that in Spenser's poem.

We should also note that, since he marked line 80 of
Spenser's poem, Jonson seems to have regarded Spenser's
version of the medieval bird mass with special interest.[32]

This passage in Spenser occurs at a moment of transition from the order of classical poetry (with its abiding interest in the Muses, nymphs, Orpheus, Hymen and their attendant thematic linking of the personal to nature) to a more Christian mode:

> The merry Larke her mattins sings aloft,
> The Thrush replie, the Mavis descant playes,
> The Ouzell shrils, the Ruddock warbles soft,
> So goodly all agree with sweet consent,
> To this daies meriment.
>
> (Spenser, lines 80–84)

Now, all the sounds of celebration make sense beneath the new order of religious harmony ("So goodly all agree") in that the universe participates in the give and take, which the liturgical movements suggest. This element is of special interest in Jonson's responsive poem: "Christians know their birth / Alone, and such a race, / We pray may grace / Your fruitfull spreading Vine" (lines 156–59). Jonson is not merely reiterating the theme of legitimacy earlier intoned in "To Penshurst,"[33] although he is surely doing that, too. Rather, he is picking up the sacramental undercurrent in Spenser's poem. Legitimacy is only one of many outward signs of the noble family's inward grace. So the poet prays in Jonson's poem, not just for "Nuptiall Sweets ... / To propagate their [the Westons's] Names" (lines 148–49), but for the "chast desires," "holy perfumes of the Mariage bed," and "those Sweet, and Sacred fires" (lines 161–63) that make human love an expression of its divine original. This thematic interest, along with its 24 stanzas ending in alexandrines, is not only reminiscent of Spenser's "Epithalamion," then, but clearly suggests Jonson's compliment to Spenser.

Although these are, we believe, telling instances of Jonson's attitude toward Spenser, no judgment of his great contemporary is better known than Jonson's famous dictum in *Discoveries*: "Spencer, in affecting the Ancients, writ no Language" (H&S 8:618). In citing this usual source to suggest Jonson's reservations,[34] J. B. Bamborough more or less invokes the casual tone of Herford and Simpson, which seems to elevate this remark to the status of established Jonsonian wisdom in the matter. But in fact, we will argue, this often quoted sentence from *Discoveries* says little about Jonson's opinion of Spenser's achievement. We would note, first, that the sentence has two members: "S*pencer*, in affecting the Ancients, writ no Language: Yet I would have him read for his matter; but as *Virgil* read *Ennius*" (H&S 8:618). In the first segment, we have a judgment accompanied by an explanation: by modeling his diction after poets of previous epochs, Spenser created a language of his own. Accordingly, Richard A. McCabe writes, correctly we think: "In a sense it is true, as Jonson said, that Spenser 'writ no Language,' following neither the accepted norm of is own day nor that of Chaucer."[35] We must remember the rhetorical situation of the work itself. Since the question under consideration at this moment in *Discoveries* is how to teach young people to communicate, Spenser's diction, presumably, an imaginary amalgam of contemporary and Chaucerian English (hence, "no [spoken] language") might present a problem, at least for younger pupils. At the same time, Jonson recalls, there is a tradition of employing the diction of precursor poets, and as Jonson would have known, Virgil was well read in Ennius. But in his use of Ennius, Virgil is worthy of study by more advanced students who have gone beyond the difficulties of learning a new language. Jonson seems to suggest that literary discussion has its own language (or, as some critics might now put it, its own domain of discourse). To follow it requires special preparation. Jonson's restrictions here, then, are among a range of such limits which he, as a tutor, would impose.

Then, too, we must bear in mind that the section containing the remark on Spenser's language concerns the art of teaching. That is, the statement cannot be taken as an account of Jonson's *poetic* judgment of Spenser, but

only of his judgment as to when, as an instructor, one
ought to introduce Spenser to students: "*It pleas'd* your
Lordship of late, to aske my opinion, touching the education of your sonnes, and especially to the advancement of
their studies" (H&S 8:613). "Advancement" in learning,
as Jonson sees it, cannot be cultivated in a random expenditure of good will and effort. Timing is important,
and recreation may be the best teacher. Youngsters need
to play: "Thence the Schoole it selfe is call'd a Play, or
Game: and all Letters are so best taught to Schollers"
(H&S 8:614). Jonson thinks of education organically, or,
as we might nowadays say, holistically: "studies have
their Infancie, as well as creatures" (H&S 8:613).

   Jonson disarms the auditory by placing himself in it:
"Ready writing makes not good writing; but good writing
brings on ready writing" (H&S 8:616). Writers see the virtues and flaws in others' writing sooner than in their
own. Thus, the wise mentor counsels preceptors to reach
beyond their own practice:

> For the mind, and memory are more sharpely exercis'd
> in comprehending an other mans things, then our owne;
> and such as accustome themselves, and are familiar with
> the best Authors, shall ever and anon find somewhat of
> them in themselves, and in the expression of their minds,
> even when they feele it not, be able to utter something
> like theirs, which hath an Authority above their owne.
> (8:616)

With experience, the writer's critique of others' work reflects a self-conscious recognition of "other mans things"
in one's own writing. Thus, Jonson as preceptor is able to
praise a practice in a young writer that he must repre-
hend in more mature authors. The instructor knows that
in finding their own style young writers must read "the
best Authors" (H&S 8:616) in order to develop their own
"*Genius.*"

   Although important, the selection of "the best Authors" will not, in and of itself, produce the desired skill.

Reading must proceed in an orderly sequence. For one to write well, one must weigh matter *and* words in "their beginnings" with "care, and industry." But how does one find the balance between emptiness and affectation? One of the difficulties of teaching is that it is hard to explain to young writers the difference between the two categories. So the issue of maturity—that is, of how to gauge it—may determine the teacher's success or failure:

> No more would I tell a greene Writer all his faults, lest I should make him grieve and faint, and at last despaire. For nothing doth more hurt, then to make him so afraid of all things, as hee can endeavour nothing. Therefore youth ought to be instructed betimes, and in the best things: for we hold those longest, wee take soonest. As the first sent of a Vessell lasts: and that tinct the wooll first receives. Therefore a Master should temper his owne powers, and descend to the others infirmity. . . . And as it is fit to read the best Authors to youth first, so let them be of the openest, and clearest. (H&S 8:618)

Jonson is not saying that "the openest, and the clearest" are also "the best Authors." Rather, he is saying that two criteria must be simultaneously imposed. Because the student retains best what is learned first, it is important that "the best Authors" be presented "to youth first." But at the same time, those "best Authors" distinguished by openness and clarity should precede those distinguished for other stylistic achievements. Thus, in the interest of pedagogical success, Jonson urges that beginners not be introduced to Spenser, because the matter, although worthy, is obscured by (to carry on with Jonson's figures) a "closed, and obscure" style. Spenser's diction, with its pronounced invocation of ancient dialect, will not contribute to the requisite grammar and vocabulary.

But, since Jonson recognizes that even the young will learn something valuable from Spenser in due time, he "would have him read for his matter" (H&S 8:618). This is precisely how Virgil read Ennius: as a preparatory step toward his own composition. Thus, the mentor proceeds to explain, his method follows Quintilian's directive:

> The reading of *Homer* and *Virgil* is counsell'd by *Quin-tilian*, as the best way of informing youth, and confirm-ing man. For besides, that the mind is rais'd with the height, and sublimity of such a verse, it takes spirit from the greatnesse of the matter, and is tincted with the best things. (H&S 8:618)

It is one thing to urge "*Livy* before *Salust*" or "*Sydney* before *Donne*" (H&S 8:618), but quite another to set young minds to the reading of "*Gower,* or *Chaucer*" at the outset of their studies. The one sequence concerns the ease and openness of the texts of Livy and Sidney in contrast to the relative obscurity of Sallust and Donne. Diction is important, too. If at a too-early date students fall in love with Chaucer and Gower, they might by imi-tation make their ancient diction their own: "and not apprehending the weight, they grow rough and barren in language onely" (H&S 8:618). Yes, "*Chaucerismes*" (H&S 8:622) can get in the way, and Jonson admires a "plaine, and pleasing" diction: a middle style (H&S 8:625). But he is also uneasy with the idea that rules or precepts might be thought to guarantee a performance when the "matter" is of the greatest importance. For Jonson, the building is the poet's character: "a goodnes of naturall wit" (H&S 8:637). And yet the poet can be en-dowed as such and still need an understanding of the po-etic ancestors in order to complete the creative task:

> The third requisite in our *Poet,* or Maker, is *Imitation,* to bee able to convert the substance, or Riches of an other *Poet,* to his owne use. To make choise of one excel-lent man above the rest, and so to follow him, till he grow very *Hee*: or, so like him, as the Copie may be mistaken for the Principall. Not, as a Creature, that swallowes, what it takes in, crude, raw, or indigested; but, that feedes with an Appetite, and hath a Stomacke to concoct, divide, and turne all into nourishment. (H&S 8:638)

The end of educational nourishment is, then, not ran-
domly achieved by consuming whatever food is at hand.
The wise teacher and the good poet choose appropriate
models to emulate. Whether one is teaching criticism or
composition, Jonson's organicism suggests an overrid-
ing insistence on the propriety of a certain sequence of
development.

For Jonson, imitation, which entails elements of reading as well as of writing, functions rather like the diges-
tive system. Nourishment, individual vitality—*enar-
geia*—is the end-product of this individual part in a
generic process. Hence, it is not Chaucer's poetry that
makes "*Chaucerismes.*" How Spenser stands in relation
to Chaucer depends upon how he uses what he finds in
the predecessor's text. Consider, for instance, another example of Jonson's treatment of the Chaucer/Spenser literary relation. *The Golden Age Restored* (H&S 7:421–29),
one of Jonson's more successful masques, was presented
during Twelfth Night festivities at Whitehall in 1615.
This event was remembered largely because of those in
attendance; tension existed between ambassadors of
Spain and Venice, and both were invited (H&S 10:553–
57n). In addition to the complexities of seating arrange-
ments, Queen Anne rather openly supported the Spanish
cause (H&S 10:558). The masque itself is an allegory of
Wisdom's sponsorship of poetry· as servants of Astraea's
restoration, Astraea having descended, sent by Jove, with
Golden Age as her consort. When the duo ask how their
"state" on earth can be sustained, Pallas answers that
both she and Jove will see to that. And, as if to offer pro-
leptic evidence of their endurance, the stage direction in-
structs, "she calls the poets":

> Expect a while.
> You farre-fam'd spirits of this happie Ile,
> That, for your sacred songs have gain'd the stile,
> Of PHOEBUS sons: whose notes the[y] aire aspire
> Of th'old *Ægyptian*, or the *Thracian* lyre,

> That *Chaucer, Gower, Lidgate, Spencer* hight,
> Put on your better flames, and larger light,
> To waite upon the age that shall your names new
> > nourish,
> Since vertue prest shall grow, and buried arts shall
> > flourish.
> > > (lines 112–20)

Declaring themselves the inevitable victors over strife, hate, fear and pain, the poets recall the harmony between the sexes that marked the Golden Age, which extends from the exterior landscape to the "libertie" within and between lovers:

> The male and female us'd to joyne,
> And into all delight did coyne
> > That pure simplicitie.
> Then feature did to forme advance,
> And youth call'd beautie forth to dance,
> > And everie grace was by.
> It was a time of no distrust,
> So much of love had nought of lust,
> > None fear'd a jealous eye.
> The language melted in the eare,
> Yet all without a blush might heare,
> > They liv'd with open vow.
> > > (lines 182–93)

In the context of the assembly at Whitehall, the text—which elsewhere casts a dark glance at the ominous drawing to a close of the Somerset trial—now points to the harmony of the court, and especially to the harmony of man and woman, seen, for instance, in the contrast between James and Anne and the predecessor sovereign. One stage direction fits: "*Dance with Ladies.*"

This stage direction is indicative of the symmetry in the masque, which has been somewhat beclouded by editorial misunderstanding of the proper ending of *The Golden Age Restored.* Jonson intended a symmetrical contrast between Astraea and Pallas. Thus, with Jove's intentions realized at the conclusion of the masque, the goddesses move in opposite directions. With Astraea once more on earth, Pallas ascends. The last portion of the masque—about the last two-fifths of the text, contains three dances, all of which celebrate the return of Astraea to earth:

> But, as of old, all now be gold.
> Move, move, then to these sounds.
> And, doe, not onely, walke your solemne rounds,
> But give those light and ayrie bounds,
> That fit the *Genii* of these gladder grounds.
>
> (lines 148–52)

After the first dance there are lines spoken or sung by Pallas, Astraea, Age, Pallas and the Quire. There follows *"The maine dance,"* then lines spoken or sung by the Pallas, Poets and the Quire, and, finally *"Dance with ladies"* before lines spoken or sung by Astraea, Pallas and the Quire. The Quire's concluding prayer, which touches the spatial contrast mentioned above ("To *Jove*, to *Jove*, be all the honour given, / That thankefull hearts can raise from earth to heaven"), suggests, as does the orthographic evidence, that Herford and Simpson—and Stephen Orgel and others as well—got the sequences of speeches at the close reversed. Jonson intended the Astraea/Pallas ending. All but three of Jonson's masques before *The Golden Age Restored* end with songs, and all of them that *could* end with a song do so.[36] The symmetry of the Astraea/Pallas ending, which is buttressed by the textual evidence,[37] not only makes greater artistic sense, but it heightens the compliment to the Stuarts as well.

But what of Herford's and Simpson's claim regarding this extraordinary bit of theatrical poetics? Jonson includes Spenser in a quartet of English poets; but he appears, also, to afford Spenser particular honor. We note, for instance, that the presentation of Pallas concludes with a couplet of hexameter lines. Considering Jonson's keen eye and ear for such poetic details, it is hard to believe that he did not intend the added feet as an imitation of the long line which, after hundreds of years, we still associate with Spenser. But, as if he would make the connection unmistakable, Jonson has Pallas respond to the poets' arrival in a sestet of alexandrines:

> Then see you yonder soules, set far within the shade,
>   And in *Elysian* bowres the blessed seates doe keepe,
> That for their living good, now semigods are made,
>   And went away from earth, as if but tam'd with sleepe:
> These we must joyne to wake; for these are of the straine
> That justice dare defend, and will the age sustaine.
>
> (lines 126–31)

David Riggs has shown how effectively these lines draw attention to the central character in the audience, young George Villiers, whose presentation to James (the Jove of Whitehall's heaven) had been made at Althorp the year before.[38] The social maneuvering should not deter us from seeing that, amid all the clamor (Somerset tried to frustrate plans of the performance by inviting the Spanish and Venetian envoys, parties at the time tactfully kept apart), we should recognize that this passage attributes to English poets the power to enliven suitors for courtly position. It is, in effect, the English literary tradition that calls the slumberers to center stage.

In view of the honor and power Jonson attributes to poetry, and of the way in which Jonson singles out Spenser among the distinguished chorus (including also Chaucer, Gower and Lydgate), we are constrained to challenge this remark by Herford and Simpson:

> None of the four enjoyed, elsewhere, any peculiar marks of Jonson's esteem. The recovery of the 'buried art' of John Lydgate can hardly have seemed a prospect for which it was worth while to obliterate the living art of Shakespeare and Donne; and Spenser, whose matter and

manner he equally disliked, doubtless owes his inclusion among the poets of Elysium to the flavour of an older day conveyed by his antique phrase, rather than to his poetry. But that the restored Golden Age should be led on by English poets—'farre-fam'd spirits of this happie Ile'— instead of by the inmates of the classic Elysium, marks another step in the gradual assimilation of the Masque to English circumstance and scenery. Beyond these names and phrases, however, there is little that is English in this Golden Age. (H&S 2:298–99)

At the very least, this statement requires reconsideration. First, in effect, the lines attribute international fame to poets of this elect choir. Even if Jonson did not elsewhere give "any peculiar marks of [his] esteem," these generous remarks suggest they had less need for it: other critics in other lands know and admire their works. Then, too, the situation in which Jonson's lyrics summon Villiers to the fore of the king's attention is English to the core, perhaps even parochially so. As Herford and Simpson point out (2:298), the antimasque alludes to the scandalous Somerset trial, not yet over, which wracked the court and threatened even to involve King James himself: "JOVE can endure no longer, / Your great ones should your lesse invade" (lines 5–6). Jonson, who had once dwelled within the Somerset penumbra, now rebukes his former friends for their presumption in their relationship to royalty. Jonson now identifies himself with Villiers. The favorite is dead; long live the favorite.

Second, here, Herford and Simpson imply that only the works of living poets "live," and in this view they separate themselves from many poets and critics—including Jonson. Jonson's text attributes not just "life" to the formative figures of the English literary tradition, but a power to "enliven" as well. Even if one were praised so highly only once, it would not mean that the praise is therefore, in some way, diminished or false.

Our argument is that Herford and Simpson overlook much that Jonson thinks the four poets share. Perhaps this point can be clarified by simply extending the logic of their statement. Suppose one tries try to have it Herford's and Simpson's way: "*Chaucer, Gower, Lidgate, and Donne* hight?" One would find, we think, that more is lost than half of the last metrical foot. The passage loses much of its coherence. On the other hand, Donne belongs here more than would, say, Thomas Watson or Barnaby Barnes. Jonson recognized Donne as a major poet; Donne contributed to the sense of an English tradition. Indeed, according to Drummond, Jonson thought him "the first poet in the world in some things," and the two epigrams (23 and 96) that Jonson addresses to Donne demonstrate this high opinion. Yet narrative verse was apparently not one of the "some things"; hence, the thematic wrenching of the revised series. And, although it would fill out the line, it would not otherwise help to replace "Donne" with "Shakespeare." Although Jonson held Shakespeare to be in a class by himself and surely worthy of inclusion in a choir of the four most notable English poets, Jonson thought of him as a poet who wrote for the stage.

Again, the series draws together the great names of the English tradition in narrative verse. Spenser is what Donne and Shakespeare are not: primarily a narrative poet. Jonson has the Golden Age present a chorus of English narrative voices, as we remember them from *Troilus and Criseyde, The Canterbury Tales, Confessio Amantis, The Fall of Princes, The Pilgrimage of Man's Life, The Life of Mary, The Destruction of Troy* and *The Faerie Queene*. The arrangement, then, is not a dismissal of Donne, much less of Shakespeare. It is, rather, an expression of high praise for English achievement in a poetic genre that Jonson much admired. (We recognize also, of course, that neither Donne nor Shakespeare was yet quite ready to be represented as dwelling in heaven.) If we may believe Drummond, Jonson planned to write his own Horoologia, presumably, a narrative poem in couplets on a national theme. In *The Golden Age Restored*, given the shift of Pallas to hexameter lines, we do find, in the words of Herford and Simpson, "peculiar marks of Jonson's esteem" for Spenser.

Further, Jonson remarks on many poets in *The Golden Age Restored* while denying them even the faintest hint of praise (John Taylor, for instance). But does Jonson set Donne and Shakespeare, here or elsewhere, in opposition to Spenser and the trio of poetic progenitors? On the contrary, the poetic foursome is in opposition to the quartet of evils metamorphosed moments earlier onstage; they are frozen—turned to statues—before the scene changes. They are the opposites of their successors onstage because they are the enemies of life. It should be noted that Iron-age appears alone, while Golden Age appears with Astraea, as if the sexual pairing coincides with a resurgence of life. The poets' song is about a bygone age, but it also concerns sexual union between male and female. It is not enough that the earth, seemingly without effort, burgeons with new growth: "But here's not all: you must doe more,/ Or else you doe but halfe restore / The *ages* libertie" (lines 178–80). That "more" is, of course, represented onstage in the recitative of Astraea and Golden Age ("1. Now peace, 2. and love, 1. faith, 2. joyes, 1. 2. all, all, increase" [line 142]) to which the poets, first in a divided chorus, then in unison, reply: "2. And strife, 2. and hate, 2. and feare, 2. and paine, 4. all cease" (line 144).

Herford and Simpson may think of of Jonson's chorus as a group of dead poets, but that is not Jonson's point. They are in the heaven from which, at Minerva's bidding, Astraea and the Golden Age are sent by Jove. Moreover, it is doubtful that Jonson's text polarizes, as Herford and Simpson would have it, the living art of Shakespeare and Donne against that of Chaucer, Gower, Lydgate and Spenser: "None of the four enjoyed, elsewhere, any peculiar marks of Jonson's esteem." Critics should remember that, although Jonson admired Donne and Shakespeare, he did not tender them unreserved praise. His critical style was, we reiterate, one of attempted balance and measure, a calculated evenhandedness in judgment.

In this vein we suggest that, while it is true that Donne and Shakespeare were living contemporaries at the time Jonson composed *The Golden Age Restored,* he does not place Spenser in his choir of poets because Spenser wrote "old English" poetry. From a literary point of view, we could argue that Spenser *was* Jonson's contemporary. Jonson was probably born on 11 June 1572 (or, perhaps, 1573). At the time, Spenser was probably 20 years old. When Jonson took up writing in the 1590s, Spenser was still alive, only 12 years older than his "living" contemporary, Shakespeare. John Donne, who lived to age 58, was a year younger than Jonson, who lived to age 65. To link Spenser with his three poetic companions by asserting their status as ancients is clearly inappropriate. Indeed, until critics recognize the rhetorical purpose of the grouping, Spenser might even seem out of place in the choir, poets whose achievements in narrative verse transcend epochal distance. Jonson thought of Spenser as he did Sidney and Sir Henry Morison: as a poet who died before his time (we will return to this point in the following chapter).

There is certainly additional evidence that Jonson admired all four poets—Chaucer, Gower, Lydgate, Spenser—if perhaps in different ways and for different reasons. Modern criticism has not been kind to John Gower, but in the Renaissance, some critics considered him on a par with Chaucer. This is how Sidney thought of him, and John Foxe as well. In 1919, G. Gregory Smith pointed out that, in *English Grammar,* Jonson quotes Gower "in his illustrations oftener than any other author."[39] And Jonson links Chaucer with Spenser in an apposite manner again in "To the Memory of . . . Shakespeare": "I will not lodge thee by / *Chaucer* or *Spenser,* or bid *Beaumont* lye / A little further, to make thee a roome." Here, the trio represent those memorialized in Westminster Abbey, but the conjunctions clearly set

Beaumont apart from the two great narrative poets. Interestingly, the proposal is not that Beaumont be moved to permit interment of the playwright with the strongest claim to their shared national eminence. In contrast to Camille Paglia (see chapter 3), Jonson pairs Chaucer and Spenser as shaping figures in the establishment of the English literary tradition, and he imagines, while dismissing, the idea of moving Beaumont's remains to allow Shakespeare inclusion in a trinity of great English poets. But the dismissal is as important as the engagement of the idea, for it is replaced by another, arresting figure. Shakespeare is not just a great poet, not just one among many enabling voices in a national culture—this is a Bloomian-by-way-of-Paglia modernist or postmodernist or post-postmodernist way of explaining poetic interrelations—but the "Soule," "applause! delight! the wonder of [the] Stage." As "Stage" rhymes with "Age," we may perceive an implosion of discrete, complimentary meanings into one, comprehensive figure: wonder = delight = applause = "Soule." To Jonson, Shakespeare is the living spirit of the epoch—or in Donne's figure, "The intelligence that moves" the "Spheares" of the poetic cosmos of Renaissance England. But Spenser alone of contemporary poets is the equal of Chaucer in narrative verse.

2

The Poet's Vocation

Jonson and Spenser's Shorter Poems

Or who would ever care to doe brave deed,
Or strive in vertue others to excell;
If none should yeeld him his deserved meed,
Due praise, that is the spur of dooing well;
For if good were not praised more than ill,
None would chuse goodnes of his owne free-will.
                "The Teares of the Muses," 1617 Folio

I n her landmark study of some 50 years ago, *Two Centuries of Spenserian Scholarship (1609–1805)*, Jewel
Wurtsbaugh describes Sir Kenelm Digby's *Observations*
(1643) "as one of the earliest attempts to interpret
Spenser's text, having been written prior to the publication of Ware's annotated edition of *A View of Ireland*

(1633) and printed almost a century before Jortin's *Remarks on Spenser's Poems* (1734)."[1] Her passing reference to the oft-repeated assertion that "Spencer, in affecting the Ancients, writ no Language" (H&S 8:618) is about all we get on the subject of Jonson's judgment of Spenser. William R. Mueller is more generous to the Elizabethans in his concession that "Spenser criticism began in 1579 with E. K.'s prefatory apology to the *Shepheardes Calender*," but he gives the Stuart period even shorter shrift than Wurtsbaugh does by asserting that Spenser criticism "was at its best in the half century between 1715 and 1762, and again during the past half century."[2] As for the Elizabethans, Jacobeans and Carolines—with the exception of Digby who provides the "only extended treatment of Spenser prior to the eighteenth century"—they are remembered only for "incidental remarks on Spenser... by Sidney, Jonson, Milton, and others." No one doubts the importance of anything a major contemporary poet may have thought about Spenser, especially as that might be reflected in commentary on specific texts, and this is *a fortiori* the case with a major poet, who, like Jonson, is also a major critic. Although Spenser was one of the most admired and imitated of English poets in the early seventeenth century, the story of Jonson's evaluation of his work has so far eluded scholarship. Understandably, with so glaring a gap facing them, critics, past and present, have either ignored the issue or felt justified in turning to the mid-seventeenth century or later for a sense of coherent reactions to Spenser in commentary from Milton on.

As for Spenser's contemporaries, in the closing decades of the sixteenth century, Sidney, Webbe and others registered now well-known opinions of Spenser's place in the English pantheon of poets, and it appears that Jonson went along with the general wisdom. For instance, in *The Masque of Queenes* (1609), he quotes lines in "The Ruines of Time" from "the graue and diligent Spenser" (H&S 7:310),[3] and, as we saw in chapter 1, in *The Golden*

Age Restored (1615), he includes Spenser in a quartet of England's greatest narrative poets. Together, the poets proclaim that their best poetry was written under the inspiration of Pallas rather than that of the Muses. But, until recently, Digby's remarks of 1643[4] stood virtually alone as specific glosses on Spenser's poetry. In 1964, Graham Hough published *The first commentary of the Fairie Queene, being an analysis of the annotations in Lord Bessborough's copy of the first edition of the Faerie queene*. Apparently, the first owner of this volume (and so it appears the first "practical critic" of *The Faerie Queene*), was one John Dixon.[5] Hough demonstrates by internal evidence that Dixon made his notes in 1597 (Hough, 19), some 45 years before the appearance of Digby's little book. So Lord Bessborough's copy appears to be the earliest example we have yet of specific commentary on the text of *The Faerie Queene*, which would be reason enough for critical interest. But Dixon entered his remarks on a copy of the first edition (1590), and then only on parts of the first two books.

Naturally, the Spenser *Variorum* makes no mention of Dixon's annotations to Spenser's text. Like Spenser criticism generally, the *Variorum* lends credence to the notion that Spenser was overlooked by critics at the turn of the century, including Ben Jonson. If we take Jonson as Drummond presumably did—at face value—we might easily suppose, as far as Spenser's talents were concerned (the confusion between Cuddie and Colin aside), that Jonson admired only a few lines from the October Eclogue: "he hath by Heart some verses of Spensers Calender about wyne between Coline and percye" (H&S 1:136).

But if we turn from Jonson's reported attitudes to his annotations in the Spenser Folio, we find in *The Shepheardes Calender* a number of markings (see Appendix B). Those markings are confined to E. K.'s introductory matter and, Spenser and E. K. alike, to the months of January, April, May, June, July, September and October, with only the last two and E. K.'s "Generall Argument" having more than a couple of marks each, those for the most part small dashes in the margins of the text and underlinings in the "glosse." If, however, there were no marks but those in the "Generall Argument," they would be worth our attention. These marks, both in pencil and in ink, show, on at least two occasions—judging from the two kinds of markings—that Jonson paused to reflect on E. K.'s discussion of ways that the year is accounted for. Very few underlinings are in pencil; a couple of them may be significant. Within a few years of the earliest date that Jonson could have obtained this edition of Spenser (1617), he shifted his own practice in citing the beginning of the year from the "Calendar date" (1 January) to the "Legal date" (25 March). On signature A5, a part of E. K.'s text is: "*GOD* (as is sayde in Scripture) commaunded the people of the Jewes to count the Moneth *Abib*, that which wee call March, for the first Moneth, in remembrance that in that Moneth hee brought them out of the Land of Aegypt" (*YSP*, 24). In pencil Jonson underlines the words "Moneth *Abib*" and "wee call March." (The other pencil marks, on sig. A5ᵛ, underscore text in which E. K. points out that the Egyptians began their year in September.) If we are correct in our assessment that the pencil marks antedate ink where the two coincide, as we argued in the introduction, it would seem that some of Jonson's earlier markings were made within a few years of this copy's printing. As we assert this, we are aware of Greg's strictures as well as his conclusion:

> Completely consistent Jonson's practice certainly was not. But the survey we have taken I think does point to a definite change at a particular date. If we assume that about 1620 Jonson abandoned his former habit of using Calendar dates and adopted the Legal reckoning, we shall find in the earlier period only two certain exceptions, which may be accounted for without much violence, and in the later period one, which may not be an exception at

all. The change would synchronize with his visit to
Scotland, though the connexion is not obvious.[6]

Without either forcing the significance of Jonson's visit
to Scotland or concerning ourselves with the consistency
of his practice, we can suggest that his markings in his
Spenser support the idea that Jonson was particularly interested in the calendar around 1620.

Of Jonson's other markings in *The Shepheardes Calender*, the most instructive, as one would expect, are
those in October; however, these are not in the poem,
but rather in the Argument and in the Glosse. In the Argument, Jonson underlines the observation that "Poetrie
[is] . . . a divine gift," the sometimes neglected one-half of
a Jonsonian judgment of Shakespeare: "a good *Poet's*
made, as well as borne." Some markings in the Glosse
bring our attention more particularly to Jonson's interests. We might recall that in October Piers attempts to
persuade Cuddie of the loftiness of the poet's calling. At
one point in his response to Piers, Cuddie laments:

> But ah Mecoenas is yclad in claye,
> And great Augustus long ygoe is dead:
> And all the Worthies liggen wrapt in lead,
> That matter made for Poets on to play.
> For ever, who in derring doe were dead,
> The loftie verse of hem was loved aye.
>
> But after vertue gan for age to stoupe,
> And mighty manhood brought a bedde of ease.
>
> (lines 61–68)

E. K. devotes two paragraphs to line 65, the entire second
of which is set off by Jonson:

> And that such account hath been alway made of
> Poetes, as wel sheweth this, that the worthy Scipio in all
> his warres against Carthage and Numanita, had evermore
> in his company, and that in a most familiar sort, the good
> olde Poet Enniuo: as also that Alexander destroying
> Thebes, when he was enformed, that the famous Lyricke

Poet Pindarus was borne in that City, not onely commaunded straightly, that no man should upon pain of
death, do any violence to that house, or otherwise: but
also specially spared most, and some highly rewarded
that were of his kinne. So favoured he the only name of
Poet. Which prayse otherwise was in the same man no
lesse famous, then when he came to ransacking of King
Darius coffers, whom he lately had overthrowne, he
found in a little coffer of silver, the two bookes of
Homers workes, as layde up there for speciall Jewells and
riches: which hee taking thence, put one of them dayly in
his bosome, and the other every night lay under his
pillow. Such honour have Poets alwayes found in the
sight of Princes and noble men, which this Authour heere
very well sheweth, as else where more notably. (*YSP*,
180–81)

Jonson also marks the next comment in the Glosse,
which refers to line 67: "he sheweth the cause of contempt of Poetrie to be idlenesse and basenesse of mind."
Taken together, these form several elements of a theme
that interested Jonson throughout his career, one he
treated thoroughly, as we discuss later in this chapter, in
his Cary/Morison ode. There we see notions of Pindar (or
Pindaric ode) and of Spenser's and Jonson's shared concept of the role of the poet in society. These themes are
brought together with E. K.'s observation (in the paragraph just above the one Jonson marks) that Alexander
was aware "that Achilles had never bin so famous, as
he is, but for Homers immortall verses," which Jonson
echoes in one of his marginal notations to "The Ruines
of Time."

   As we will show in the next chapter, we need no
longer depend on surmise in discussing Jonson's reaction
to *The Faerie Queene*. But at the same time, we might
concede that Jonson's remarks as recorded by Drummond
("Spencers stanzaes pleased him not") could refer to stanzaic patterns in Spenser's minor poems. Although his
markings in *The Shepheardes Calender* demonstrate his
interest in that poem, they do nothing to support, one

way or the other, conclusions about his opinion of Spenser's prosody. Let us turn our attention briefly to representative markings in other of Spenser's shorter poems, most of which bear some sign of Jonson's attention. We omit here poems or parts of poems we discuss elsewhere in the study; for instance, "Epithalamion" in chapter 1 and "The Teares of the Muses" in chapters 1 and 3. As in *The Shepheardes Calender,* Jonson's markings elsewhere in the shorter poems are both in pencil and in ink, chiefly the latter. And in these poems there are not any notations, except for "Mother Hubberds Tale," where the hand may not be Jonson's. Jonson's characteristic flowers and descending wavy lines appear a number of times in "The Teares of the Muses" (figs. 7, 8, 9), without exception in pencil, although there are also a few ink underlinings as well. The section most fully marked is "Calliope," in which Jonson sets off passages that call attention to Calliope's twin offices of castigating corruption and praising virtue; the same considerations are central to "The Ruines of Time," as we will discuss shortly. Figure 9 shows that at one time or another Jonson marked fully one half of the stanzas of "Calliope," including the last three lines of the stanza that appears as the epigraph for this chapter.

There are a few dashes in the margins and underlinings in other poems: "Colin Clouts Come Home Againe," "An Hymne in Honour of Beautie," "An Hymne of Heavenly Beautie," "Daphnaida," "Muiopotmos," "Visions of the Worlds Vanitie" and "The Visions of Bellay," and even a few underlinings in "A Letter of the Authors." There are a couple of marks in *Amoretti,* which may come as a surprise to those who still erroneously believe that Jonson had no time for the sonnet form.[7] The only notations in the minor poems, as we said, are in "Mother Hubberds Tale." We cannot altogether rule out the hand in this poem as being Jonson's, for one's hand can vary greatly from time to time, but it is doubtful. The notation in the text in which the hand most nearly resembles Jonson's is that reproduced in figure 10. The words "Lord treserors" have been written next to line 1148 to identify the "false Fox" of whom the poet says:

All offices, all Leases by him lept,
And of them all what-so he likte, he kept.
Justice he solde injustice for to buy,
And for to purchase for his progeny.

(lines 1145–48)

In his introduction to "Mother Hubberds Tale," William Oram observes that "modern commentators agree that the picture of the Fox as a courtier in the last two episodes of the poem glances at Lord Burghley," but Oram, sensibly cautious, continues: "What we know of contemporary reference to *Mother Hubberds Tale* suggests that the particular political targets of the allegory were obscure even when it was published" (*YSP*, 327). Burghley, the least obscure of the targets for modern observers, was apparently not at all obscure for one early observer. We call attention to one additional marking of the poem. Lines 891 to 919, characterized by Greenlaw as "the bitter passage on suitors' delays,"[8] are set as a verse paragraph in the 1617 Folio. They are called to attention by a broken vertical line; within the break is written the word "sutors" (with the "t" not crossed). It is worth noting that Jonson spelled "sute" or "sutor" about as often without the "i" as with it.

In "The Ruines of Time," evidence of Jonson's reading appears in two forms: 1) in Jonsonian echoes of this poem in his own work; and 2) in specific marks and annotations in Jonson's copy of the 1617 Folio. In "The Ruines of Time," there are markings in ink and, much less frequently, in pencil (fig. 11); the flower to the right of the second stanza in column 1 and the flowers and lines at the left of the last four stanzas in column 1 are in ink; all of the other markings (in the bottom half of the page, both column 1 and column 2) are in pencil, which leads one to believe that Jonson marked certain parts of this poem, as well as others in the volume, at least twice. Where ink and pencil marks coincide, again, the ink appears to be on top of the pencil.[9] "The Ruines of Time" merits special illustrative treatment for two reasons. First, it is one of Spenser's minor works, and therefore scholars may find the annotations surprising and even illuminating with respect to Spenser's perceived poetic purpose. Second (setting Spenser's impact on Milton aside for the moment), if the issue is how Spenser's work was read in its own time, then Jonson's perspective—or even Digby's, for that matter (we return to this question in detail in chapter 4)—must be of more immediate concern than Jortin's, whose perspective tells us more about the interest of a contemporary of Dr. Johnson in Spenser's "sources" and in his grammatical "correctness" (or lack of it) than about the way Renaissance readers responded to Spenser's poetry.[10]

   In 1985, Timothy Cook reviewed remarks of Ian Donaldson and G. A. E. Parfitt concerning the "major source" of the Cary/Morison ode, namely, "Seneca's consolatory 113th Epistle."[11] As Cook points out, Jonson's echo of the description of the "Stirrer," whose auspicious beginning in no way presaged his later, stifling growth, bears the unmistakable traces, also, of "The Ruines of Time":

> Hee entred well, by vertuous parts,
> Got up and thriv'd with honest arts.
>
> (*Und* 70, lines 33–34; H&S 7:244)

The idea is that the Stirrer's early promise—his "vertuous parts"—in fact preceded uncontrolled development, a protracted longevity unallayed by ethical or artistic improvement:

> It is not growing like a tree
> In bulke, doth make man better bee;
> Or standing long an Oake, three hundred yeare,

To fall a logge at last, dry, bald, and seare:
A Lillie of a Day,
Is fairer farre, in May,
Although it fall, and die that night;
It was the Plant, and flowre of light.
In small proportions, we just beautie see:
And in short measures, life may perfect bee.

(lines 65–74)

Cook acknowledges the way Jonson employs the outlook of Seneca's consoler in Epistle 113, but he finds the echo from Spenser's "The Ruines of Time" to be an important element as well:

O griefe of griefes! ô gall of all good harts!
To see that vertue should dispised bee
Of such as first were raisd for vertuous parts,
And now broad spreading, like an aged tree,
Let none shoote up that nigh them planted bee.

(lines 449–53)

Here, as Cook rightly suggests, Jonson echoes Spenser's locution, "vertuous parts," in an comparable effort to stress the devolution of a talented individual from promising youth to disappointing age.

Even more than Seneca, whose influence on the Cary/Morison ode has always seemed obvious to critics, Spenser provides Jonson with the vehicle to elicit a sense of bitter irony. For Jonson, "The Ruines of Time" provides a thematic link between the premature demise of the "Brave Infant" and the fate of poets in a hostile world. With Seneca, length of life presents a philosophical issue. Jonson's poem not only extends Seneca's argument to its powerful and logical (if absurd) conclusion, but it also draws on Spenser's set-piece to drive the theme of monstrous horror home with a poetic corollary. For in a world dominated by corrupt leaders, the young are not given the chance to achieve wisdom, which, for

Seneca, is the *sine qua non* of the perfect life. For him, wisdom, not duration, renders life valuable and opens the way to perfection.

Thus, the Cary/Morison ode gives a wry answer to Seneca, who advises Lucilius that quality, not length, of life is what counts. Since life is valuable only insofar as one learns wisdom, so the "Brave Infant of *Saguntum*" (line 1) is the "Wise child" (line 7), wise because, having recognized the intolerable conditions of prolonged existence, he chooses to cut life short at birth, and by this choice achieves the end and perfection of life: "How summ'd a circle didst thou leave man-kind / Of deepest lore, could we the Center find!" (lines 9–10). Addressing the child whose brief life foreshadows the case of "*Morison*," the speaker affirms the Infant's brief span as a monstrous effect of Hannibal's horrific assault, and the event that made Saguntum an "immortall Towne" (line 4).

Jonson opens his "Ode" to "immortall memorie" of a friendship cut short by pursuing Seneca's argument to its logical conclusion. If the end of life is wisdom, and if wisdom lies in recognizing the intractable horror of one's circumstance, then, supposing that such recognition comprehends the totality of wisdom, the shortest life is also the most nearly perfect. For, Seneca argued (and Jonson agrees), once wisdom has been achieved, the soul can no longer improve, but only diminish itself by repetition. And since change perforce entails departure from wisdom, therefore, prolongation of life inclines toward imperfection. Since repetition vitiates the quality of life, it follows, too, once wisdom has been perfected, that longevity diminishes the value of life. In the case of the "Brave Infant of *Saguntum*," wisdom and birth temporally coincide. Wisdom advises the "Wise child" to quit life, which he does, and by so doing, he adds all that is required for the perfect circle by subtracting whatever is extraneous to wisdom, namely, length of life beyond the moment of illumination. The poet does the computation by excluding the unwise ("could we the Center find"). The center is equidistant from all points on the circumference, which the poet imagines as an imploding sphere. When the extraneous lengths of radii are eliminated, only the essential perfection remains: wisdom minus pernicious repetition of longevity.

Cook also notes the analogous "Februarie" Eclogue, with its allegory of the briar striving against the "Aged Tree." But Jonson's echo of the stanza from "The Ruines of Time" explicitly links Jonson with Cary, who, like Spenser and Jonson, sought to commemorate a fallen warrior and talented friend. In both poems, the survivor has lost more than a friend. English poetry also suffers a significant loss, which, because both are poets, intensifies the survivors' shared grief. And, since Cary can be expected to write an elegy for Morison, too, the speaking poet is united with his audience in grief, just as his auditory was united with the fallen hero in friendship. Jonson's echo of Spenser reminds his reader of the recurring motif of friendships and poetic interests as private values. As S. K. Heninger has recently argued, in the case of Spenser, this poetic connection existed even in the absence of close acquaintance:[12] "Sidney was the cynosure of his generation" (11), and Spenser's love for and admiration of Sidney became a shaping force in his work. Thus, these elegists celebrate real or imagined friendship between poets: Spenser/Sidney, Cary/Morison, Jonson/Morison. The connection between the two poems concerns the poignancy of their speakers' relation to the surviving poet, who remains to endure the "whips and scorns" of a doltish world: "O! let not those, of whom the Muse is scorned, / Alive nor dead, be of the Muse adorned" (lines 454–55).[13] For now Jonson joins with Cary in grief, not only as a grieving friend, but also as a poet aware that the craft of poetry has been weakened by the loss of a potential contributor to the art.

As a glance at figure 12 shows, Cook's literary instincts are good. Jonson marks four of the five lines that Cook finds echoed in the Cary/Morison ode (note the lines beneath the exclamation mark of line 1, and the three parallel marks below lines 2, 3 and 4). Further, his attention to this stanza fits with similar marks and annotations to the preceding and following stanzas. Jonson brackets the stanza beginning with line 442, underlining the ends of lines 1 through 3 (just as he does in the succeeding stanza), with the bracket suggesting that the comment ("Salomon was greived w<ith> this consideration") applies to the entire stanza:

> These two be those two great calamities,
> That long agoe did grieve the noble spright
> Of SALOMON, with great indignities;
> Who whilome was alive the wisest wight.
> But now his wisedome is disproved quight:
> For, such as now have most the World at will,
> Scorne th'one and th'other in their deeper skill.
>
> (442–48)

Here, Jonson may have remembered the 1591 version of the two stanzas,[14] which pointedly single Burghley out for his heavy-handed abuse of power ("For he that now welds all things at his will" [line 447]); and he finds the perfect analogue to Morison as a victim of the social order. The *Variorum* points to Ecclesiasticus 26.29:

> There be two things that grieve mine heart, and the thirde maketh me angrie: a man of warre that suffreth povertie: and men of understanding that are not set by: and when one departeth from righteousnes unto sinne: the Lord appointeth suche to the sworde. (Geneva Bible)

Solomon, "who whilome was alive the wisest wight," bitterly observed that the world as he found it represented "two great calamities." Wisdom taught that too often in the world "men of understanding" went unnoticed and powerless; and in the world of politics a correlative paradox obtained: the state rewards the brave soldier by arranging his irrevocable descent into poverty. In Jonson's copy of the 1617 Folio, the topical reference is transformed from the more specific indictment of Burghley. But, Jonson's remark suggests, it is the thought—"this consideration" itself—that grieves. Solomon's perspective on the whole of life is like that of the "Brave Infant of *Saguntum*." For even though Verlame designates a class of men rather than Burghley as the historic instantiation of this vice, the effect is the same: "men of Armes doe wander unrewarded" (441). Jonson appreciates Spenser's bittersweet tone, as the spirit of Verulam turns from recalling Watson's commemoration of Walsingham ("that hath a Poet got") to Leicester's case. Done in by Burghley (at least from this speaker's point of view), Leicester is an example of the mistreatment of virtue in the world. And yet Spenser, Jonson, and Cary remain to reinforce the truth of Scripture, by understanding and grieving as Solomon had before them.

To Jonson, not only is Cary's funeral elegy "On Dr. Donne" impressive, but Cary remains behind as both a friend and a poet, who, like Jonson, remembers as only friends who are poets can: by public, poetic commemoration. Hence, as Jonson's poet prepares to apotheosize Morison, he also crowns his younger peer, Cary, with the garland reserved only for the gifted and dedicated of their kind:

> Call, noble *Lucius*, then for Wine,
> And let thy lookes with gladnesse shine:
> Accept this garland, plant it on thy head,
> And thinke, nay know, thy *Morison's* not dead.
> Hee leap'd the present age,
> Possesst with holy rage,
> To see that bright eternall Day:
> Of which we *Priests*, and *Poëts* say
> Such truths, as we expect for happy men,
> And there he lives with memorie; and *Ben* . . .
>
> (75–84)

Jonson, speaking *in propria persona*, implies that he and his understanding audience belong to a fraternity of *"Priests,* and *Poëts."* It is in this peculiar relationship that Jonson finds his answer to Seneca: a poetic rather than a philosophic counterpart to the Senecan insight of the preceding *"Turne,"* in which the speaker grapples with the age-old agony of survivors who witness the death of the very young. It is one thing to concede that length of life is not an intrinsic value, but quite another to know how the very brief life attains any value at all, much less the *summum bonum.* In Morison's life—that perfection of human character that is a necessary requisite to the writing of poetry—Jonson's poet finds consolation for himself and Cary: "For, if men will impartially, and not à-squint, looke toward the offices, and function of a Poet, they will easily conclude to themselves, the impossibility of any mans being the good Poet, without first being a good man" (H&S 5:17).

Perhaps more salient than the notion of Cary's being a poet is that of Morison's being one. Opinions about Morison as a poet are varied, even contradictory, at least insofar as modern commentators are concerned. In 1938 Kenneth B. Murdock published from a manuscript in the Harvard College Library "An Elegie on the death of my dearest (and allmost only) friend Syr Henry Moryson."[15] Here, Cary seems to praise Morison for his accomplishments as a poet:

> Dun did feare (more then feare, for he did know it)
> That he [Morison] was like to arise the maister poet,
> And though he was so admired in his time,
> T'would scarce a loude be shortly he did rime.
>   (Murdock, "Elegie," lines 217–20)

Murdock writes: "The reference here is clearly to John Donne, and the suggestion is that he [Donne] knew something of Morison's poetry, which was so good that Donne feared for his own laurels and reputation in the future" (Murdock, 38n). Although this statement seems plausible enough, it does entail difficulty when we try to reconcile the passage with another in which Cary discusses Morison as a poet. A year or two after Morison's death, Cary wrote an anniversary poem, in which he praises Morison by claiming him to be the youthful epitome of poetry itself: "Hee was a living Epick Poëme, soe / leading us on, to what we did not knowe."[16] Morison is situated in contrast to those who scorn what they cannot understand, who

> hate all Antiquitie, for they not knowe
> Whether the Talmud be a towne, or noe.
> 'Count Poëtrie, worse, then any Cross-rung Chime:
> because they never could arrive at Rime.
> (Weber, 283–84)

But then, in the next line, we are told: "Hee [Morison] lov'd, yet made no verse" (284). This could be construed to mean that Morison wrote no love poetry, but probably Weber is right in saying that Morison attempted no verse at all (Weber, 48). In this context, Cary's praise of Morison unfolds in a series of exclusions. Morison wrote no poetry: "Neither was hee, / One of those Puritanes in Poësie / that scorne the Fathers" (284). Cary's point seems to be that Morison was not the kind of poet who rushes to express indecorous personal or religious feelings. Rather, he had internalized the values of Virgil in such a way as to become "no more his Reader, but his booke!" When the Jonson and Cary passages are taken together, it is clear that the point of the earlier passage is that Donne could discern in Morison the idea of the poet, one who "shortly" would rime, would "arise the maister poet." Morison, it seems, was in the matter of his unfulfilled, indeed unattempted, poetic creation very much like the "Brave Infant of *Saguntum*." Neither the verse of the one nor the existence of the other was weighed, so neither could be found wanting.

In his extensive and learned analysis of the Cary/
Morison ode, where he argues that the prodigy's circle of
life "is a grotesquely inadequate extreme, and not the
conventional symbol of perfection," Richard S. Peterson
sees in the ode a working out of grief and stoic reconciliation through "the turn or transformation of circumstances that Jonson celebrates in the poem."[17] Peterson
contends that the "Infant" is "really neither 'brave' nor
'wise,'" in part because his rejection of life "would
scarcely be manly" (205). Aside from the curious notion
that an infant should be manly, this reading requires that
"brave" mean "courageous"; however, Jonson most often
uses the word, either straight-forwardly or ironically, in a
sense noticed by Dr. Johnson: "it is an indeterminate
word, used to express the superabundance of any valuable quality in men or things." We suggest that this definition is the relevant one. The extraordinary "Infant" is
contrasted with the "Prodigious [monstrous, truly gro-
tesque] Hannibal"; the "wise" (not only having good
sense, but 'skilled in magic or hidden arts' [*OED*] child"
has left the living, if they could but find the center, "a
summ'd circle ... of deepest lore." The ideas of the perfect life and of poetry, with their profoundly moral implications, are the legacies of the too-brief lives of the "Infant" and of Morison.[18]

Not only are the two youths alike in their wisdom, but
they are also alike in their effect as individuals on the
world:

> Death to eternity hath helpt a towne
> Had else beene buried in oblivion;
> I see that from the smallest townes doe spring
> My gretest good hap, and gretest sorrowinge:
> Our Saviour at thach't Bethlehem borne is,
> Whoe is both mine and the world's generall bliss,
> And at Carmarthan, full as poorely built,
> My joyes are irramediably spilt

By looseinge thee. Now't may be esily showne
Carmarthan will as long as Troy be knowen
With out blind Homer's helpe; when every stone
Is gon, the memory will not be gonn.

("Elegie," 275–86)

Like Christ, who immortalized the town of Bethlehem, and like the "Brave Infant of *Saguntum*," Morison bestows eternal fame on a small town, which will be remembered for only one thing: the spectacular demise of a very young paragon of virtue. Thus, Cary's aside on literary history asserts much more than it takes away. Carmarthan needs no blind poet to write an epic about Morison, for it has an elegist who has seen that his friend and poetic subject embodied the very essence of poetry. Thus, Morison is the perfect man ("His life was of Humanitie the Spheare"), and part of that perfection lies in the fact that he had, like the Lord and Lady of Penshurst, mastered "The mysteries of manners, armes and arts" (H&S 8:96). Like Jonson and Cary, he was—if only in the poetic imagination of those who carry on the tradition—a poet, perfected by "first being a good man," albeit one who was cut off before he could deliver on that literary promise.[19]

It is worth noting here that Jonson's markings in another volume shed light on the vexed question concerning Jonson's well-known headings for the three parts of the Cary/Morison ode, which are *"Turne," "Counterturne"* and *"Stand."* Richard Peterson discusses the terms, and, following Carol Maddison, notes the precedent for them in Minturno's *volta*, *rivolta* and *stanza*, headings in his odes in Italian on Charles V's conquest of Tunis;[20] in his very useful edition of Jonson's poems, Ian Donaldson unaccountably gives the Italian terms to J. C. Scaliger.[21] There is, however, another source that needs to be considered, not for headings of parts of the ode, but, rather, for an association of terms. Jonson's copy of

George Puttenham's *The Arte of English Poesie* (1589), now in the British Library,[22] bears a number of Jonson's markings in the first few pages and, more sparsely, other markings scattered throughout. On signature Z1, a typical Jonsonian flower is set against Puttenham's final example of "Anaphora" (repetition of words at the beginnings of lines of verse). Just below this begins Puttenham's discussion of "Antistrophe." Now, this "antistrophe" has nothing to do with the stanzaic pattern of the ode, but rather, like "anaphora," with the repetition of words in lines of verse. Puttenham says of it: "Ye have another sort of repetition quite contrary to the former [i. e., anaphora] where ye make one word finish many verses in sute, and that which is harder, to finish many clauses in the middest of your verses" (in fact, Puttenham's examples illustrate only the latter). In the margin next to the beginning of Puttenham's explanation—that is, immediately below Jonson's flower—is the note *"Antistrophe*, or the Counterturne." Even though "Counterturne" has nothing to do with the ode and even though Puttenham doesn't mention either "Turne" or "Stand," "Counterturne" as a translation is striking. There are, of course, many possible translations of either *antistrophe* or *rivolta*. If Jonson had Puttenham's in mind, "Turne" would be the only sensible translation for *volta*. And that Jonson did have Puttenham's Englishing of antistrophe in mind seems at least likely, for we know that Jonson's eye rested on the page where it occurs.

Turning now from Jonsonian echoes of "The Ruines of Time" in the Cary/Morison ode to evidence of his actual reading of that poem, we note that Jonson's markings on the text are of three kinds: underlinings, devices in the margins (flowers, lines, brackets, etc.) and annotations. For instance, we know now that these stanzas on Sidney drew Jonson's special attention:

> Most gentle spirit breathed from above,
> Out of the bosome of the makers blis,
> In whom all bountie and all vertuous love

Appeared in their native properties,
And did enrich that noble breast of his,
With treasure passing all this worldes worth,
Worthy of heaven it selfe, which brought it forth.

His blessed spirit, full of power divine,
And influence of all celestiall grace,
Loathing this sinfull earth and earthly slime,
Fled backe too soone unto his native place;
Too soone for all that did his love embrace,
Too soone for all this wretched world, whom he
Robd of all right and true nobilitie.

(lines 281–94)

We know these lines arrested his attention because, as we see in figure 13, Jonson marks, brackets and underlines parts of the stanzas, and then, in the left-hand margin, inscribes one of his typical flowers. In the context of our previous discussion, Jonson's focus on the connection between the poet's virtue and talent is evident here. Further, Spenser remembers Sidney's youth. The poet's death at an early age returned a noble spirit to its original abiding place in heaven. Thus, Jonson marks two lines of a stanza, as the poet addresses Sidney's departed spirit: "O noble spirit, live there ever blessed, / The worlds late wonder, and the heavens new joy" (lines 302–03).

Spenser's stanzas on Sidney begin the section of the poem which, it appears, were the most important to Jonson. These are the stanzas that affirm the value of poetry. As we see in the markings to the texts in the right-hand column (fig. 13), Jonson brackets and/or comments on five stanzas, which imagine Sidney as a divine Orpheus, accompanied in the afterlife with his brother, singing "their heavenly layes" (line 335):

So there thou livest, singing evermore,
And here thou livest, beeing ever song
Of us, which living, loved thee afore,
And now thee worship, mongst that blessed throng

Of heavenly Poets, and Heroës strong.
So thou both here and there immortall art,
And everie where through excellent desart.

But such as neither of themselves can sing,
Nor yet are sung of others for reward,
Die in obscure oblivion, as the thing
Which never was; ne ever with regard,
Their names shall of the later age be heard,
But shall in rustie darknes ever lie,
Unlesse they mentioned be with infamie.

What booteth it to have beene rich alive?
What to be great? what to be gracious?
When after death no token doth survive,
Of former beeing in this mortall hous,
But sleepes in dust dead and inglorious,
Like beast, whose breath but in his nostrils is,
And hath no hope of happinesse or blis.

How many great ones may remembred be,
Which in their daies most famously did florish:
Of whom no word we heare, nor signe now see,
But as things wipt out with a spunge do perish,
Because they living, cared not to cherish
No gentle wits, through pride or covetize,
Which might their names for ever memorize.

Provide therefore (ye Princes) whilst ye live,
That of the Muses ye may friended bee;
Which unto men eternitie doe give:
For they be daughters of Dame Memorie,
And JOVE, the Father of eternitie,
And doe those men in golden thrones repose,
Whose merits they to glorifie doe chose.

(lines 337–71)

Notice the close attention evident here, with markings
to both the left and right of the column. Not only does

Jonson bracket four of the five stanzas, but in two instances, he double-brackets lines. And his critical remarks in the margin make abundantly clear what poetic motif the reader perceives Spenser's text to emphasize:

> the immortality of vertue;
> oblivion is the rewarde of the vitious;
> the eternity of the Muses.

We know that, for Jonson, "The Ruines of Time" stands out among the poems in *Complaints*. But within "The Ruines of Time" these stanzas in particular affirm that virtue is a contingent value. As Jonson reads Spenser, without the poet, virtue dies "in obscure oblivion." And Jonson comments that "oblivion is the rewarde of the vitious." But the vicious and the virtuous are alike in one respect: both are subject to the depredation of Time. So what difference does one's ethical character make in the scheme of things? Spenser's lines suggest an answer in the stanza Jonson notes with a double-bracket. Great ones, even those who are "gracious," are no more than signs easily erased by a sponge, unless they take care to encourage the sole source of "the immortality of vertue," namely, the "gentle wits . . . / Which might their names for ever memorize" (lines 363–64).

The shift of Spenser's speaker to the imperative mode has been neatly prepared. If they know how to evade ruin, then enlightened princes will act in their own interest. Poetry is the divine vehicle of eternal memory, the means by which those who merit glory are glorified. Hence, patronage is more than an act of self-interest; it is also the means by which poets, who follow descendants of Jove and of Mnemosyne, are enabled to extend the gift of "eternitie."

Jonson proceeds to mark several succeeding stanzas which, likewise, delineate the power of poetry:

For deeds doe die, how ever noblie donne,
And thoughts of men doe in themselves decay:
But wise words taught in numbers for to runne,
Recorded by the Muses, live for aye;
Ne may with storming showers be washt away,
Ne bitter breathing winds with harmfull blast,
Nor age, nor envie shall them ever wast.

(lines 400–06)

In figure 12, we see that Jonson brackets the stanzas, writing: "verses eternise the vertuous." So, again, Jonson emphasizes Spenser's theme of virtue's dependence upon poetry for life. Similarly, further down in the same column, Jonson read these lines with special interest:

For not to have been dipt in LETHE lake,
Could save the sonne of THETIS from to die;
But that blind Bard did him immortall make,
With verses, dipt in deaw of CASTALIE:
Which made the Easterne Conqueror to crie,
O fortunate young man whose vertue found
So brave a Trompe, thy noble acts to sound.

(lines 428–34)

Spenser's speaker continues his praise of poetry, affirming that, although Thetis failed in her attempt to place her son beyond the ruin of time, Homer, whose lines were "dipt in deaw of CASTALIE," succeeded in making Achilles immortal. The stanza prompts Jonson to pen a response with brackets and a comment: "Achilles eternised by Homer: and for that envie'd by Alexander." Modern editors refer the reader to E. K.'s gloss to the October Eclogue for another example of the observation (*YSP*, 251; *Var*). As Jonson also marked a portion of that passage in his copy of Spenser's works, the connections between Spenser's ideas and Jonson's become ever more clear. For instance, Jonson also marks in the gloss the next line that E. K. explicates: "[Spenser] sheweth the cause of contempt of Poetrie to be idlenesse and base-nesse of mind" (*YSP*, 181). Thus, the part of the poet in immortalizing Achilles is just that claimed for himself by Jonson in the Cary/Morison ode, and pervasive contempt for poetry by the ignorant seems to be as inevitable and perhaps as necessary to the immortalizing power of poetry as is the poet himself.

These stanzas on poetry that so much interest Jonson suggest a tension between the poet and the world, especially the world of "great ones," who ignore the gentle, talented voices of eternity in their midst. It is not surprising that Jonson also makes special note of the stanzas that follow. Although Walsingham ("Good MELIBAE" [line 436]) has been remembered for having done service to poetry and learning while he lived, the poet's indignation toward powerful but ungenerous contemporaries of Walsingham suggests that they deserve a different fate: "These two be those two great calamities." Clearly, Verlame is moving now to represent her ruin by Time as a diatribe against still living political corruptors, who make life difficult for those surviving poets who have not yet earned the apotheosis given Sidney. Jonson may or may not have thought of Burghley (though, if indeed the markings to this poem are Jonson's,[23] we do know that he catches the allusion to him in "Mother Hubberds Tale"), but he notes the development of Spenser's theme of contrast between the spirit of poetry and that of the sublunary world of politics. We have already discussed the two stanzas revised before inclusion in the Folio of 1611, which precede the speaker's renunciation of the world:

> O vile worlds trust, that with such vaine illusion,
> Hath so wise men bewitcht, and overkest,
> That they see not the way of their confusion:
> O vainenesse to be added to the rest,
> That doth my soule with inward griefe infest.

Lct them behold the pitious fall of mee,
And in my case their owne ensample see.

(lines 456–62)

Here, Jonson comments: "the Inconstancy of this worlds Felicity." That is, Jonson construes Spenser's text as amplifying the theme of poetry's ultimate sway over time, which victimizes even unassisted moral virtue—that is, virtue unattended by the Muses. Walsingham, with all his accomplishments, required the service of a poet (Thomas Watson) to be transformed into transcendent substance: "But," Watson's speaker affirms, drawing on the same figure that Spenser would employ, "neither are his [Walsingham's] vertues drenchd in *Leath*,"[24] and this because of the poet's good offices. Further, although poetry immortalizes the worthy, not all celebrants of virtue are equally graced by the Muses. For it is Spenser who renders both Walsingham and Watson immortal, as the poetry celebrates poetry celebrating virtue; and, while doing so, Jonson's notations emphasize, he also suggests that even "Felicity" is not the sure reward of earnest service to the kingdom. Virtue needs great poetry to conquer time.[25]

Thus, in Spenser, Verlame presents herself as an emblem of a "pitious fall," one in which the "ensample" of even "wise men" may be seen. We cannot be certain Jonson noted the earlier, explicit reference to Burghley. But he does notice the connection between the grief of Solomon and the destiny of supposedly "wise men" of his and every time. Without the poet to remember them, even the greatest—even the most virtuous—simply vanish.

Analysis of Ben Jonson's annotations to the 1617 version of "The Ruines of Time," in view of his markings to the other *Complaints*, suggests that he read Spenser's text very closely, and read it more than once. Rather than indicating reservations about its stanzaic form,

Jonson's markings exhibit his strong interest in the poetics represented. Jonson read "The Ruines of Time" as a coherent defense of poesy. We find no evidence here of any perception of the disjointedness argued by modern critics.[26] The apotheosis of Sidney was, for Jonson, consistent with the implicit comparison between Spenser and Thomas Watson. Here, the test of Walsingham's memory to withstand the assault of Time depends entirely on the greatness of the poet who celebrates the principal's virtue: the author of *"Meliboeus"* contra the poet of "The Ruines of Time." But the rhetorical drift implied by Jonson's reading does not, finally, pit poet against poet. Rather, the objects of Verlame's ire are the powerful to whom all practitioners of the art must look for sustenance. But, by an act of poetic legerdemain, Jonson and Spenser turn the tables on their aristocratic masters, either giving or withholding the substance of survival in the afterlife of the world's memory. Patrons of poetry and heroic defenders of the bastions of England are one and the same. Richard Helgerson and others have shown that Jonson and Spenser present themselves as poet laureates.[27] Our interpretation suggests that, as such, Jonson's reading of "The Ruines of Time" perceives its poet laureate as a heroic defender of the nation, praising the qualities of leadership on which the preservation of England depends.

A reading of "The Ruines of Time" in the context of Jonson's annotations requires renewed attention to Jonson's echo of that poem in his Cary/Morison ode. For Jonson, the two poems are apposite representations of the ultimate place of poetry in relation to a society that nurtures or fails to nurture poets. Those who are politically powerful control immediate circumstances, and so have an impact on Seneca's question of whether, ideally, the poet's life should be usefully long or mercifully short. But, in the end, the poetry that governs the fate of reputations lies beyond the reach of secular power, in the "eternising" favor of the Muses. Jonson's reading of "The Ruines of Time" can be traced in his own marks and comments on Spenser's poem; even more important, the uses he makes of his reading can be traced in his Pindaric ode "To the immortall memorie, and friendship of that noble paire, Sir *Lucius Cary* and Sir H. Morison."

3

Jonson Reads
The Faerie Queene

Yet I would have him read for his matter; but as *Virgil* read *Ennius*.

Discoveries

I n the preceding pages we examined some recent Spenser criticism and considered evidence of Jonson's opinion of Spenser as represented in his criticism, poetry, plays, masques, entertainments, and in his poetic and critical responses to "The Ruines of Time." This focus on Jonson's responses to the minor works of Spenser should suggest an alternative to the predominant opinions of Jonson's judgment of Spenser. Yet, any account of Jonson's critique of Spenser that did not consider his reaction to *The Faerie Queene* would probably, and justifiably, be thought incomplete. Remove *The Faerie Queene* from the annals, and the Spenser canon would look very different, as indeed would the English literary tradition. If we may believe Camille Paglia (whose commentary is not everywhere marked by understatement), "English literary distinction begins in the Renaissance and is the creation of one man, Edmund Spenser."[1] And here Paglia refers to Spenser's *magnum opus*: "His epic poem, *The Faerie Queene* (1590, 1596), does for the English Renaissance what painting and sculpture did for the Italian" (170). Paglia thinks that Spenser criticism is largely misdirected from its "Apollonian brilliance" (171), which derives from an original treatment of sex and aggression, but moves away from the work's "mystic hieraticism of power latent in western sexual personae" toward a bland and obtuse moralism. When Milton referred to his famous predecessor as "our sage and serious poet *Spencer*,"[2] he was reading *The Faerie Queene* much as critics like Ronald Horton do today. Horton argues that the structural principle of the poem cannot be separated from the work's ethical perspective: "The price of understanding *The Faerie Queene* is to take seriously the moral allegory."[3]

Paglia's rhetoric, although refreshing (eccentric? ideologically bent?), is as much at odds with Spenser's aims (set out in the Letter to Ralegh) as it is with Jonson's understanding of those aims. In fact, as we shall see, Jonson's contemporary reactions to *The Faerie Queene* are not far from Milton's. Milton characterized Spenser not as the progenitor of a great national epic (although he probably regarded him as having been so), but as a model "teacher" "better [than] ... *Scotus* or *Aquinas*." Milton was thinking not only of the literary heritage he shared with his mid-century readers, but of the way in which he, they and Spenser formed a corporate body of Protestant resolve against such texts and understandings as might encourage the new licensing law. Milton conceives of Spenser as the great English poet and teacher who created, in the Cave of Mammon and Acrasia's

Bower episodes, memorable scenes of "sage and serious" ethical instruction.

So we turn to Jonson's reading of *The Faerie Queene*, having earlier touched on negative opinions ascribed to Jonson by Herford and Simpson and many critics since them. According to these critics, Jonson did not like its allegorical features. He did not like its stanzaic form. He disliked its "cross rhymes" so much that he designed his own poetic style in reaction to such Spenserian excesses. Furthermore, like Donne, Jonson turned away from Spenser's meter and verse narrative, but while Donne reacted against the Petrarchism of predecessors—including Spenser—Jonson went a step further, rejecting love poetry as well. Hence, the first poem in *The Forrest*, "Why I write not of Love," appears as a manifesto of and prelude to a volume of verse liberated from the limitations of contemporaries by a reversal: he would "binde" Love, who has bound other poets "to reherse" the same old theme with its limited cast of characters and predictable situations.

As we have already seen, the cleavage between Jonson and Spenserian poetic practice is not so neat and clean. Even Jonson's repudiation of love is not so simple a matter. At one time, for instance, as he was reading through "The Teares of the Muses," Jonson penciled, with flowers and vertical lines, these two stanzas from the section "Erato":

> Love wont to be schoole-master of my skill,
> And the divicefull matter of my song;
> Sweete Love devoyd of villanie or ill,
> But pure and spotlesse, as at first he sprong
> Out of th'Almighties bosome where he nests;
> From thence infused into mortall brests.
>
> Such high conceit of that celestiall fire,
> The base-borne brood of blindnes cannot ghesse,
> Ne ever dare their dunghill thoughts aspire
> Unto so loftie pitch of perfectnesse,

> But rime at riot, and doe rage in love;
> Yet little wote what doth thereto behove.

(lines 385–96)

It would seem, if anything, that Jonson is struck by Spenser's admiration of Love's power. Indeed, insofar as these two stanzas interested him, they did so, not for their repudiation of love, not even for their ambivalent attitude toward it, but for their typically Spenserian recognition of the divine power of this strong and sometimes unruly human emotion.

Similarly, Claude J. Summers and Ted-Larry Pebworth sensibly point out, in fact, that rather than expressing persistent hostility to love as a poetic subject, Jonson repudiates the love motif only in rhetorical flourishes. Even then, as in "Why I write not of Love," while supposedly rejecting love as a theme for writing, Jonson makes love his subject. Besides, as Summers and Pebworth remind us, Jonson "actually writes of erotic love fairly often and most movingly about failed love, as in the witty but poignant 'My Picture Left in Scotland.'"[4] Summers and Pebworth rightly single out this eminently Jonsonian *jeu d'esprit*, for here the poet, at his own expense, wittily registers doubt that Love is so much blind as deaf—rendered so by more than a slight glimpse of his physical features: "My mountaine belly, and my rockie face, / And all these through her eyes, have stopt her eares" (*Und* 9, lines 17–18).

With the discovery of Jonson's own, copiously annotated copy of the 1617 Folio of *The Faerie Queen: The Shepheards Calendar: Together with the other Works of England's Arch-Poët, Edm. Spenser,*[5] we now have hard evidence of Jonson's immediate reactions to Spenser's *magnum opus*, and to many of his minor works as well, and can better address Jonson's views. This new evidence justifies a careful reexamination of many of the assumptions of traditional literary history of the period—those, for instance, concerning a split between poets at the turn of the century along Spenserian/Jonsonian lines.

The range of Jonson's markings in the 1617 Spenser Folio is rather broad, extending from factual observation to allegorical interpretation, some of the more elaborate of which are illustrated in this study. A commentary that augments Spenser's allegory, as in 2.12.3–4 ("gulfe of gredinesse" and "Rocke of prodigallity"), is discussed later in this chapter (see 97–98); some of Jonson's "acknowledged" conjectures about Spenser's description, as in 2.9.21, "By this I conceiv he [Spenser] meanethe the skinne of the Body of man," as well as that which otherwise dilates upon Spenser's observation are discussed at length in chapter 4.

Before turning to other kinds of Jonson's commentaries in *The Faerie Queene*—not fully to describe them, but, for the most part, simply to give examples of them— we wish first to discuss those markings we have characterized as "notations" ("identifications" and "figures"), here divided into three categories. First, one- or two-word (noun phrases, etc.) descriptions: these are virtually the only kinds of marks in book 1; they continue throughout *The Faerie Queene*. Second, descriptions in which Jonson uses the word "simile":[6] these appear in the first three books of *The Faerie Queene*, mostly (13 out of 14 examples) in books 1 and 2. Third, descriptions in which Jonson uses the word "description":[7] these appear in books 2, 3 and 4 of *The Faerie Queene*, mostly (14 of 18 examples) in book 2. In the cases of both "simile" and "description," Jonson sometimes modifies his key term with the word "excellent." For instance, in book 2, canto 3, Spenser describes the consort of Sans-loy:

> As fearefull fowle, that long in secret Cave,
> > For dread of soaring hauke herselfe hath hid,
> > Not caring how, her silly life to save,
> > She her gay painted plumes disorderid,
> > Seeing at last herselfe from danger rid,
> > Peepes forth, and soone renewes her native pride;

> She gins her feathers foule disfigured
> Proudly to prune, and set on every side,
> So shakes off shame, ne thinks how erst shee did
> her hide.
> (1617 Folio, *FQ* 2.3.36)

In the margin Jonson writes: "An excell. Simile to expresse cowardnesse."[8] The remark does more, of course, than catalog a rhetorical trope; it also ventures an evaluation, given the subject, of its propriety.

With one exception,[9] when Jonson uses the word "excellent," he has marked off large passages, from one to four stanzas. Also, we note that "simile" is qualified by "excellent" only in those passages where the simile could be called an epic simile. It seems that Jonson, under some circumstances at least, had no particular objection to copiousness. When Herford and Simpson declare that "the splendid torso of the *Faerie Queene*, . . . 'writ in no language' and in Italianate stanzas, can never have been to [Jonson's] mind" (1:10), the term "splendid torso" must refer to the bulk, the copiousness, of Spenser's achievement (as distinct from its language and its verse form). We have dealt with language and verse form elsewhere. Now, the remaining third of the Herford and Simpson assessment can be laid to rest; these markings, which Jonson could never have expected to have been of much concern to anyone but himself, suggest he must have thought that he admired even lengthy descriptive passages in *The Faerie Queene*.

Of the "factual" and other matter that Jonson noted in Spenser's text, not so much can always be made. In book 2, canto 10, for example, Jonson's marks reflect his interest in the etymology of English place names, hardly surprising for the sometime pupil of William Camden. In the margin next to stanza 6, Jonson has written: "England was first n<amed> Albion ab Alpis Rup<ertis> from the white rocks on <the> Southerne coast," and next to stanza 12: "<Cor>iueus had the west <cou>ntry assigned

him <by> Brutus. and from him <it> was called
Cornew=<all>. Debons share <was> Devonsheire and

utus had Canutium <no>w called Kent."[10]

The explications or allegorical significations of a passage are generally straightforward, and, along with précis
of the narrative, are the most common kind of markings
in book 2, as, for instance, in canto 6: "Sir Guyon carried
by the Lady Vaine deligh<t> into the Iland of plesu<re>"
(stanza 19). Or, similarly, as Jonson echoes Spenser's elu-
cidation of the allegory: "Vaine delight cha<nges> the
senses of frail<e> man into a sec<ure> carelessenesse"
(2.6.15). As these are so numerous, we give but few examples here, but do remind the reader that Jonson often
makes explicit that which Spenser has left implicit. Although book 2 is, by far, the most heavily annotated part
of *The Faerie Queene*—and for that reason alone the
most interesting—some of the most remarkable of
Jonson's annotations are to be found elsewhere, as in
book 5, when Astraea leaves Talus behind her to execute
justice, Jonson explicates: "That is Like for Li<ke>"
(5.1.12)

Closely related to such remarks are direct assertions of
allegorical interpretation: "the dainger of Fury that it
woundes it selfe" (2.4.7). One instance of this type will
be of particular importance to critics interested in book
1. Stanzas 46 and 48 of canto 11 have been the focus of
much commentary, and both of these receive attention,
not only from Jonson but from his contemporary John
Dixon, whom we mentioned in chapter 2, as well.
Clearly, the two readers find in these heavily under-
marked as well as annotated lines expression of the doc-
trinal aspect of Spenser's description:

> There grew a goodly tree him faire beside,
>   Loaden with fruit and apples rosie red,
>   As they in pure Vermilion had been dide,
>   Whereof great vertues over all were red:
>   For, happy life to all which thereon fed,

And life eke, everlasting did befall:
Great God it planted in that blessed sted
With his almighty hand, and did it call
The tree of Life, the crime of our first fathers fall.
(1617 Folio, *FQ* 1.11.46)

Dixon reiterates (*"the tree of Lyfe"*)[11] and, in the margin of the following stanza, writes: *"the garden of Eden"* and *"Adams fall"* (8). Then, in the margin of Dixon's text of stanza 48, we find an asterisk, and this remark: "a fiction of the incarnation of Christe" (9). Jonson's reaction to stanza 48 is even more telling. This is the stanza describing the liquid issuing from that tree:

From that first tree forth flow'd, as from a Well,
    A trickling streame of Balme, most soveraine
And daintie deare, which on the ground still fell,
And overflowed all the fertill Plaine,
    As it had deawed been with timely raine:
Life and long health that gracious oyntment gave;
    And deadly wounds could heale, and reare againe
The senselesse corse appointed for the Grave.
Into that same he fell: which did from deeath him save.
(1617 Folio, *FQ* 1.11.48)

At the end of line 1 of this stanza, Jonson has placed an asterisk, and in the margin a bracket extending downward. Then, he interprets the "Well," not as John Hankins does (in the sense of "Extreme Unction"),[12] but as (writing, with underlining) *The Euch<arist>*." This difference not only emphasizes the particular sacrament entailed by Jonson's reading, but is also significant for his choice of words. Then, as now, some religious sentiment insists upon a serious difference between the meaning of the "Lord's Supper" and "The Eucharist." At this point, in any case—and in marked contrast to Dixon, who makes no association with the communion table at all—Jonson thinks of a not very Protestant locution to describe Spenser's figure.

Perhaps none of Jonson's individual annotations is more interesting than his marginal remarks on the first stanza of canto 2 of book 3. This stanza marks the narrator's intrusion to protest the literary suppression of historical facts, namely, those concerning the martial feats of women:

> Here have I cause, in men just blame to find,
>> That in their proper praise too partiall be,
>> And not indifferent to woman-kind,
>> To whom, no share in armes and chevalrie
>> They doe impart, ne maken memorie
>> Of their brave gests and prowesse Martiall;
>> Scarse doe they spare to one, or two, or three,
>> Roome in their writs; yet the same writing small
> Does all their deeds deface, and dims their glories all.
>> (1617 Folio, *FQ* 3.2.1)

In the margin, Jonson writes:

> \<W>omen in former
> \<a>ges have excelld in
> \<b>old deeds of armes.
> \<S>ee. Sands Ovid.

Jonson notes that Spenser addresses differences between past and present activities of women. At one time they excelled on the battlefield. But in noting Spenser's interest here, Jonson adds an instructive imperative:"\<S>ee. Sands Ovid." But, we might ask, why Sandys's Ovid rather than any of the many Latin versions? We know that Jonson owned a copy of the complete works of Ovid (actually, a binding together of two volumes published separately at Basle and Venice),[13] so the instruction entails a particular relevance of the Sandys translation.

The answer to this question, in fact, helps establish the date of this particular entry, and, further, it tells us something about Jonson's poetic and intellectual energy in the years just preceding his death. First, Jonson refers to Sandys's translation of Ovid, so, given the context of women and war, we may justly infer that he is thinking of the *Metamorphosis* rather than of the *Heroides* or *Fasti*. Then, too, Jonson singles out one of three English translations available at the time—that is, between 1617, when Jonson's copy of the Spenser Folio was published, and the time of his death in 1637. There was, of course, the Arthur Golding translation (1565); and, in 1618, J. B[rinsley] published another version, this eight years before the first edition of Sandys's translation. But once one examines the three translations and asks, "Why Sandys?" one must focus on the particular passage in the poem that brings Ovid to Jonson's mind. If one takes Jonson's reference at face value, one must infer that what differentiates the volumes is not the translation it-self, but Sandys's commentary on Ovid's text. Further-more, since no commentary accompanied the 1626 edi-tion, and since that edition printed only Sandys's translation of the first five books, we can therefore nar-row the time span during which this particular notation could have been written. Although Sandys's translation of the whole of the *Metamorphosis* came in 1628, that edition did not have his commentary either.

Sandys's translation and his extensive critical appara-tus appeared in the handsome, illustrated Folio of 1632.[14] Jonson had a copy of this 1632 Folio in his possession. As noted by David McPherson (no. 137), this copy, a gift to Jonson from Sir Kenelm Digby, is described in H. M. Fletcher Catalogue 88 (1936). McPherson did not have space to include Fletcher's full description of the volume, one part of which bears upon the present point: "The book was acquired by me [Fletcher explains] at a sale by auction of the effects of 'King's Ford' near Colchester, sold by order of the owner, a wife of a descendant of Sir Kenelm Digby, and of the same surname." Fletcher goes on to say that the copy he is selling brings with it a let-ter, no doubt solicited by Fletcher, in which the owner regrets "that she is unable to give any further particu-lars, ... [except] 'I think however it has been in the

Digby Family (of whom Sir Kenelm Digby is an Ancestor) for a long time, though whether straight from Ben Jonson I do not know.'"[15] On the title page of the Sandys (illustrated in the Fletcher Catalogue) is Jonson's typical signature "Sum Ben: Jonsonii," followed by a Latin note in Jonson's hand saying that he received the book from his good friend Kenelm Digby. It is reasonable to assume that the gift came back to Digby himself a few years after it was given, for Digby was Jonson's literary executor, and, as such, he was in a position to acquire numerous books and papers.

Although we return to this matter in our discussion of Digby's *Observations* (chapter 4), it is important to our argument here to recognize the particular text Jonson had in mind as he entered this reference to Sandys in his copy of the 1617 Folio Spenser. Jonson was probably thinking about one of two passages in the 1632 Folio, one from book 8, the other from book 9, of the *Metamorphosis*. The latter passage, a comment on the line, "You got the golden belt of *Thermodon*"[16] (that is "*Hippolita's* rich Belt" [sig. 2P2ᵛ]), describes the "race of warlike women; who suffered no men to live among them, but such as they imployed in their drudgeries" (sig. 2P2ᵛ). It addresses the martial accomplishments of women, including their training and skill in "military exercises," which were enhanced by the searing of their right breasts "that [they] might not hinder their shooting, nor the throwing of their javelins." But this commentary on the Amazons' treatment of men would seem on its face more fitted to the Radigund episode later in book 5 of *The Faerie Queene*.

Jonson, it appears, perceives a connection between Spenser's opening stanza to canto 2 of book 3 and Sandys's commentary on the lines describing Atalanta in book 8 of the *Metamorphosis*. She is the "*Tegeaean Atalant'*, a maid / Of passing beauty" (sig. 2H4ᵛ), who, like Diana, carries "a bow well strung," and who somewhat resembles a young boy. Perhaps for this reason,

Melaegher is attracted to her, but before he can press his suit for her affections, the Caledonian boar threatens. These lines draw Sandys's attention:

> While *Pelaeus* lifts him up, a winged flight
> *Tegaea* drew, which flew as swift as sight:
> Below his eare the fixed arrow stood,
> And stain'd his bristles with a little blood.
>
> (sig. 2I1ᵛ)

Sandys comments:

> *Atalanta*, a Virago of excellent beauty, first wounded this thiefe. Nor is there any history almost, that makes mention of warlike women, who have conducted armes successefully, and fought in their owne persons. Not onely allowed off, but commaunded in *Platos* Republique [Laws]: whose opinions since not a little poetically expressed, are best apparelled in numbers.
>
> (sig. 2L2ᵛ)

Before returning to what he calls "the fable," Sandys supplies what he thinks literary tradition sorely lacks—namely, a tribute to women warriors:

> But heare we him whom men doe call divine.
> I dare affirme that martiall Discipline
> As well to women as to men pertaines.
> And now where *Saramatian* shore restraines
> The *Pontick* floods, we know a people dwell;
> Where women in bolde deedes of armes excell:
> Who mannage steedes, subdue the stubborne Bow;
> And severall use of every weapon know.
>
> (sig. 2L2ᵛ)

Here, in verse paraphrase, the poet (presumably, Sandys himself) intones the wisdom of Plato, who would impose laws to equip and train women, right along with men, to fight for their nation. Although men supply the model of the warrior, women reflect the same image of martial power. So the imperative makes sense: "Their weapons therefore let them exercise." Sandys would let women dance in armor, indeed, let them practice all the arts of search, assault, fortification and retreat. By these endeavors the state can only be doubled in strength; and, contrariwise, the alternative, "sloth and servill breeding," will be a debased and demoralized nation, and a "humane race" commensurately "poore in spirit" (sig. 2L3).

This is not to claim Ovid's text as the source of Jonson's annotation, but only to suggest that Jonson perceived a connection between Sandys's translation and *The Faerie Queene.* Jonson died in 1637, and, if our analysis is correct, these comments had to have been written during or after 1632—that is, at a time in Jonson's life marked by illness, public controversy, hard feelings and financial difficulty.[17] Jonson was reading *The Faerie Queene* with considerable diligence, and was, moreover, exercising fastidious discrimination regarding its intertextual relations, as well. By associating this stanza from Spenser with Ovid's characterization of Atalanta, and with Sandys's expansive commentary on it, Jonson demonstrates that in the first half of the seventeenth century this passage from canto 2 of book 3 was given, at least by one knowledgeable reader, what today might be called a "feminist reading"—that is, a reading that links Spenser's text to an ancient egalitarian scheme laid out in Plato's *Laws* and, to a lesser extent, in *The Republic.*

Given the current drift of Spenser criticism, this point requires special emphasis. The tendency has been for feminist critics (Camille Paglia and Philippa Berry, for instance) to assume that Spenser's feminist motifs were hidden from the view of Spenser's contemporary readers, and even from Spenser himself.[18] Yet the evidence of Jonson's annotations points in exactly the opposite direction. The misconception of critics such as Paglia and Berry emerges, we think, from their insistence on "unconscious" meanings of Spenser's texts. Critics who exhibit belief in "unconscious meanings" seem to show a

concurrent opposition to the "conscious" meanings laid
out in the Letter to Ralegh. For instance, Camille Paglia
is scornful of critics who take the document seriously. In
her account, Spenser-as-critic and his ethically oriented
critical descendants attend only to the dull and uninter-
esting conscious intention of the author: "Spenser wants
good to come out of noble action. But sexual personae
have a will of their own" (192). If Spenser failed in his
"generall end," this is not a sign of fault but of greatness.
It need not concern us that the wills of "sexual personae" are directed by critics who imagine their hidden ori-
gins to be rooted in a generic human psyche. The critical
assumption here is that Spenser's "whole intention" in
writing *The Faerie Queene* entails elements he may not
have imparted—or, rather, may not have *thought* to im-
part—in his own conception of the "generall end . . . to
fashion a gentleman." Indeed, as this argument goes,
Spenser may not even have recognized the part of the
"whole" that now emerges as the dominant value in his
efforts to include or exclude subject matter from his
"whole intention." Paglia explains why this is so: "Criticism assumes that what Spenser says is what he means.
But a poet is not always master of his own poem, for
imagination can overwhelm moral intention" (191).
Thus, Paglia insists that Spenser criticism must come to
terms with an "unspoken"—that is, psychological—di-
mension, of both authorial intent and reader inference.

Supposing we have this argument straight, we must
then ask: what author and what reader? The evidence indicates that Spenser's contemporary reader, Jonson, read
Spenser's text in much the same way that Sandys read
Ovid's *Metamorphosis*. And if this is a just inference,
then, for the two seventeenth century literary figures
(poets and critics alike), the issue of gender-based rivalry
was *not* hidden, but recognized and explicit. For Jonson,
Spenser's text—like Sandys's commentary on the passage
from Ovid—is seen to indict men for weakening the state
by refusing to recognize the martial power of women.

Indeed, Jonson seems interested in the political aspect of this passage from book 3, which purports to be about love between the sexes. We must either infer that these thematic interests were a conscious part of the linguistic system at the time, or we must single Jonson out as a contemporary reader who was blessed with the capacity to perceive unconscious meanings before the system of their decoding had been invented (in which case decoding is only another instance of encoding).

But there is, in our imperative to consult the 1632 Sandys translation of Ovid's *Metamorphosis*, more than evidence of a perceived intertextual relation. The possibility that Jonson entered at least some of the annotations, including this one, in his advanced years has several important implications, which require a reevaluation of our understanding of Drummond's account of the poet's attitude toward both Spenser and narrative verse. For such a dating of this notation would indicate that, even after his strokes,[19] Jonson paid close attention to long passages of *The Faerie Queene*. Although it is possible that Jonson could also have entered some of the marks and annotations as early as 1617, prior to his walking trip to Scotland,[20] clearly that pertaining to the Atalanta passage must be later than 1632. Furthermore, although Jonson makes no mention of the volume in "An Execration upon *Vulcan*," it is still possible that this copy of the 1617 Folio survived the famous fire in Jonson's study in 1623.[21] We know, too, that the annotations were probably not entered at the same time, for some are in pen, some in pencil, and some in pen over pencil. Hence, the evidence allows us to infer that Jonson may have read and reread Spenser during the last 20 years of his life, and that, even during the last five years before his death, his interest in Spenser remained strong.

We have already mentioned Jonson's practice of memorizing passages of poetry. We recall that some years earlier Drummond, mistakenly substituting Colin for Cuddie as the singer of the blazon to wine in the October

Eclogue, said that Jonson had "by Heart some verses of Spensers Calender" (H&S 1:136), making no claims about the capacity of his own memory. The evidence of Jonson's annotations indicates that Jonson intended, perhaps even in his later years, in fact, to commit long passages of Spenser's *magnum opus* to memory.

To make this point clear, certain of Jonson's abbreviations and marks must be clarified. In addition to the comments and flowers and other signs with which he has marked *The Faerie Queene*, three times in book 2, Jonson seems to indicate particular interest in committing passages to memory. At canto 6 (fig. 14), stanzas 16, 17 and 18, in addition to an inverted pyramid of five flowers and a line in the margin, he has written "Reminisc^e," presumably standing for *reminiscentia*. In the next canto, in two stanzas (canto 7, stanza 33, lines 8 and 9, and canto 8, stanza 50, lines 2, 3 and 4), he has written "M.," perhaps an abbreviation for *memoria*. In her excellent study of a medieval habit of mind, *The Book of Memory*,[22] Mary Carruthers points out a number of considerations that are relevant here. Two have immediate bearing: first, her observation that the medieval practice of setting out florilegia, or extracts from readings, continued well into the Renaissance, and, indeed, that florilegia "retained their immense popularity until this present century" (178); second, part of her introduction to her second chapter, "Descriptions of the Neuropsychology of Memory":

> All accounts of the workings of memory written after Aristotle separate its activities into two basic processes: that of storage (in a strictly defined context, the activity to which the words *memoria* and *mnesis* are applied); and that of recollection (*reminiscentia* and *anamnesis*). . . . Though the two activities are obviously closely related, the one being dependent upon the other, I prefer to follow ancient example and discuss *memoria*, at least to some extent, separately from *reminiscentia*. Thus, this chapter is concerned first with the nature of memory-storage, of

what is stored and how, and then with the question of what recollection is and how it was thought to proceed. (Carruthers, 46)

This is exactly the distinction Jonson makes in introducing his discussion of memory in *Discoveries*:

> *Memory*, of all the *powers* of the mind, is the most *delicate*, and *fraile*: it is the first of our *faculties*, that Age invades. *Seneca*, the father, the *Rhetorician*, confesseth of himselfe, hee had a miraculous one; not only to receive, but to hold. I my selfe could, in my youth, have repeated all, that ever I had made; and so continued till I was past fortie: Since, it is much decay'd in me. Yet I can repeate whole books that I have read, and *Poems*, of some selected friends, which I have lik'd to charge my memory with. (H&S 8:578)

There is modesty here. Although Jonson claims to have slipped in his capacity, we can infer from even the claim of reduced capacity that he possessed an exceptional ability to memorize, if he wished, long passages of poetry. And even allowing for some self-serving exaggeration here (imported by the trope of modesty), Jonson's interest in and powers of memorization must have been, even late in life, quite active. Evidence indicates that he was trying to memorize, if not "whole books," long sections of *The Faerie Queene*.

If we are to accept that such considerations were in Jonson's mind when he annotated his 1617 edition of Spenser, we open up ways of assessing *Discoveries* as well. In his valuable discussion of *Discoveries* and its relation to the critical thought of Heinsius,[23] Paul Sellin demonstrates that at least some of the "commonplaces" must have been collected near the end of Jonson's career—that is, after 1629. Sellin offers this appraisal:

> By now, it should be clear that the material assembled in the *Discoveries* cannot be regarded as fused into an integrated doctrine of poetry which Jonson 'made his own' out of the snippets gathered from his reading; and it is

obvious, particularly from the isolated statements on the magnitude and unity of the fable which he took from Chapter IV of *De Tragoediae Constitutione*, that he has not tried to preserve the assumptions of his original. The *Discoveries* does not present a system of ideas on poetry, and the treatise seems to be little more than a mere collection of ideas, a common-place book. As far as the trends indicated in his statements are concerned, it is clear—if the *Discoveries* in any way reflects Jonson's critical position—that he is not a Heinsian critic. (Sellin, 162)

The implications of Sellin's remarks are significant, and some require further investigation. Although we have reservations about Sellin's overall thesis, he puts discussion on the right track. *Discoveries* is not a "treatise," and was never meant to be. Rather, it is a collection of sayings analogous to the matter that Jonson, as a younger man, could hold in his head. Again, Mary Carruthers's study is helpful, as she so carefully traces out as an established mode of memorization, established in the medieval period but used well into the Renaissance, so Jonson sets down subjects of *memoria* and *reminiscentia*.

Differences in the kinds of markings found in books 1 and 2 indicate just such a function. The florilegia, which predominate in book 1, suggest a vast, ambitious plan to mark even very lengthy passages of *The Faerie Queene* for memorization. In the "memory" section of *Discoveries*, Jonson's complaint and boast in the long passage cited above ("he confesseth of himselfe") is: "I my selfe could, in my youth, have repeated all," etc.[24] There is no reason to suspect the veracity of Jonson's boast here, especially given the evidence of Drummond, whose claim that Jonson had "by Heart some verses of Spensers Calender about wyne between Coline and percye" (H&S 1:136) refers to Jonson as he nears the age of 50.

In attempting to account for the apparent want of coherence in *Discoveries*, Herford and Simpson say that "the . . . arrangement of the [printed] text is haphazard. It is clear that Sir Kenelm Digby gathered up Jonson's loose papers and handed them over to the publishers just as he found them" (H&S 8:558). Perhaps so. The purpose of such a collection, however, entails the probability that some readers—for whose use it was not intended—may find its arrangement haphazard, just as matter retained word-for-word in the memory is "haphazard." It is in the recollection and reordering of ideas that "originality" (not a notable concern of Renaissance critics) springs forth. As one imposes one's own interests, one employs the understood method of florilegia. If we are correct, then, Herford and Simpson impose an irrelevant criterion of unity that might not have interested Jonson's readers: "The discoveries were made by other men. [Jonson] fuses, rearranges, and adapts his borrowed matter; the weakness of the collection is that he seems to have thought out little or nothing for himself" (H&S 11:213). It seems that Herford and Simpson, and to some extent, Sellin, look too keenly for a "modern" value. Carruthers points out, in a way relevant to Jonson's practice, that "Perhaps no advice is as common in medieval writing on the subject, and yet so foreign, when one thinks about it, to the habits of modern scholarship as this notion of 'making one's own' what one reads in someone else's work" (Carruthers, 164). Jonson's thinking could have been tempered by just such a pre-Romantic tradition. If so, the argument that in *Discoveries* we find evidence of an older man striving to create a written equivalent to what, in his younger days, he could perform entirely in his memory, would seem to be justified.

Accordingly, in books 1 and 2 of *The Faerie Queene*, Jonson at first follows the habitual practice of setting out matter to be memorized (though, to be sure, with any number of verbal indices), succeeded by a more fully elaborated set of notations, not unlike those one finds in *Discoveries*. The alternative titles of *Discoveries*, *Explorata* and *Timber*, emphasize the nature of this collection; the second of them both relates this collection to collections of Jonson's poems (*The Forrest, Under-woods*) and to a passage from Caspar Gavartius's commentaries on Statius, which explains Statius's title, *Sylvae* (H&S 8:557–58). Furthermore, *Timber* echoes an idea that fits very conveniently into our argument: "Hugh of St. Victor writes of walking through the forest ("silva") of Scripture, 'whose ideas [*sententias*] like so many sweetest fruits we pick as we read and chew [*ruminamus*] as we consider them'" (Carruthers, 164–65). Another clue to the meaning of Jonson's collection, and also a confirmation that the title page is his,[25] is the epigraph from Persius, the last line of Satire IV, *Tecum habita, ut noris quam sit tibi curta supellex* ("live in your own house and recognize how poorly it is furnished").[26] Is this not a rueful acknowledgment that a once-reliable, perhaps even extraordinary, memory is no longer able to retain enough of what has been read into it?

We cannot, of course, be certain that the flowers in book 1 and elsewhere were intended to mark off passages that Jonson intended to memorize,[27] but, given what we know of Jonson's practices, this possibility cannot be overlooked. Petrarch, who was regarded as an authority on memory in the Renaissance, advised: "When you come to any passages that seem to you useful, impress secure marks against them, which may serve as hooks in your memory [*uncis memoria*], lest otherwise they might fly away."[28] The evidence suggests that Jonson used flowers as just such "hooks"—that is, that he employed the figurative concept of florilegia quite literally.

A different kind of hook, but a hook nonetheless, can be discerned in Jonson's use of one of Spenser's chief sources. The *Mythologiae*, of Natale Conti (Natalis Comes), the most widely used mythological handbook of the sixteenth century,[29] as Douglas Bush observes, summarized "mythological tales in easy Latin, assembled abundant references, quoted and translated Greek authors." And, Bush adds, Conti "provided the means which enabled many men, such as Chapman, to appear more learned than they were."[30] But we must remember that not only intellectual pretenders read Conti. As C. W. Lemmi has shown, Spenser and Jonson had no need to appear more learned than they were, and yet they not only read Conti, but they also understood Conti's systematic allegorizing of classical myths, including his incorporation of ethical and moral precepts. It is in these moralized readings of classical myth that one can trace, first, Spenser's use of Conti, and then Jonson's reading of Spenser through Conti. Thanks to the work of Lemmi and H. G. Lotspeich,[31] we are aware of Spenser's indebtedness to Conti; and Herford and Simpson have demonstrated Jonson's similar indebtedness, and so enabled us now to recognize certain ways in which Jonson brings Conti to bear in his own reading of Spenser.

For instance, in book 2, Jonson's markings more than once suggest that he was relying on the same comments in Conti that Spenser seems to have employed. The first two of three examples are not in themselves convincing, but taken in conjunction with the third, they form a pattern that carries its own weight as evidence:

> There, as in glistring glory she did sit,
>> She held a great gold chaine ylinked well,
>> Whose upper end to highest heaven was knit,
>> And lower part did reach to lowest hell;
>> And all that preace did round about her swell,
>> To catchen hold of that long chaine, thereby
>> To climbe aloft, and others to excell:
>> That was *Ambition*, rash desire to stie,
> And every linke thereof a step of dignitie.

> Some thought to raise themselves to high degree,
>> By riches and unrighteous reward,
>> Some by close shouldring, some by flatteree;
>> Others through friends, others for base regard;
>> And all, by wrong wayes, for themselves prepar'd.
>> Those that were up themselves, kept others lowe,
>> Those that were lowe themselves, held others hard,

> Ne suffred them to rise or greater growe,
> But every one did strive his fellow downe to throwe.
>
> Which, when as *Guyon* saw, he gan enquire,
>   What meant that preace about that Ladies throne,
>   And what she was that did so high aspire.
>   Him *Mammon* answered; That goodly one,
>   Whom all that folke with such contention
>   Doe flock about, my deare, my daughter is;
>   Honour and dignitie from her alone,
>   Derived are, and all this worldes blis
> For which ye men doe strive, few get, but many miss.
>
> And faire *Philotimè* she rightly hight,
>   The fairest wight that wonneth under sky,
>   But that this darksome neather world her light
>   Doth dim with horrour and deformitie,
>   Worthy of heaven and high felicitie,
>   From whence the gods have her for envie thrust:
>   But sith thou has found favour in mine eye,
>   Thy spouse I will her make, if that thou lust,
> That she may thee advaunce for works and merites
>   just.[32]
>   (1617 Folio, *FQ* 2.7.46–49)

Referring to these stanzas, Lemmi cites *Mythologiae* 2.4, where we find Conti's comments on "the golden chaine" in book 8 of the *Iliad* "by which all the gods were unable to pull Jove down from heaven" (Lemmi, 277). Conti writes:

> I should judge it to mean sometimes avarice and some- times ambition, which although it is very potent, and has drawn many from the true faith of God to false dog- mas . . . nevertheless will not be able to move a good man. (Lemmi, 277)

In the margin next to stanza 46, Jonson writes: "Am- bitions chaine is fastned to Heaven and reacheth to Hell <—> it is of gold and every Linkeroad a step of Honor." Jonson's identification of the golden chain could be the result of his having read a few stanzas further; or he could simply have gone back and made the notation. In view, however, of the other two examples below, where Jonson almost certainly has Spenser's source in mind, it is reasonable to infer that Jonson also does so here.

This is not to say that Jonson knew that Spenser had relied on Conti, but that Jonson, for whatever reason, recalled Conti's observation and made it his own. Although we believe this modest assertion to be accurate, we concede that any reading that attempts to locate the influence of *one* source—either for Spenser or for Jonson (let alone for both)—must remain speculative. At the same time, we must recognize that virtually all Renaissance writers conflated and consolidated a variety of sources, as many and as often as they could, and that this practice, although not contrived to baffle modern critics, in many instances has had just that effect. In the case of the golden chain, for instance, Herford and Simpson (10:425) call attention to Jonson's debt in *Hymenaei* to Macrobius's commentary on *The Dream of Scipio*. In a sidenote to line 320 of the masque, Jonson does in fact refer to "*In Som[nium] Scip[ionis] libr.* I. *cap.* 14 [15]":

> Since Mind emanates from the Supreme God and Soul from Mind, and Mind, indeed, forms and suffuses all below with life, ... all follow ... degenerating step by step in their downward course, the close observer will find that from the Supreme God even to the bottommost dregs of the universe there is one tie, binding at every link and never broken. This is the golden chain of Homer which, he tells us, God ordered to hang down from the sky to the earth.[33]

Jonson was quite able to see entirely various meanings of the "Golden Chaine," depending upon his interest: claiming profound implications for the marriage of a pair of children from two noble English families, or following Spenser's allegorizing in *The Faerie Queene*. While it may be impossible to prove the influence of only one source, we nevertheless suggest that Conti was probably one of Jonson's sources.

In the second instance of these notations, Guyon, having "lost his trusty guide," proceeds on his own and, after a while, discovers Mammon in a glade:

> At last, he [Guyon] came unto a gloomie glade,
> Cover'd with boughes and shrubs from heavens light,
> Where-as he sitting found, in secret shade,
> An uncouth, salvage, and uncivill wight,
> Of griesly hew, and foule ill favour'd sight;
> His face with smoake was tand, and eyes were bleard,
> His head and beard with sout were ill bedight,
> His coale-blacke hands did seeme to have been seard
> In Smithes fire-spetting forge, and nailes like clawes
> appeard.
> (1617 Folio, *FQ* 2.7.3)

Jonson's interpretation of Spenser's description is placed in the margin next to the stanza: "Descr. of a covitous man." Lemmi points out the relevant passage in *Mythologiae* 3.5: "Conti, interpreting Cerberus as a symbol of avarice, declares that the monster 'is said to live in a dark cavern because avarice is the most stupid of vices'" (278). As with the first example, it is possible that here, too, Jonson simply read further into the poem and then came back to mark the stanza. But if such were the case, it seems likely that Jonson would have been more specific in his interpretation; he would have identified the cave's inhabitant as Mammon. What seems most to have interested Jonson here, as in other parts of the poem as well, is the *picture*, in this case that of avarice, and this because of his familiarity with Conti. These markings, then, clearly suggest a congruence of opinion among Conti, Spenser and Jonson.

The third example presents the strongest evidence of Jonson's dependence on Conti for his interpretation of Spenser. Indeed there is nothing in Spenser's text, in itself, that seems to support Jonson's reading:

Said then the *Boatman*, Palmer steere aright,
   And keepe an even course; for yonder way
   We needs must pass (God do us well acquight):
   That is the *Gulfe of Greedinesse*, they say,
   That deepe engorgeth all this worlds pray:
   Which having swallowed up excessively,
   He soone in vomit up againe doth lay,
   And belcheth forth his superfluitie,
That all the seas for feare doe seeme away to fly.

On th'other side an hideous Rock is pight,
   Of mighty *Magnes* stone, whose craggy clift
   Depending from on high, dredfull to sight,
   Over the waves his rugged armes doth lift,
   And threatneth down to throwe his rugged rift
   On who so commeth nigh; yet nigh it drawes
   All passengers, that none from it can shift:
   For whiles they fly that Gulfes devouring jawes,
They on this rock are rent, and sunk in helplesse wawes.
             (1617 Folio, *FQ* 2.12.3–4)

As A. C. Hamilton observes,[34] Spenser's "*Gulfe of Greedinesse*" and the "hideous Rock" are drawn from Homer "by way of Virgil"; Lotspeich, Hamilton reminds us, "argues for the direct influence" of Conti. And yet, Hamilton points out, Spenser "would not need Comes for the proverbial description of the twin perils of the sea." On the contrary, Lotspeich insists, "It seems significant that nearly all Sp[enser]'s affinities with these passages are with such parts of them as are quoted by N.C., 8.12."[35] Hamilton does allow that Conti may be relevant to the notion of "virtues mean between two extremes."

Jonson's response to this passage seems to show that he definitely had Conti in mind,[36] and that he employs Conti much as Spenser did. Both poets follow Conti in interpreting myth in a highly imaginative way; and they allow each element of myth to have more than one signification, those significations varying with each interpreter. Thus, in Spenser the rock (Scylla) is both a magnet ("*Magnes* stone" [4.2]) to tempt men and a "*Rocke* of vile *Reproach*" (8.1) to punish them for having been tempted. In Conti's commentary, Scylla represents voluptuousness, and also "excessive expenditure" (*Mythologiae* 8.12, Lemmi's trans.; see *Var* 2:355). In the latter connection, Jonson's comment on stanza 3 identifies the "Gulfe of gredinesse and . . . the Rocke of dispaire." So, at stanza 4, Jonson writes: "Eschewing the gulfe of gredinesse men fall upon the Rocke of prodigallity."[37] It seems clear that the "Rocke of prodigallity" is more than coincidentally like Conti's "excessive expenditure," the punishment for which is, in both Conti and Jonson, self-contained. Thus, Jonson's remarks here point toward those soon afterward on "the misery of prodigality."[38]

4

The Legacy of
the Text

Jonson's House of Alma

But it was Fortune that made me fall upon it, when first
this *Stanza* was read to me for an indissoluble Riddle.
                              Sir Kenelm Digby, *Observations*

U ntil now, we have for the most part been discussing
literary relations between Spenser and Jonson. In
this chapter we turn to slightly different matter, which
should alter the customary way of looking at an important passage of *The Faerie Queene*—namely, the famous
"mathematical stanza" of book 2, canto 9. In glossing
this text, the editors of the *Variorum* direct readers
(2:289) to an appendix, "The Twenty-second Stanza of
Canto 9" (2:472–85), where we read: "This recondite

stanza called forth the earliest learned commentary on Spenser, Sir Kenelm Digby's *Observations"* (2:272), which was published in 1643. With the appearance of John Dixon's and Ben Jonson's annotations to *The Faerie Queene* as well as *Spenser Allusions In the Sixteenth and Seventeenth Centuries,*[1] we can now say that Digby's remarks definitely were not "the earliest commentary" on *The Faerie Queene.* Moreover, evidence from Jonson's copy of the 1617 Spenser Folio indicates that many of the key ideas and even specific critical locutions in Digby's *Observations* were not, strictly speaking, his. This is demonstrated not only by Jonson's markings to stanza 22, but also by his treatment of a number of subsequent stanzas describing the House of Alma. In considering the context of this description, one should recall that, after Guyon has been stripped of his armor, Arthur takes up his cause, defeating "the Paynim brethren," setting Archimago and Atin to flight. Soon thereafter, Arthur and Guyon come upon a castle which has, it turns out, been under siege for seven years. Since they need rest, Arthur and Guyon accept the hospitality of Alma, who shows them about the castle, which Spenser's narrator then describes in elaborate detail.

In his remarks (quoted in full in the *Variorum*), Digby in a short space makes repeated claims of originality; these have been accepted by all authorities,[2] for until now there has been no reason not to accept them. However, close study of Jonson's annotations suggests that the most significant parts of the *Observations*—namely, the identification of the details of the allegory—are not Digby's, but Jonson's. The elaboration—the dilation on the allegory—appears to be Digby's, as does the repetition of details. Indeed, once one recognizes the ideas for what they are—namely, Jonson's—the most striking quality of the *Observations* becomes the extent of Digby's repetition of them.

Let us demonstrate this point by examining the earliest example in the work of Digby's "borrowing." He quotes the first line and a half of book 2, canto 9, stanza 22:

The Frame thereof seem'd partly Circular,
And part Triangular.[3]

Then Digby asserts that this stanza is unlike all others
in the "whole Book" (3), in that elsewhere, although
Spenser's text begins in an "Allegory or mysticall sense,"
Spenser invariably declares "his own conceptions in
such sort as they are obvious to any ordinarie capacitie."
But here, Digby claims, Spenser ventures into "the pro-
foundest" of scientific mysteries:

> By these Figures, I conceive that he means the mind
> and body of Man; the first being by him compared to a
> Circle, and the latter to a Triangle.... a Body made of
> such compounded earth as in the preceding *Stanza* the
> Author describes.... But mans soul is a Circle.... By the
> Triangular Figure he very aptly designes the body. (6–8;
> *Var* 2:473)

Consulting Jonson's copy of the 1617 Folio (fig. 2), we see
that he has placed a star by "Castle wall" in line 1 of
"the preceding *Stanza*," and next to that line he has written: "By this I conceiv he meanethe the skinne of the
Body of man." Further, Jonson has placed a star above the
first word of stanza 22, and next to and just above the
first lines we read: "the circular signe represents th<e>
Soule the Triangular the body <of> Man." In short, the
conceptual analysis is virtually identical to the one we
find in Digby's *Observations*.

There is more. Interlarded among, and extending
somewhat beyond, Digby's remarks just cited are such
explanations as the following rationale for a hierarchy of
geometric figures:

> For as a Circle of all Figures is the most perfect,
> and includeth the greatest space, and is every way full
> and without Angles, made by the continuance of one
> onely line: so mans soul is the noblest and most
> beautifull Creature, that God hath created.... For as a

circumference doth in all parts alike respect that indivis-
ible Point, and as all lines drawn from the inner side of
it, do make right Angles within it, when they meet
therein ... for as the Circle is of all other Figures the
most perfect and most capacious: so the Triangle is most
imperfect, and includes least space. It is the first and low-
est of all Figures. (6–8; *Var* 2:473)

Returning to stanza 22, Digby quotes lines four and five:

The one imperfect, Mortall, Feminine:
Th'other immortall, perfect, Masculine,

and he observes:

Mans Body hath all the proprieties of imperfect matter.
It is ... liable to corruption and dissolution if it once be
deprived of the form which actuates it, and which is in-
corruptible and immortall. And as the feminine Sex is
imperfect, and receives perfection from the masculine: so
doth the Body from the Soul, which to it is in lieu of a
male. ... And as there is a mutuall appetence between
the Male and the Female, betweene matter and forme; So
there is betweene the bodie and the soul of Man. (14–15;
Var 2:475)

It is important to note that Digby emphasizes difference here. He is carried away by the neatness and clarity
of the perceived opposition in Spenser's text. And yet, in
the context of Jonson's annotations on the same passage,
it is not the nascent Platonism of Digby's contrastive
analysis, but the relatively undeveloped figure of the
vivifying agency that conjoins body to soul, that grasps
our attention. Look, for instance, at Jonson's markings to
the "mathematical stanza" (fig. 2). Jonson has placed a
star above and slightly before line 4; next to that line he
has written: "The Body is mortall and of it<selfe>
imperfecte without the Soule <which> is in lewe of a
maker and actu<ator of> it."[4] It seems that Jonson notices, not the opposition between the sexes here, but
rather the dependence of the body on the soul for its

capacity to change—that is, to act, to improve. The soul makes, or "actuates" (is the agency of) perfection. This Jonsonian focus points up an emphasis on agency lacking in Digby; it informs us, too, that the most striking figure in the passage from Digby is that of the soul as "actuator," which is the form of the unusual word used by Jonson.

The Oxford English Dictionary (OED) tells us that the verb, to "actuate," which in the sixteenth century meant "to perform" or "carry out," could by 1642 mean "to inspire [a thing] with active properties, to quicken, enliven, or vivify." This seems to be the sense employed in both of the above contexts. The OED further credits James Howell with the first recorded use of this sense in *Forreine Travels* (82): "What kind of soule doth inform, actuat, govern, and conserve that vast empire." It is perhaps more than coincidental that, in Jonson's later years, he and Howell were intimate friends, and, moreover, that for more than 30 years, Digby and Howell were closely associated.[5] As an aspect of dialect, diction exhibits its local variations. In other words, authors learn their vocabularies from each other. But even so, usage begins somewhere for everyone. We must recall that the latest possible date that Jonson could have made his comment on the "mathematical stanza" (the year of his death, 1637) justifies the inference that the figure of the soul as "actuator" of the body was Jonson's, not Digby's; and, as we shall argue, this is surely the case when we consider that Digby probably had the good "Fortune" of access to Jonson's annotations to Spenser's *Faerie Queene* prior to his composition of the *Observations*.

The unusual usage of "actuator" in both Jonson's annotations and Digby's *Observations*, in precisely the same context, is by no means the only such coincidence found in the *Observations*. For instance, after quoting line six of the "mathematical stanza" ("*And twixt them both, a Quadrate was the Base*"), Digby writes:

> By which Quadrate, I conceive, that he meaneth the
> foure principall humors in mans Bodie, viz. *Choler,*
> *Blood, Phleme,* and *Melancholy:* which if they be distem-
> pered and unfitly mingled, dissolution of the whole doth
> immediately ensue: like to a building which falls to
> ruine, if the foundation and Base of it be unsound or dis-
> ordered. (15; *Var* 2:475–76)

Again, despite Digby's protestations of original conception, this reproduces Jonson's comment almost verbatim:
"By this Quadrat is meant <the> principall Humours
in man<s> body." Delete the breakdown of humours that
ends Digby's sentence, replace "which" by "this," and
note that Digby's phrase enumerates the humours (Jonson's doesn't); this produces virtually identical sentences:

By	this / which	quadrate	is meant / he meaneth	the / foure	principall humours in mans body.

We may ignore Digby's "I conceive that," not because it
is gratuitously self-serving, but because, as an editorial
remark, it is subject to challenge. (For instance, to whom
does the "I" in fact refer?) The negligible semantic shift
from "that" to "which" does not change the meaning of
the utterance at all. Indeed, what Digby *does* add to the
passage is an extended definition of the function of
the "base" or foundation of a building. Thus, Jonson's
figurative analysis remains intact, as, in the earlier instance, did his figure of the soul as "actuator." Although
Digby volunteers to number and name the humours,
they are still the "principall humours." Digby expands
upon the Jonsonian marginalia.

As for line 7 of the famous stanza (*"Proportion'd*
equally by seven and nine"), Digby writes:

> In which words, I understand he meanes the influences
> of the superior substances (which governe the inferiour)
> into the two differing parts of Man; to wit, of the *Starres*

(the most powerfull of which, are the seven Planets, into his body: and of the Angels divided into nine Hierarchies or Orders) into his soul. (16; *Var* 2:476)

When we examine Jonson's comments, the similarity is striking. Jonson has placed a star above the word "seaven" and in the margin has written: "By seven and 9 are ment <the> Planetes and the Angells which ar<e> distributed into a Hierarch<y> which governe the body." In both his and Digby's expressions, "seven" refers to the planets, and "nine" to the angelic orders; these figures, in turn, accord with the governance of man's body. Again, the diction as well as the conceptual analysis suggests a strong connection between the two interpretations.

Jonson's explication of Spenser's elaborate device continues with a persistence that is striking well past the twenty-second stanza. Notice, for instance, Jonson's extended description of the Castle of Alma in the next stanza:

> Therein two gates were placed seemly well:
>   The one before, by which all in did passe,
>   Did th'other far in workmanship excell.
>
> (1617 Folio)

One of the most relevant commentaries, particularly with respect to the criterion of conteporaneity, is Jonson's. In stanza 23, as we have seen, Jonson identifies the "two*gates"[6] as "*the Mouth and funda[ment]." The parts described in line 6 as "Doubly disparted*" he construes as "*the upper and lower Jawe." Similarly, in stanza 24, Jonson places asterisks next to the "hewen* stone," "Ivie twine,*" and "Portcullis*" in lines 1, 5 and 6, and then inscribes in the margin: "*the Jawe bones," "*the beard of a man," and "*the Nose." Again, next to the first line of stanza 25, "Within the Barbican a Porter sate,*" Jonson writes: "*the Tounge." The last three lines of the stanza are:

His [the Porter's] larum-bell might loud and wide
bc heard,
When cause requir'd, but never out of time;
*Early and late it rong, at evening and at prime.

In explication of the perceived allegory, Jonson writes in
the margin next to the last line (but this time without
starring his comment): "He praide morning and eve<ning>."

It is, of course, possible that Digby borrowed neither
his diction nor his notions from Jonson—that the borrowing went the other way around. But this is not likely.
Observations ends in a crescendo of Digby's claims for
originality. After his purportedly spontaneous reply to a
request for help in puzzling out a difficult patch in *The
Faerie Queene* ("And now I return to you also the Book
that contains my Text, which yesterday you sent me, to
fit this part of it with a Comment"), Digby veers into but
then recovers from a stroke of humility:

> I perswade my self very strongly, that in what I have said
> there's nothing contradictory to it [the "Authors Inten-
> tion"], and that an intelligent and well learned man pro-
> ceeding on my grounds might compose a worthie and
> true Commentarie on this Theme: Upon which I wonder
> how I stumbled, considering how many learned men have
> failed in the Interpretation of it, and have all at the first
> hearing, approved my opinion.
>
> But it was Fortune that made me fall upon it, when
> first this *Stanza* was read to me for an indissoluble
> Riddle. And the same Discourse I made upon it, the first
> halfe quarter of an houre that I saw it, I send you here. . . .
> (24–25; *Var* 2:478)

These remarks on *The Faerie Queene* are "worthie and
true," and they came about through serendipity: Digby
stumbled. Even if we ignore the double edge of this
figure, with its potentially confessional implications, we
are left with a self-serving claim that "Fortune" imposed
on the matter an "Interpretation" that has led to the ap-
proval of all, this despite the hard fact that "many

learned men" had already failed in this regard.

Sir Kenelm Digby's intellect and talent were considerable, yet we must question his claim of spontaneity, as
well as his figure of serendipity. Evidence and analysis
allows for explanation of the same "worthie and true
Commentarie" without resort to unusual occurrences,
either personal or cosmic. In the matter of a prodigious
spurt of creative energy, first of all, it is safe to say that
Digby's "halfe quarter of an houre"[7] is a palpable fiction.
As for the intervention of "Fortune" as the agent of
"worthie and true" originality, is seems no less probable
that Digby's claim here, likewise, considerably overstates
the case. Why, we would ask, would anyone credit the
claim that Digby wrote the *Observations* for a friend?
Manuscript versions of the treatise confirm that it was
meant for Sir Edward Stradling, dated "From aboord [his]
Ship the Eagle the XIII of June, 1628."[8] It seems more
likely that the entire enterprise was a device to get ideas
of a greater critic (Jonson) into print. For it is surely more
than "Fortune" or happenstance that Digby was Jonson's
literary executor long after the episode on the Eagle, and
yet before Digby sought to have the *Observations* published. If this analysis is inaccurate, then why did Digby
wait 15 or 16 years *after* it was written, and two or three
years *after* the death of Stradling for whom it was supposedly intended,[9] to publish it? It seems more than coincidence that Sir Kenelm Digby presents *Observations
on the 22. Stanza in the 9th. Canto of the 2d. Book of
Spencers Faery Queen* in the form of an extended "Letter
of the Authors" to "a Friend," who, purportedly made a
"request" (title page) during a discussion some days before Digby took up composition of the exposition on the
famous mathematical stanza (2). Although Digby tenders
a rather typical disclaimer of his ignorance and diffidence
in addressing his august friend, Edward Stradling, he nevertheless claims that his views are merely a response to
the previous discussion.

Fiction or not, of course, the story is harmless. Digby's

claim about the casual nature of his composing the *Observations* is like his similar claim in the Postscript to his *Loose Fantasies*.[10] As Vittorio Gabrielli says of that postscript, it is "quite in keeping with the honoured Renaissance convention according to which a gentleman-courtier looked down, or affected to put low estimate upon, his literary productions" (xviii). The time it took Digby to compose his piece on stanza 22 can be thus accounted for, and so too can the place of composition, and even, perhaps, the "recipient," Sir Edward Stradling. But the date of 1643 or 1644 gives scope for the harmless posturing to extend into mere fraud. The invocation of Stradling's by-this-time ghost no doubt pays a kind of oblique compliment to Digby's old friend, but that friend is no longer in a position either to have private doubts or to raise public questions about Digby's veracity. It is hard to resist suspecting that Digby employed an "honoured Renaissance convention" for reasons that are more self-interested than "worthie and true."[11]

The foregoing remarks are not to suggest that Digby's work lacks merit. Indeed, in the context of much recent criticism, it has potential corrective value, in that it illustrates how Spenser's text possibly could and probably could not have been read in its own time. Contemporary readings are potential anodynes against anachronistic ones. Consider David Lee Miller's reading of stanza 22, for instance.[12] Miller's analysis fails to come to terms with Spenser's "quadrate," which is, of course, for Jonson and for Digby, critical to the passage. And this shift away from that figure would suggest that, in the last quarter of the twentieth century, such a shift has become current in critical "Commentarie." But the *Observations* can help correct not only what is omitted, but what is not omitted in post-seventeenth century criticism. Miller argues that the circle (masculine) and the triangle (feminine) constitute the significant figures of the mathematical stanza. As they are merged, he thinks, they create an "image of transcendence and reconciliation," and one finds "masculine authority hierarchically privileged" (182), this, presumably, because the circle is thought to represent the head, and the head only, and the triangle the legs.

This interpretation is not only not a Renaissance interpretation, but it is a narrowly literal interpretation as well. It leaves no room at all for the Jonsonian perspective that "the circular signe represents th<e> Soule the Triangular the body <of> Man."[13] So we must question whether Spenser *could* possibly have meant, as Miller suggests, that in the stanza "what is offered [presumably by Spenser] as an explicit image of the higher unity of man and woman in a single body, *figura* of the risen body 'in which there is neither male nor female,' also represents the castration of both genders" (182). And we are skeptical of what follows as well:

> Woman is symbolically castrated in that she is at once excluded from the perfect closure of the divine circle and subordinated within a deceptively symmetrical unity. Her bodily specificity is in effect converted into a sign of all that is fallen in nature, just as man's is converted into a sign of the self-sufficient perfection from which we fell. This allegorical reinscription of the body is repeated in our tour of the castle, which begins and ends in the divine masculine circle of the head. . . . (182–83)

The contemporaneity of these assertions must be questioned. Would Spenser's contemporaries have construed the passage in this way? For that matter, is this how they used the term "castration"? Times change, and the lexicon changes with them. So we must admit that confusions regarding historical and linguistic particulars may be variously derived.

Analysis might help. The implication of Miller's remarks seems to be that "woman," by virtue of being "castrated," is, *ipso facto*, capable of being castrated. Now, the OED lists many uses of this term, but many of these seem to derive from the Latin *castrare*, meaning to remove the testicles of, to geld, to emasculate. Hence, the substantive: "A castrated man, a eunuch." A figurative use, meaning to mutilate, might work: to cut down or to expurgate, as in the case of a literary artifact. Here, the gender issue might work, for the OED records that, because Queen Elizabeth didn't like certain passages of Holinshed's Scottish *Chronicles,* "several sheets . . . were castrated" (but later restored, so more like a vasectomy than a castration).[14] But even this would seem to stretch the application well beyond Miller's psychoanalytic purpose.

It goes without saying that neither Miller nor any other critic should be faulted for not having consulted Jonson's annotations to *The Faerie Queene.* (Neither did compilers of the OED.) And yet Miller could have had at least second-hand access to Jonson's ideas (without, of course, knowing that they were Jonson's) by looking at Kenelm Digby's *Observations.* The circular-feminine-soul and triangular-masculine-body associations are quite clear in Digby. Had Miller consulted Digby's *Observations* seriously, and applied its figurative understanding to the text at hand, it is unlikely that he would have concluded that in stanza 22 anyone is "symbolically castrated." Digby's text informs our understanding of the way in which this Spenser passage was in fact interpreted in the seventeenth century.

On the other hand, the figurative interpretation of stanza 22 certainly does not depend on one and only one instance of contemporary reaction. Digby—and Miller, for that matter—might also have been familiar with another seventeenth century critic who had much to say about Spenser's figure of the Castle of Alma. In 1943 Carroll Camden called attention to William Austin's *Haec Homo, Wherein the Excellency of the Creation of Woman is described, By way of an Essay,*[15] which was published the year of Jonson's death in 1637, and so, like Jonson's literary estate, was available to Digby as he compiled his *Observations.* Austin cannot be linked to

Jonson's Spenser in the way that Digby can, but at the very least we can assume that Austin and Jonson were acquainted over a period of years. Austin contributed a commendatory poem for Coryate's *Crudities* (1611), for which Jonson is traditionally supposed to have been the editor (H&S 11:131). Austin was one of the 84 eminent men (Digby and Jonson were others) who were named by Jonson's close friend Edmund Bolton as proposed members for the Royal Academy that Bolton tried to establish, starting in 1616 or 1617.[16] Like Digby and Jonson, Austin was an intimate of James Howell, who claimed to have been much inspired by a poem Austin had written on "the Passion of Christ."[17] He may have been the "Master Austinn" who was the author of "A verse-contest at a tavern. / m^r Austinn to his friend Benn Johnsonn," preserved in a manuscript in St. John's College, Cambridge (H&S, 11:412–15). Whether Austin knew of Jonson's Spenser or not, it is a least possible that he knew something of Jonson's opinion of Spenser. In any case, what he has to say about stanza 22 certainly is compatible with Jonson's (and Digby's) observations. That Austin has anything to say about the stanza means that, apparently unlike any other passage in *The Faerie Queene*, it received particular attention from at least three men who were members of the same literary circle in the late 1620s and early 1630s.

In his interesting little prose work, Austin construes the body of woman (fig. 15) as "a *perfect Square,*"[18] in which "*Geometricall proportion*" it represents "the *form* of the *Temple,* and of the *mysticall Church,* in the *Revelation.*" But with her arms slightly raised (fig. 16), the same body conforms to "a just *Triangle:* which is a *figure* of the *Trinitie*" (sig. E3^v). Then "let the hands fall" (fig. 17), Austin observes, and the legs "*somewhat*" part, and the woman's body approximates the circumference of "a just *circle*" (sig. E3^v), with the navel at the exact center, "which is a *true figure* of the *Earth.*" Finally (fig. 18), "elevate the *hands* againe," with the feet even wider apart, and the woman's body forms "a Saint *Andrews Crosse*," from which one might draw the "true form of the *twelve houses* of the *seven Planets* in Heaven" (sigs. E3ᵛ–E4).

On its face, this sequence might not appear to be an interpretation of Spenser's mathematical stanza. And yet it is clear that Austin thinks of his commentary on these designs as relevant to Spenser's *Faerie Queene*, just as Digby thought of his mathematical figurations as an unfolding of Spenser's meaning. In fact, Austin thought that "All" of his figures were relevant, for they:

> are very elegantly and briefly contracted, by the *late dead Spencer*, in his *everliving Fairy Queen;* where, coming to describe the *house of Alma*, (which, indeed, is no *other* but the *body;* the *habitation* of the Soule,) he saith. *The frame thereof seem'd partly circular, and part triangular; (O worke Divine!)* (sigs. E4–E4ᵛ)

After quoting the rest of the stanza, Austin offers this assessment:

> Besides these proportions, which in the *Geometricall* art signifie things both *divine*, and *humane* (as you have heard;) there is scarce a *figure*, or character of a *letter*) in the whole *Alphabet* (which are the grounds and elements of all *Arts*, and *Sciences*, whatsover) but may be aptly figured and expressed by some S*tation, motion, or action* of the Body. All which were too long to particularize: but hee that will make an ingenious triall may soone see the truth of it. And *all these* forms are expressible in the *body of Woman* and *man, equally.* (Sigs. E4ᵛ–E5)

According to Austin, anything that can be expressed—the totality of linguistic possibilities—can be expressed in terms of bodily behavior or attitude. The body is either in motion or at rest; and in these two attitudes, the body is capable of reflecting, as in a cosmic mime, every configuration in the cosmos. It is not enough to say that this passage is just another instance of the Renaissance theory of correspondences between the macrocosm and the microcosm. Here, Austin's inclusive diction ("the whole *Alphabet*," "*all these* forms") suggests that, as he read Spenser's mathematical stanza, he perceived a comprehensiveness that eludes convenient description. And yet if one were to exercise the requisite discipline, one would "see the truth of it," namely, that "*all these* forms" can be accurately portrayed in the human body, whether male or female.

Although comprehensive, Austin's figurative catalogue of devices would include only what is shared by the sexes. Hence, we infer that Austin would not think of the figure of castration as "both divine, and humane," nor even as male and female. For him, such a figurative construction would be too "specie" and "gender" specific to represent Spenser's text. So it is that Austin thoughtfully writes:

> Seeing therefore, to circumscribe the *forme* to certaine limits, were but to *disgrace* the worke: wee will not compare it in *particular* to any *one* thing, but speaking *generally* (as of a *curious building*) follow the *Allegory* of a *house*. Which *name*, it naturally (without any *crushing*) deriveth from the word in Scripture, [*Aedificium*] a building. (Sigs. E6ᵛ–E7)

Citing Isidore, Austin notes that, like Alma's castle, "All buildings consist of *three parts*" (sig. E7), but these in no way represent an upright human figure. Rather, they depict the foundation, the frame (including joists and roof) and the "ornament" (sig. E7). Beauty points up the difference between man and woman ("she is but *Mulier homo*" [sig. E7ᵛ]). The base, Spenser's "quadrate," is the foundation, which constitutes the bottom of the structure. Austin argues that the best foundation is of the same substance as the rest of the building. It is this "perfection" of one substance that links Spenser's description to Austin's notion of the foundation.

And yet we must not forget that Alma is, after all, a woman whose body shares—as man's body does not—

certain attributes of the Deity, namely, comprehensiveness. Austin thinks of woman ("*Thy legs are like pillars
of marble, set upon sockets of fine gold*" [sig. E9ᵛ]) in
terms of the Song of Songs, for woman's legs are built for
support and for succour:

> The *reason* (for the largenesse and firmeness of *this*
> foundation, above *that* of mans) may be easily gathered
> from the observation of the *Constructio*, the *frame* or
> *fabrick* of the rest of her body. . . . (sig. E10)

Woman's body is larger, rounder, and more spacious than
man's. Hence, it appropriately represents the function of
upholding and support. This is so because, although
woman has everything that a man possesses in his body,
she has also greater capaciousness in her body, this "because shee must contain *another house* within her,
with an *unruly* ghest, and all *provision* necessarie for
him" (sig. E11).

Again, woman is known for grace as well as for com-
modiousness. And it is in this connection that Austin
thinks of stanza 32 of canto 9:

> But all the *liquor* that was foule and waste;
> Not good nor serviceable, else for ought:
> They in an other great round vessell plast;
> Till by a conduit pipe, it thence was brought.
> And all the *rest*, that noyous was and nought,
> By *secret wayes* (that none might it espye)
> Was close conceiv'd, and to the *backe gate* brought
> That cleped was *Porte Esquiline*; whereby
> It was avoided quite, and throwne out *privily*.
>
> (sig. E11ᵛ)[19]

Now, as Austin understands this structure, description
proceeds from the body, including the legs, to the neck,
which is like a tower. And here Austin thinks of the
Canticles again: "*Thy neck is like the tower of David*"
(sig. E12). As for the head, Austin thinks of it, not as a
circle, but as "a faire *turret*" (sig. E12). And to elucidate

his analogy, he turns again to Spenser: "Up to a *stately Turret* she them brought, / Ascending by *tenne steps* of *Alablaster wrought*" (sig. E12ᵛ). And he interrupts himself to say that he can spare expense of time by quoting from stanza 46 Spenser's "description of the *Turret* it selfe":

> The *roofe* thereof was arched over head,
> And deckt with *flowers*, and harbours daintily:
> *Two goodly Beacons*, set in watches stead,
> Therein gave light and flam'd continually.
> For they of *living fire*, most subtilly
> Were made, and set in *silver sockets* bright;
> Covered with *lidds* devis'd of Substance slie,
> That readily they *shut* and open might;
> *Oh who can tell the praises of that Makers might!*
> (sigs. E12ᵛ–F1)

We have examined this figurative context to draw attention to a practice or predisposition current with members of the reading audience of Spenser's contemporaries. We do this, not to be polemical, or even because we find Miller's alternative method of reading Spenser's text to be uniquely, or even unusually, off the mark. Rather, it is because Miller's practice is, in a number of ways, representative, particularly as he insists upon a kind of literal reading of the Castle of Alma: circle = head, square = body, triangle = legs. We think, on the contrary, that making a strict allegorical representation of the figures in this famous passage does not work very well. We simply cannot make a picture of Alma's Castle *and* a human body at the same time. Moreover, we believe that Spenser renders it virtually impossible for an attentive reader to compose a picture of either. Instead, as Walter Davis acutely observes, "The descriptive procedure is by function rather than by simple toe-to-top anatomy."[20] In strong agreement with Davis, we would point, for illustration, to one line of the stanza ("And twixt them both a quadrate was the base") for evidence

of the inconvenience of the picture theory when applied
to stanza 22. If we imagine a picture, then the "base"
must be the bottom; and, being the bottom, it cannot
therefore literally be "twixt" anything (unless, of course,
we insist that the square is on the same plane as the
circle and the triangle, not simply between them; but in
this case, the figure "base" would not mean anything because it would not distinguish one part from another).
That is, if "base" is construed to be figurative, such as
"the essential quality" of such-and-such, then it cannot
be pictured at all.

But if, instead, we consider this perspective only a par-
tial explanation, we can deal with the attempt of Digby
and others to extrapolate a literal picture of the Castle of
Alma. This line of thought can be traced at least as far
back as Francis Webb in his *Panharmonicon* (1815).
Webb includes in his study an appendix, "A letter from
the author . . . to a friend. *On the 22nd Stanza of the 9th
canto of the 2nd book of Spenser's Faerie Queen* (33)," in
which he speculates on Digby's essay and on how Digby
"stumbled upon" (34) the solution to the riddle of stanza
22. The three geometric forms Webb treats as follows:

> [The Platonic] philosophy considered the Quadrat as a
> principle of union between numbers and proportions. . . .
> [Thus] the quadrat [is] placed as a mean, or connecting
> principle, between the circle and triangle; and therefore
> may properly be considered . . . in the same manner as
> the Platonists did the *tertiam quandam naturam*, which
> partaking of the quality of body and mind, was the bond
> by which these were united.[21]

Webb considers the passage, "The *frame* thereof seem's
partly *circulare* / And part *triangulare*," agreeing with
"Sir Kenelm Digby, [who] very properly observes, '*that
the Poet; means the mind and body of man: and it was
by these the Platonists explained it.*[']" But in the end,
the circle is "the divine mind, [which] has thereby
been aptly signified, whose centre is every where, but its

circumference is no where." When Webb invokes Aristotle and Clement, who state "that principles and conclusions must be within the sphere of the same science; and that leaping à genre ad genus, and transferring principles into sciences to which they do not belong, may be prejudicial to knowledge," he is "rather inclined to suppose, that the application of these [principles and conclusions are] not altogether within the Aristotelean rule or observation" (36). Webb's point is that needless confusion can descend upon a discussion when one insists that differing things can be substituted one for another—for instance, the assertion that soul = mind = divine mind. A similar caveat may be registered about the dangers of making Spenser's allegory literal, as when a critic argues that circle = head, square = body, triangle = legs.

Some Spenser critics, including James Nohrnberg and Leonard Barkan, have suggested how deeply Elizabethans were imbued with ideas of imitation, and how extensively those ideas affected their creative efforts.[22] Ideas of spatial design were not rigorously distinguished from "myth" or "allegory," but rather formed one among many categories of artistic expression. As S. K. Heninger, Jr. observes (quoting Wittgenstein): "'An entirely different game is played in different ages'";[23] and he implies, of course, that we must acquaint ourselves with the rules of the game in play. In the context of our discussion, the game of attitudes might have changed in such a way as to reward our resistance to or weariness with a system of thought which presupposes system, which is only to say that today we might win a game by perceiving disorder in the same arrangement of pieces on the board which would have drawn from, say, Vitruvius and Spenser, a seemingly valid perception of ordered analogy. The issue is an empirical one. Applying "modern" or "postmodern" attitudes to the underlying analogy between a well designed edifice and the human body may, if we think we are talking about "the same thing," mislead us into thinking that the two things with dissimilar features are the same. Our error would derive simply from over-emphasizing similarity to the exclusion of dissimilarity. But we should be attentive to discontinuity as well as continuity in the literary record.

Let us look more closely, now, at the famous crux of book 2, canto 9:

> The frame thereof seem'd partly circulare,
>   And part triangulare, ô worke divine!
> Those two the first and last proportions are,
> The one imperfect, mortall, foeminine;
> Th'other immortall, perfect, masculine;
> And twixt them both a quadrat was the base,
> Proportiond equally by seaven and nine;
> Nine was the circle set in heavens place,
> All which compacted, made a goodly *Diapase*.
>
> (1617 Folio)

After centuries of commentary, what are we now, nearing the twenty-first century, to make of this passage? A. C. Hamilton's notation to the passage reads: "The simplest physical explanation is that **circulare** refers to the head, the **quadrate** to the body, and **triangulare** to the lower body with legs astride."[24] Accordingly, the quadrate is "the trunk of the body," one of three souls. But this physical analogy between head (circle); trunk (square); and legs, presumably spread (triangularly) appears to require a vertical structure. We imagine the figure from top to bottom, from circle (head) downward through quadrate (torso) to triangle (legs outspread). The problem with the figure thus construed is that, like the compass in Donne's "A Valediction: forbidding Mourning" (as John Frecerro pointed out some time ago),[25] such a vertical assembly does not quite work out. Consider: the divinity of "the frame" inheres in its seeming. Although it "seem'd" at one moment to be partly one shape and partly another, in fact, the single frame is neither the one nor the other. For "twixt" these figures is a base, namely, a "quadrat." Then how can the base exist "twixt" the top and the bottom and still be a base? And what would be "divine" about so woefully confused a figure?

Again, literary genealogy helps. As S. K. Heninger, Jr. observes,[26] the *locus classicus* for such a use (and perhaps of the layout of Spenser's Temple of Isis) is Pollio Vitruvius, in particular books 1 and 3 of *De architectura*. The main principle in "The Planning of Temples" (namely symmetry), Vitruvius states, "arises from proportion, (which in Greek is called *analogia*)."[27] And this proportion, which must be exact, is worked out "after the fashion of the members of a finely shaped human body." In this famous tableau, Vitruvius discusses the way in which the human body is distributed in parts regulated by the number ten, which the proper temple emulates. It is worth noting that Vitruvius thinks of these ratios as derived from a body that is lying prone:

> Now the navel is naturally the exact centre of the body. For if a man lies on his back with hands and feet outspread, and the centre of a circle is placed on his navel, his figure [fingers?] and toes will be touched by the circumference. (3.1.3)

Thus, the finger is one inch, the palm, the fist, the cubit, and so on, as Plato considered it, a perfect harmony: $10 = 1 + 2 + 3 + 4$ (3.1.5).

When Jonson read the twenty-second stanza of book 2, canto 9, he may very well have done so with a thorough knowledge of this mathematical scheme and of its architectural application—in short, of Vitruvius, in particular. We infer this acquaintance from Jonson's snide dig at Inigo Jones, whom he accuses of not getting the "names" in Vitruvius right. (Albeit that Jones probably had more Latin than Shakespeare had Greek [H&S 11:152–53].) We know that Jonson owned at least two copies of Vitruvius:[28] the Danielo Barbaro Italian translation (1556), which bears Jonson's markings, and the Lyons edition of 1586, in which Jonson has "glossed technical terms in English, and [given] Latin equivalents to Greek words" (H&S 11:600). Thus, although it is possible that Spenser composed his text with no firsthand knowledge of Vitruvius, it is more likely that Jonson's reading of that text was informed by his firm understanding of Vitruvius.

So even though it cannot be said with certainty that Spenser had Vitruvius in mind when he penned his verse description of the House of Alma, Vitruvius was closely read and admired by such readers of Spenser as Ben Jonson, as Heninger points out. As a result, whether we are talking about encoding or decoding of *The Faerie Queene*, the ideas of Vitruvius might serve a helpful function. Not only does the bibliographic record allow us to infer Jonson's knowledge of Vitruvius, but his notations jibe closely with Vitruvius. For instance, they seem to assume the body's position on a horizontal rather than a vertical plane. But—and this, we think, is an important restraint—again the design is neither upward nor outward alone, but intermixed. Even in the imagination, everything is in proportion: "For nature has so planned the human body that the face from the chin to the top of the forehead and the roots of the hair is a tenth part, . . . (3.1.2)" and so on. But the head is not the circle. The body, when extended, touches the circumference of a circle (perfection: the ceiling of the Sistine Chapel): "Also a square will be found described *within* [non minus . . . item quadrata designatio . . .] the figure, in the same way as a round figure is produced" [our italics] (3.1.3).

A glance at pertinent Renaissance illustrations in Vitruvius may help elucidate the way in which the whole body approximates all three geometric forms. In figure 19, we see a man with arms and legs outstretched. If he is standing, he is doing so very precariously, with toes "on point," so to speak, on the circumference of the circle. On the page opposite (fig. 20) we see that, if he were indeed standing, his genitals, not his navel, would

mark the equidistant spot from top to bottom, and from
side to side. This explains why Vitruvius depicts a man
lying down with his arms and legs outstretched. In figure
21, we can easily imagine a triangle formed by the outstretched limbs intersecting at the navel, especially if we
recall the "base" of the building laid out previously (fig.
22). Although the nodes of the radii are slightly different,
we seem to have the same interposition of body and geometric form.

As André Chastel has pointed out, in the Renaissance
Vitruvius was construed according to an "anthropometry
of figures,"[29] a "symbolism of numbers" in which,"
drawing on Vitruvius, such theorists as Leo Battista
Alberti and Francesco di Giorgio Martini tried to bring
together theory and practice.[30] Francesco di Giorgio, who
helped design the famous palace of Urbino and whose
S. Maria del Calcinaio in Cortona is considered one of
the masterpieces of the High Renaissance, recognized
"the human figure as a key or clue for the proportion of
architectural forms" (Chastel 143). Accordingly, in the
Codex Magliabechiano (fol. 42[v]), the human body forms
the outline of the cruciform design of a basilica.[31]

Without arguing for Vitruvius as a specific source for
the arithmetical stanza, then, we can say that it is likely
that Spenser had a rather typical Renaissance geometric
system of analogy in mind, which surely entails the human body, but which does so in a subtle and complex
way. As in Vitruvius, so in Spenser, the figure of the
base need not refer to a literal bottom, but may as its pri-
mary function suggest a figurative foundation or plan
(OED). The point is not so much that the emphasis on
symmetry in Vitruvius seems to argue against the analogy between the upright human figure and the divine
edifice, but rather that Spenser's figurative description
seems to resist such a univocal spatial understanding. In
the same way and for the same reason, Spenser's description of the Castle of Alma has a good deal in common
with his description of the three Graces in book 6, and it

seems that his intention in each case is to make it impossible for readers to form in their minds a single, "literal," picture.

The Graces, we will recall, appear to Sir Calidore as he approaches Mount Acidale, while hearing the sound "Of a shrill pipe":

> Unto this place when as the Elfin knight
>   Approacht, him seemed that the merry sound
>   Of a shrill pipe he playing heard on hight,
>   And many feete fast thumping th'hollow ground,
>   That through the woods their Eccho did rebound.
>   He nigher drew, to weet what mote it bee;
>   There he a troupe of Ladies dancing found
>   Full merrily, and making gladfull glee,
> And in the midst a Shepheard [Colin] piping he
>   did see.
>   (1617 Folio, *FQ* 10.10)

In the next stanza, Calidore sees "the naked maydens lilly white, / All ranged in a ring, and dancing in delight" who are in number "An hundred." It is not so much that Calidore is counting; A. C. Hamilton notes that the number "signifies completeness," or it may explain why Calidore, whose being cannot be limited to any one of his five senses, "his eyes envide." And yet, depending on his focus from moment to moment—that is, upon which "ring" of dancers his eye rests—the number varies from 100 to 3 to 1. Again, the traditional view seems to be reversed as two of the three Graces face toward Calidore, while one faces away. In her comment on this complex array of dancing figures, Lila Geller points out the incompatibility of the various "pictures" and even of the various points of view:

> Perhaps Spenser is thinking of the Graces, as in Pico, as mediatrixes between the higher and lower beings. If so, then the one Grace, showing herself afore, goes towards God, who sends back double, the two 'froward' Graces,

doubling what man has given in an overflowing of divine grace. . . . We are not to think that Colin, as maker, associates himself with this point of view, however, for he humbly places himself with the "us" from whom the single grace flows. Obviously the portrait here is iconographic, and does not describe what Colin and Calidore see, which, being in perpetual motion, could not admit of the stationary stance implied in the two-one relationship. Neither does this picture allow for the inclusion of the fourth Grace which is so central to the total meaning of the episode. Yet it is important for Colin to introduce this second picture, as a set-piece to stress the philosophical elevation of the group.[32]

This sounds right to us. The "picture" of the Graces is not a picture at all, for it must be at least two pictures, and more likely three. Furthermore, it is a picture that vanishes or several that vanish. We find here the same kind of anti-literalism that, if our analysis is correct, pervades Spenser's description of the Castle of Alma, and it functions here in much the same way. Spenser goes to considerable lengths to make it impossible for an attentive reader to form in his mind one "picture" of the circle = head, square = body, triangle = legs, much less one picture that can accommodate circle, square, triangle, body and the various parts of a castle.[33]

The foregoing remarks are not aimed at diminishing the importance of the body in Jonson's reading of canto 9. His annotations to stanzas following stanza 22 make this point clear, even though he is not uniform in distributing his markings, or even in using stars in the text or adjacent to his notes.[34] In stanza 26, for instance, line 2 begins with "*Twice sixteene warders," and in the margin we read: "*the Teethe." Stanza 27, line 1, "Thence she them brought into a stately Hall," has next to it: "the Mouth." Stanza 29, line 1, "It was a vaut ybuilt for great dispence," has next to it "<th>e Stomacke." Likewise, in stanza 30, line 4, "*An huge great paire of bellowes," is identified as "The Lunges."

In stanza 33, line 6, Jonson's inscription stating that "a goodly Parlour*" is "the Minde" marks the beginning of a transition in Spenser's treatment of the body, as all stanzas from 33 on concern the inner functions of reason, passion and intellect. These topics require attention. Next to the first several lines of stanza 34 Jonson has written: "the Ladies were named praise desire and shamefastnesse." One could say that, in a sense, Jonson is being too specific here, for Spenser talks, not of two, but of a "bevy of faire Ladies," and from stanza 35 it is clear that they cannot number fewer than five. But Jonson focuses on the only two whom Spenser will name. We can see that, after Jonson has read further in the poem, he has turned back, perhaps in two stages, to note identifications that Spenser postponed making. In stanza 39, line 8, Spenser first names *Praise-desire*, and in stanza 43, line 9, *Shamefastnesse*. Jonson does not mark 39; however, he does place a dash next to the line where *Shamefastnesse* is first named (the only example but one of his using a dash in canto 9; for the other, see below, in the discussion of stanza 51). Jonson does identify each of the figures near the place where she is first described by Spenser. Stanza 37 opens with these lines: "*In a long purple pall, whose skirt with gold / Was fretted all about, she was arrayd." In the margin, Jonson notes "*Desire of praise." In stanza 40, the opening lines are: "The whiles, the *Faerie* knight did entertaine / *Another Damsell of that gentle crew." In the margin is "Shamefastnesse." It would seem that Jonson has worked backward from stanzas 39 and 43 to stanzas 37 and 40, and then further backward to 34 to "undo" Spenser's practice of introducing characters but naming them only after several or even many stanzas. In his note on stanza 40, Hamilton observes:

> The two ladies are associated in Elyot, *Governour* I ix, as shamefastness and the desire for praise, two of the most necesary qualities in a youth: 'By shamfastnes, as it were

with a bridell, they rule as well theyr dedes as their appe-
tites. And desire of prayse addeth to a sharpe spurrre to
their disposition towarde lernyng and vertue.' (The bridle
and spur indicate contrary states.) Elyot's source is Aristotle, Ethics III vii 1116ᵃ, on the balance between shame
and the desire for honour in courageous men. (Hamilton,
255n)

Consonant with our emphasis on the body/soul implications of Jonson's figurative reading of the Castle of Alma,
we would point out that Jonson marks off the next stanza
(35) entirely. He not only places a star before the line, but
he also brackets the stanza with a line to the left side. In
the margin, near the top of the stanza, we read: "the Passions of the minde." This phrase must have had a special
ring for Jonson, and it could easily inform psychological
theses such as those of David Lee Miller. In 1604, Jonson
had contributed a commendatory poem for the second
edition of Thomas Wright's *The Passions of the Minde in
Generall*. According to Theodore A. Stroud, Wright was
the priest who converted him to Roman Catholicism.[35]
Even if Jonson's connection with Wright was not so intimate as Stroud suggests, Jonson certainly knew the man
for whom he wrote the poem, and, from the evidence of
the poem itself, Jonson knew Wright's book.[36] It has been
argued that Jonson's "notions about dramatic character"
owe much to Wright's work.[37] Surely Jonson's commendatory poem indicates that, from Jonson's point of view,
Wright had meticulously and accurately portrayed "In
picture" the "subt'lest Passion, with her source, and
spring" (*UV* 7, line 7). What Jonson admires here is
Wright's discernment on the claims of sense (the subject
of the sequence in book 2 of *The Faerie Queene* is discipline of the five senses) and reason (the ethical content of
Guyon's check on sense, namely, the understanding of
sensation's limits): "'Tis not your fault, if they [your
readers] shall sense preferre, / Being tould there, Reason
cannot, Sense may erre" (lines 13–14).

In the last chapter, we saw how Jonson's direction,

"See Sandys Ovid," indicated his recognition that Spenser's treatment of women was comparable to Sandys's appreciation of the feminist flourish in book 9 of the *Metamorphosis*. We tried to elucidate something of the complexity of Jonson's reading of that passage. In a similar way, Jonson's placement of the title of Wright's book here implies a thematic link between *The Passions of the Minde* and Spenser's representation of the pastimes of the "bevy of faire Ladies":

> Diverse delights they found themselves to please;
>> Some sung in sweet consort, some laught for joy,
>> Some plaid with strawes, some idle sate at ease;
>> But othersome could not abide to toy,
>> All pleasance was to them griefe and annoy:
>> This fround, that faund, the third for shame did blush,
>> Another seemed envious, or coy,
>> Another in her teeth did gnaw a rush:
> But at these strangers presence every one did hush.
>> (1617 Folio, *FQ* 2.9.35)

Thomas Wright insists that passions feed upon the passions, even to the point of "an insatiable desire of pleasure."[38] They can, if not kept under the sway of reason, become like "hungry vipers gnawing uppon the heartstrings of the soule" (sig. F5). In this passage, Spenser emphasizes the breadth of the range of stimulations—even the desire to do nothing—to which the women are inclined. Wright emphasizes the manifold ways in which the passions are revealed: "Words and deeds, speech and action" (sig. H5). Words are the "very image of the mind and soule" (sig. H5), but, as expressions on the face often indicate, even silence can expose the passions. Games, pastimes, feasting, drinking, slothfulness, lechery. Indeed, the tableau struck in stanza 35 may easily remind Spenserians of the engraving in *A Theatre for Voluptuous Worldlings*, the text of which Spenser translated, and which serves David O. Frantz as one example of what Joseph Hall thinks of as the "'experimentall Baudery'" indicative of "the general state of literature in England."[39] Implicitly, Jonson's annotation would seem to suggest Wright's text as a similar gloss on this stanza from book 2.

We have already mentioned stanzas 37 and 40, the next two to be marked by Jonson, who goes on to comment on six more stanzas in the canto. In 45 he identifies the "Turret" of line one as "the Heade" and in 46, line three, "Two goodly Beacons*" as "*the Eyes." In stanza 47, the last four lines are:

> Therein were diverse roomes, and diverse stages,
> But three the chiefest, and of greatest powre,
> In which there dwelt three* honourable sages,
> The wisest men (I weene) that lived in their ages.

Jonson identifies the "three* honourable sages" as: "1 Phantesy. 2 Judg<ment.> 3 memory." Just as Spenser dilates upon the three sages for the remainder of the canto, Jonson apparently follows the practice indicated when he wrote in stanza 34, "the Ladies were named praise desire and shamefastnesse," only here he has taken the terms identified in stanzas 49 ("Phantesey"), 53 ("<Ju>dgment or discre=<t>ion") and 55 ("<M>emory"), and has used them to identify the three sages at the place where they are first introduced into the poem.

Jonson marks only two other stanzas in canto 9. In stanza 48, he identifies *"Phylian*"* as "Nestor"; in the remaining stanza 51, Spenser elaborates on a proverbial expression for a head full of idle thoughts[40] before explaining his metaphor.

> And all the chamber filled was with flyes,
>> Which buzzed all about, and made such sound,
>> That they encombred all mens eares and eyes,
>> Like many swarmes of Bees assembled round,
>> After their hives with honny doe abound:
>> All those were idle thoughts and fantasies,
>> Devices, dreames, opinions unsound,

Shewes, visions, sooth-sayes, and prophecies;
And all that fained it, as leasings, tales, and lies.
(1617 Folio, *FQ* 2.9.51)

Next to the first few lines of this stanza, Jonson
writes: "the severall imaginati<ons> which flott in our
phanse<y>." And in the margin, as though to set off the
last four lines, he places a dash which starts just above
line 6 and slants downward toward the bottom of the
stanza. This may be an instance of Jonson merely describing a passage that attracted his attention (one supposes that he could have written something like: "An
excellent description of phansey"); the explication he offers is no more than is offered in the stanza itself. On the
other hand, it is tempting to imagine that because
Jonson's observation at stanza 51 seems different from
those just before and just after that it might be the result
of a reading of a passage of *The Faerie Queene* that oc-
curred apart from that of other sections. But, since
Jonson was almost certainly going back and forth
through parts of canto 9, it is more likely that his observation at stanza 51 was made at the same time as the
others and is different from them for some other reason.
Again, it may reflect Jonson's recollection of a passage in
Wright's *Passions of the Minde*, or, at any rate, the sense
of such a passage:

> The passion of shamefastnesse brideleth us of many loose
> affections, which would otherwise bee ranging abroad.
> The appetite of honour, which followeth, yea and is due
> unto vertue, encourageth often noble spirites to attempt
> most dangerous exploytes for the benefite of their coun-
> tries: feare expelleth sinne, sadnesse bringeth repentance,
> delight pricketh forward to keepe Gods commandments:
> and to bee brief, passions are spurres that stirre up slug-
> gish and idle soules, from slouthfulnesse to diligence,
> from carelesnesse to consideration. Some questionlesse
> they (almost by force) draw to goodnesse, and others
> withdraw from vice. (sigs. C1–C1ᵛ)

Sir Kenelm Digby, then, is only one of several early shaping influences on the way critics were to read *The Faerie Queene*.

We would be remiss if we ended this discussion of Digby without responding to one objection we have received from a colleague, who perceives in our analysis a "privileging" of Jonson's interpretation over that of such other critics as David Lee Miller. First, we object to the vocabulary in which this particular objection is cast, in that the concept of "privilege" implies the existence, and even the legitimacy, of the notion that choice among alternative hypotheses entails a hierarchical arrangement (even an irrationally structured hierarchical arrangement) of interpretations, which are subject to the assertion of the "will to power" of the critics doing the "privileging." This is an unwarranted assumption. When the compilers of the OED organize the uses, say, of "actuator," or of any other linguistic item for that matter, into groups, they are not "privileging" anything or anybody except the potential user of the information compiled. People are free to ignore the "historical principles" not only of this particular dictionary but of lexicography as well. Critics who prefer to follow their own inclinations may choose to ignore historical principles, and even, in some formulations, to deny the notion of historical evidence.

Our intent throughout this study has been to show that we believe Jonson's views are instances of a reading contemporaneous with authorial usage, and so, potentially relevant to an understanding of that contemporary usage. That intention, which might "privilege" Jonson's reading in some way, affirms two postulates: first, that Jonson's heretofore unpublished remarks add to our understanding of Jonson's critical idiolect, and, so, of the history of the language; and, second, that it is, in and of itself, evidence of the possibilities—and even probabilities—concerning the way Spenser's writings were understood in the language of the period. The problem with

Miller and like-minded critics is that they often fail to address what E. D. Hirsch refers to as the "possibility" criterion of relevance (as we can see from these extant examples, such uses did occur in the Renaissance), and in so doing they peremptorily deny any question of engaging the "probability" criterion (it is or is not likely that this particular use, which was demonstrably current in the Renaissance, is in play in this particular linguistic locale).[41] Could Spenser's texts have been so construed? Were they in fact so construed? At one level, these are simply empirical questions. We must answer them by evidence of usage at the time. And, of course, the corpus of evidence is not fixed, but always expanding. If we must choose between the readings of Jonson and Miller, we would have two reasons to choose the former. Jonson was Spenser's contemporary, and so his readings were possibly relevant to a contemporary understanding of the Spenserian text. But we can say, too, that Jonson's wealth of knowledge of the poetic scene in the late Elizabethan and early Jacobean periods lends credence to the notion that his readings were not only possible in that time, but also actually extant at the time. We must add that one only need choose between a Jonson and a Miller when the question of contemporaneous relevance is invoked, or when the two perspectives appear to be irreconcilably at odds.

The ethical justification for this position should not be hard to understand. In order to avoid isolation in time, we value the voices of the past. But we were not born with sufficient knowledge of the past to grasp all past usages intuitively. That is why we consult dictionaries: to alter the limits of our previous linguistic familiarity with a particular context. Jonson was closer to Spenser, and would probably have understood the way he talked and wrote better than we, without considerable lexicographical orientation, would or do understand him. But this does not mean that either we or Jonson are "privileged," in the sense that one period of time or one locality or one dialect is *intrinsically* superior to another. This is why the term itself is more prescriptive than descriptive in the way that it is used by many critics today. Surely our myths or metanarratives—Freudian, Marxist, historicist, radical, materialist, conservative, semiologist, feminist, structuralist, poststructuralist, deconstructionist, Lacanian, humanist or antihumanist—lead to ways of reading peculiar to late-twentieth century critics. But they deserve no special "privilege," especially when we are talking about texts written prior to the importation of nomenclature from Freud, Marx, Lacan, Irigaray and so on, into literary usage. For these contexts tell us about how we think and talk about ourselves and about works of our own time. Even the pretense that they provide a general breaking of hidden codes that were there all along is only that: a claim devoid of any historical purchase on belief beyond the repetition of statements of belief. We need to know about ourselves, of course. But it is useful, also, to learn about others. For without the voice of others, we must be content to hear only the echolalia of an unchanging message. Like that of John Dixon, the voice we hear may be faint and of unclear value. Like that of James Howell, it may have but slight bearing on the object of our concern. Like that of an Austin or a Digby, it may be either obscure or well-known but deceptive. If we are fortunate, it may be the voice of Ben Jonson.

AFTERWORD

I t is one thing to express the hope of isolating "the voice of Jonson" but quite another to say how we will recognize that voice should we hear it as Jonson's and not merely as the echo of our own impressionistic musings. If one has read this far and remains doubtful on these grounds, it is unlikely that anything we say now would prove convincing. But we would like to register a few remarks on the question of Jonson's voice, and even to proffer a reasonable response to such doubts (as distinct from a "final" answer), because we think it is an important one, and one that has recently been rather given over to strangely skewed and tendentious lines of thought.

These terms are, of course, censorious, but we believe they fit. "Ripeness is all," says Edgar at just the time when it is clear to the audience at how dear a price that recognition has been purchased. A congenial temperament may be a necessary condition for some critical enterprises, but is it a sufficient condition of sensible judgment? We think that timing is essential. Perhaps in striving for a terminology to fit our unskewed, untendentious aims, we need to remind ourselves that the matter of critical propriety may be one of timeliness. When should the critic characterize evidence, before or after, it has been examined? What drives criticism, in the absence of evidence, toward judgment? At the 1991 annual meeting of the Renaissance Conference of Southern California to which we first announced our "discovery," we were surprised when, during the question and answer forum after the session, a noted participant claimed that Jonson's annotations of Spenser were "conventional." We were surprised because, in our paper, we had only alluded to the barest few of Jonson's markings. So on what basis had our interlocutor arrived at a characterization of Jonson's annotations, taken together, as "conventional"? We also knew that not many people in the world had ever seen them, and that, in fact, in the *Spenser Encyclopedia* it had just been announced that the volume in which they were alleged to have been written apparently did not exist. Moreover, we had only recently transcribed the annotations, and the characterization of them as "conventional" did not fit our experience.

We press this point because we believe it is theoretically important. The impulse to characterize evidence before it has been seen may be rooted in our instincts: fight or flight. Evidence threatens to complicate our impulse to explain the world in familiar terms. Jonson's annotations are of necessity "conventional," because the alternative might lead us to think that some remarks are not "conventional," and possibly even original. Such a possibility involves an epistemological enormity. How can annotations come into being unless they are "constructed"? And if they are "constructed," they must *be* "constructed"—that is, "conventional"—made up of material recognizably like themselves "by custom" and "according to precedent." In this way "conventionality" as a concept makes evidence bearably predictable and boring, and so, irrelevant. The world of "convention" goes on as it did before evidence appeared—that is "conventionally"—thus proving that evidence as a concept is bogus and retrograde in that it threatens theory based on "conventionality."

We see no point in saying, to the contrary, that Jonson's remarks are unconventional. Rather, we would register skepticism about this particular characterization and the theoretical assumptions it appears to embrace. The whole idea of research seems to make sense if and only if we allow for an element of discovery. Not only may something new come up, but if and when it does, it might change our characterization of the fictive work at hand. Then, with respect to certain annotations, for instance, we might say that Digby, Jonson and John Dixon appear to agree, while in another case they may register quite disparate and even irreconcilable reactions (Redcrosse Knight as Leicester; Redcrosse Knight as St. George). Although all might be "conventional," in the sense of not idiosyncratic (this matter is open to empirical inquiry), neither may be so. But these assertions remain historical evidence that such readings were in fact lively possibilities in the Elizabethan and Jacobean period.

Having said this, we have still not responded fully to the statement that Jonson's remarks on *The Faerie Queene* were "conventional." If "conventional" here means "customary" or "by precedent," it should take no more than one example to prove the historical assertion that Jonson's annotations of Spenser's poems were sometimes "unconventional" and "without precedent." Like Donne's locution "interinanimates," "actuator" may be an invention of the poet, Jonson; without doubt, the term as we see it used next to book 2, canto 9, stanza 22, apparently came into and passed out of usage roughly within the lifetime of Ben Jonson, and the evidence allows the inference that he could have coined it. We do not believe that we, or anyone else, would know this had no one ever seen Jonson's annotations of the 1617 Folio of Spenser's *The Faerie Queen: The Shepheards Calendar:*

Together With The Other Works. Further, we doubt that anyone, prior to examining these annotations, can proffer a convincing characterization. We learn from them, for instance, that although we might not "conventionally" think of Conti when reading certain passages, Jonson did. So that, if we are referring to the association of Conti with specific passages in Spenser, then in some instances the term tells us something we might want to know about Jonson's understanding of his great contemporary. And the same is true, not only of Ovid, but also of Sandys. As he read along, Jonson thought of other interpretive ventures with respect to certain passages. His marginalia, in these instances, amount to evidence of the phenomenology of reading in the period.

It is important for us to acknowledge that we did not recognize this until we actually examined the annotations, or, more accurately, until we had transcribed the annotations and looked at them in relation to the lines annotated. The same is true of Jonson's reading of Spenser's minor poetry. The development of the English elegy from the obsequies to Sidney to *Lycidas* has been no secret; the elegies commemorating the death of Sidney served as a vehicle for the expression of native poetic ambition. For Spenser, Sidney's passing was like Walsingham's and Leicester's; all were signs that courtly values celebrated by courtly poets were, by desuetude and fecklessness, disappearing from British life. And yet until we examined Jonson's annotations of "The Ruines of Time," we did not see how profoundly Jonson thought of Sidney, Spenser, Walsingham, Leicester, and, above all, Henry Morison, as cognate signs of a virtually apocalyptic decline of civilization that must accompany aristocratic defection from poetry.

We have argued that evidence defies "convention" by forcing a new characterization, in this case, of the "conventionality" of Jonson's literary reaction to Spenser's works. When evidence collides with theory, theory becomes part of the history of theory.

How, then, did Jonson understand *The Faerie Queene*? Well, in the absence of evidence, it looked to some literary historians as if Jonson, the burly stepson of a bricklayer, escapee from the executioner's rope, would not have liked the effete pretender to court favor. On the one hand, we have a poet who cultivated an aureate, elaborately ornamental, narrative style, and on the other, we have one known for a restrained classicism in theatrical and lyric modes. We know from comments that Jonson may have intended indirectly to make public (as in a lecture), but certainly intended also for his own benefit, that he admired Spenser as a poet. He particularly praised many parts of *The Faerie Queene*, which he not only read carefully and understood, but may have explicated for his friend, Sir Walter Ralegh, allegory and all. In theory, Jonson might not be a critic who would have liked Spenser's poetry, but in fact the evidence indicates that he thought highly of it.

Thus, if we pay some mind to the voice of Ben Jonson, our attention is carried away from the vagaries of current critical debate into a consideration of Spenser's text as it could have been—and in some cases was—understood by his contemporaries. Jonson's, of course, is not the only voice, but it is most compelling. Recent critics such as Camille Paglia and David Lee Miller, who may seem to be at loggerheads over *The Faerie Queene*, disagree about what Spenser said not, we suggest, because their critical methods are so different, but because they are so similar. Each bases an argument on what she or he would like the poem to mean, and both, therefore, feel free to impose upon it a personal impression, often called a "reading." We consider that in one respect they are very much like those who insist that Jonson could not have cared for Spenser's poetry at all. That is, they insist on the importance of themes and interests of which neither Spenser nor his contemporary audience were aware. In these pages we have tried, by carefully considering evidence both new and old, to let Jonson speak for himself.

ILLUSTRATIONS

The following illustrations from Ben Jonson's copy of the 1617 Folio of *The Faerie Queen: The Shepheards Calendar: Together With the Other Works of England's Arch Poët, Edm[und] Spenser* include representative annotations and markings of Ben Jonson, which figure prominently throughout this study. Four woodcuts from William Austin's *Haec Homo* (1637) support our discussion of Spenser's House of Alma in the early seventeenth century. We also discuss illustrations from three Renaissance editions of Pollio Vitruvius's *De architectura*, which, we argue, inform a proper understanding of the Spenserian and Jonsonian sense of the analogy between the human body and certain architectural forms.

Illustrations from Jonson's copy of Spenser are reproduced with the permission of J. Paul Getty, KBE. The page from Jonson's 1586 copy of Vitruvius is reproduced by permission of University College Library, London. All other illustrations—those from Austin and Vitruvius (1520, 1660)—are reproduced by permission of the Huntington Library, San Marino, California.

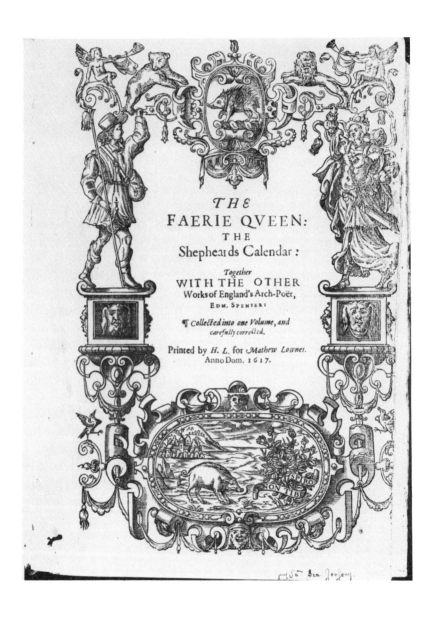

Figure 1. Jonson's Copy of 1617 Spenser Folio, Title page.

Cant.IX.   THE FAERIE QVEENE.   99

16

As when a fwarme of Gnats at euentide
  Out of the fennes of Allan doe arife,
  Their murmuring fmall trumpets founden wide,
Whiles in the ayre their cluftring armies flies,
  That as a cloud doth feeme to dim the skies;
  Ne man nor beaft may reft, or take repaft,
  For their fharpe wounds, and noyous iniuries,
  Till the fierce Northern wind with bluftring blaft
Doth blowe them quite away, and in the Ocean caft.

17

Thus when they had that troublous rout difperft,
  Vnto the Caftle gate they come againe,
  And entrance crav'd, which was denied erft.
  Now, when report of that their perilous paine,
  And combrous conflict which they did fuftaine,
  Came to the Ladies eare which there did dwell,
  She forth iffued with a goodly traine
  Of Squires and Ladies equipaged well,
And entertained them right fairely, as befell.

18

Alma she called was, a virgin bright;
  That had not yet felt *Cupids* wanton rage,
  Yet was she woo'd of many a gentle knight,
  And many a Lord of noble parentage,
  That fought with her to linke in marriage:
  For, she was faire, as faire mote euer bee,
  And in the flowre now of her frefheft age;
  Yet full of grace and goodly modeftee,
That euen heauen reioyced her fweet face to fee.

19

In robe of lilly white she was arrayd,
  That from her fhoulder to her heele downe raught,
  The traine whereof loofe far behind her ftrayd,
  Branched with gold and pearle, moft richly wrought,
  And borne of two faire Damfels, which were taught
  That feruice well. Her yellow golden haire
  Was trimly wouen, and in treffes wrought,
  Ne other tyre she on her head did weare,
But crowned with a garland of fweet Rofiere.

20

Goodly she entertaind thofe noble knights,
  And brought them vp into her caftle hall;
  Where, gentle court and gracious delight
  She to them made, with mildneffe virginall,
  Shewing her felfe both wife and liberall:
  There when they refted had a feafon dew,
  They her befought of fauour fpeciall,
  Of that faire Caftle to afford them view;
She granted, and them leading forth, the fame did fhew.

21

Firft, she them led vp to the Caftle wall,
  That was fo high, that foe might not it clime,
  And all fo faire, and fenfible withall,
  Not built of brick, ne yet of ftone and lime,
  But of thing like to that *Egyptian* flime,
  Whereof king *Nine* whilome built *Babell* towre;
  But ô great pitty, that no lenger time
  So goodly workmanfhip fhould not endure:
Soone it muft turne to earth; no earthly thing is fure.

22

The frame thereof feem'd partly circulare,
  And part triangulare: ô worke diuine!
  Thofe two the firft & laft proportions are,
  The one imperfect, mortall, fœminine;
  Th'other immortall, perfect, mafculine;
  And twixt them both a quadrat was the bafe,
  Proportioned equally by feauen and nine;
  Nine was the circle fet in heauens place,
All which compacted, made a goodly *Diapafe*.

23

Therein two gates were placed feemly well:
  The one before, by which all in did paffe,
  Did th'other far in workmanfhip excell;
  For, not of wood, nor of enduring braffe,
  But of more worthy fubftance fram'd it was;
  Doubly difparted, it did lock and clofe,
  That when it locked, none might thorough paffe,
  And when it opened, no man might it clofe,
Still open to their friends, and clofed to their foes.

24

Of hewen ftone the porch was fairely wrought,
  Stone more of value, and more fmooth and fine,
  Then let or Marble farre from Ireland brought:
  Over the which was caft a wandring Vine,
  Enchaced with a wanton Iuie twine,
  And over it a faire Portcullis hong,
  Which to the gate directly did incline,
  With comly compaffe, and greater ftrong,
Neither vnfeemely fhort, nor yet exceeding long.

25

Within the Barbican a Porter fate,
  Day and night duly keeping watch and ward:
  Nor wight, nor word mote paffe out of the gate,
  But in good order, and with due regard;
  Vtterers of fecrets he from thence debard,
  Babblers of folly, and blazers of crime.
  His larum-bell might loud and wide be heard
  When caufe requir'd, but neuer out of time;
Early and late it rong, at euening and at prime.

26

And round about the porch on euery fide
  Twice fixteene warders fate, all armed bright
  In gliftring fteele, and ftrongly fortifide:
  Tall yeomen feemed they, and of great might,
  And were enranged ready ftill for fight.
  By them as *Alma* paffed with her guefts,
  They did obeyfance, as befeemed right,
  And then againe returned to their refts:
The Porter eke to her did lout with humble gefts.

27

Thence she them brought into a ftately Hall,
  Wherein were many tables faire difpred,
  And ready dight with drapets feaftiuall,
  Againft the viands fhould be miniftred.
  At th'vpper end there fate, yclad in red
  Downe to the ground, a comely perfonage,
  That in his hand a white rod menaged:
  He Steward was, hight *Diet*; ripe of age,
And in demeanure fober, and in counfell fage.

I 3   And

Figure 2. Jonson's Copy of 1617 Spenser Folio (*FQ*), sig. I3.

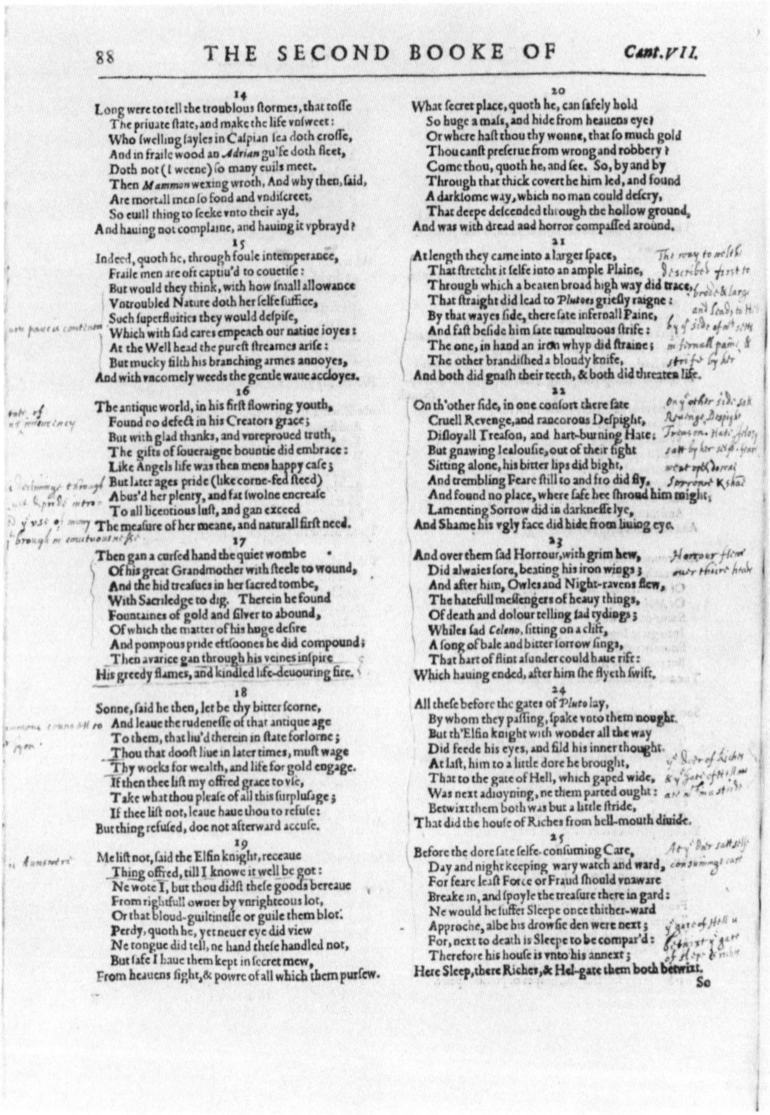

88 THE SECOND BOOKE OF *Cant.VII.*

14

Long were to tell the troublous stormes, that tosse
The priuate state, and make the life vnsweet:
Who swelling sayles in Caspian sea doth crosse,
And in fraile wood an *Adrian* gulfe doth fleet,
Doth not (I weene) so many euils meet.
Then *Mammon* wexing wroth, And why then, said,
Are mortall men so fond and vndiscreet,
So euill thing to seeke vnto their ayd,
And hauing not complaine, and hauing it vpbrayd?

15

Indeed, quoth he, through foule intemperance,
Fraile men are oft captiu'd to couetise:
But would they think, with how small allowance
Vntroubled Nature doth her selfe suffice,
Such superfluities they would despise,
Which with sad cares empeach our natiue ioyes:
At the Well head the purest streames arise:
But mucky filth his branching armes annoyes,
And with vncomely weeds the gentle waue accloyes.

16

The antique world, in his first flowring youth,
Found no defect in his Creators grace;
But with glad thanks, and vnreproued truth,
The gifts of soueraigne bountie did embrace:
Like Angels life was then mens happy case;
But later ages pride (like corne-fed steed)
Abus'd her plenty, and fat swolne encreasе
To all licentious lust, and gan exceed
The measure of her meane, and naturall first need.

17

Then gan a cursed hand the quiet wombe
Of his great Grandmother with steele to wound,
And the hid treasues in her sacred tombe,
With Sacriledge to dig. Therein he found
Fountaines of gold and silver to abound,
Of which the matter of his huge desire
And pompous pride eftsoones he did compound;
Then auarice gan through his veines inspire
His greedy flames, and kindled life-deuouring fire.

18

Sonne, said he then, let be thy bitter scorne,
And leaue the rudenesse of that antique age
To them, that liu'd therein in state forlorne;
Thou that doost liue in later times, must wage
Thy works for wealth, and life for gold engage.
If then thee list my offred grace to vse,
Take what thou please of all this surplusage;
If thee list not, leaue haue thou to refuse:
But thing refused, doe not afterward accuse.

19

Me list not, said the Elfin knight, receaue
Thing offred, till I knowe it well be got:
Ne wote I, but thou didst these goods bereaue
From rightfull owner by vnrighteous lot,
Or that bloud-guiltinesse or guile them blot.
Perdy, quoth he, yet neuer eye did view
Ne tongue did tell, ne hand these handled not,
But safe I haue them kept in secret mew,
From heauens sight, & powre of all which them pursew.

20

What secret place, quoth he, can safely hold
So huge a mass, and hide from heauens eye?
Or where hast thou thy wonne, that so much gold
Thou canst preserue from wrong and robbery?
Come thou, quoth he, and see. So, by and by
Through that thick couert he him led, and found
A darksome way, which no man could descry,
That deepe descended through the hollow ground,
And was with dread and horror compassed around.

21

At length they came into a larger space,
That stretcht it selfe into an ample Plaine,
Through which a beaten broad high way did trace,
That straight did lead to *Plutoes* griesly raigne:
By that wayes side, there sate infernall Paine,
And fast beside him sate tumultuous strife:
The one, in hand an iron whyp did straine;
The other brandished a bloudy knife,
And both did gnash their teeth, & both did threaten life.

22

On th'other side, in one consort there sate
Cruell Revenge, and rancorous Despight,
Disloyall Treason, and hart-burning Hate:
But gnawing Iealousie, out of their sight
Sitting alone, his bitter lips did bight,
And trembling Feare still to and fro did fly,
And found no place, where safe hee shroud him might,
Lamenting Sorrow did in darknesse lye,
And Shame his vgly face did hide from liuing eye.

23

And over them sad Horrour, with grim hew,
Did alwaies sore, beating his iron wings;
And after him, Owles and Night-ravens flew,
The hatefull messengers of heauy things,
Of death and dolour telling sad tydings;
Whiles sad *Celeno*, sitting on a clift,
A song of bale and bitter sorrow sings,
That hart of flint asunder could haue rift:
Which hauing ended, after him she flyeth swift.

24

All these before the gates of *Pluto* lay,
By whom they passing, spake vnto them nought.
But th'Elfin knight with wonder all the way
Did feede his eyes, and fild his inner thought.
At last, him to a little dore he brought,
That to the gate of Hell, which gaped wide,
Was next adioyning, ne them parted ought:
Betwixt them both was but a little stride,
That did the house of Riches from hell-mouth diuide.

25

Before the dore sate selfe-consuming Care,
Day and night keeping wary watch and ward,
For feare least Force or Fraud should vnaware
Breake in, and spoyle the treasure there in gard:
Ne would he suffer Sleepe once thither-ward
Approche, albe his drowsie den were next;
For, next to death is Sleepe to be compar'd:
Therefore his house is vnto his annext;
Here Sleep, there Riches, & Hel-gate them both betwixt.

So

Figure 3. Jonson's Copy of 1617 Spenser Folio (FQ), sig. A3.

46   THE FIRST BOOKE OF   *Cant. X.*

29

Whom thus recouer'd by wise *Patience*,
And true *Repentance*, they to *Vna* brought:
Who ioyous of his cured conscience,
Him dearly kist, and fairely eke besought
Himselfe to cherish, and consuming thought
To put away out of his carefull brest.
By this, *Charissa*, late in child-bed brought,
Was woxen strong, and left her fruitfull nest;
To her, faire *Vna* brought this vnacquainted guest.

30

Shee was a woman in her freshest age,
Of wondrous beauty, and of bounty rare,
With goodly grace and comely personage,
That was on earth not easie to compare;
Full of great loue: but *Cupids* wanton snare
As hell she hated, chaste in worke and will;
Her neck and breasts were euer open bare,
That aye thereof her babes might suck their fill;
The rest was all in yellow robes arraied still.

31

A multitude of babes about her hong,
Playing their sports that ioyd her to behold;
Whom still she fed, whiles they were weake and young,
But thrust them forth still as they wexed old:
And on her head she wore a tyre of gold,
Adornd with gemmes and owches wondrous faire,
Whose passing price vneath was to be told;
And by her side there sate a gentle paire
Of Turtle doues, she sitting in an Ivorie chaire.

32

The Knight and *Vna* entring, faire her greet,
And bid her ioy of that her happy brood;
Who them requites with court'sies seeming meet,
And entertaines with friendly cheerefull mood.
Then *Vna* her besought to be so good,
As in her vertuous rules to schoole her knight,
Now after all his torment well withstood,
In that sad house of *Penaunce*, where his spright
Had past the paines of Hell, and long enduring night.

33

She was right ioyous of her iust request;
And taking by the hand that Faeries sonne,
Gan him instruct in euery good beheft
Of loue and righteousnesse, and well to donne,
And wrath and hatred warily to shunne,
That drew on men Gods hatred and his wrath,
And many soules in dolours had fordonne:
In which, when him she well instructed hath,
From thence to heauen shee teacheth him the ready path.

34

Wherein his weaker wandring steps to guide,
An ancient Matrone she to her does call,
Whose sober lookes her wisedome well discride:
Her name was Mercy, well knowne ouer all,
To be both gracious, and eke liberall;
To whom the carefull charge of him she gaue,
To lead aright, that he should neuer fall
In all his waies through this wide worldes waue,
That Mercy in the end his righteous soule might saue.

35

The godly Matrone by the hand him beares
Forth from her presence, by a narrow way,
Scattred with bushy thornes, and ragged breares,
Which still before him shee remou'd away,
That nothing might his ready passage stay:
And euer when his feet encombred were,
Or gan to shinke, or from the right to stray,
Shee held him fast, and firmly did vpbeare,
As carefull Nurse her child from falling oft does reare.

36

Eftsoones vnto an holy Hospitall,
That was foreby the way, she did him bring,
In which seauen Bead-men, that had vowed all
Their life to seruice of high heauens King,
Did spend their daies in dooing godly thing:
Their gates to all were open euermore,
That by the weary way were trauailing,
And one sate waiting euer them before,
To call in commers-by, that needy were and pore.

37

The first of them that eldest was, and best,
Of all the house had charge and gouernment,
As Guardian and Steward of the rest:
His office was to giue entertainement
And lodging, vnto all that came, and went:
Not vnto such, as could him feast againe,
And double quite for that he on them spent,
But such as want of harbour did constraine:
Those for Gods sake his dutie was to entertaine.

38

The second was the Almner of the place:
His office was, the hungry for to feed,
And thirstie giue to drinke, a worke of grace:
He feard not once himselfe to be in need,
Ne car'd to hoord for those, whom he did breed:
The grace of God he laid vp still in store,
Which as a stock he left vnto his seed;
He had enough, what need him care for more?
And had he lesse; yet some he would giue to the pore.

39

The third had of their Wardrobe custodie,
In which were not rich tires, nor garments gay,
The plumes of Pride, and wings of vanity,
But clothes meet to keepe keene cold away,
And naked nature seemely to array,
With which, bare wretched wights he daily clad,
The images of God in earthly clay;
And if that no spare clothes to giue he had,
His owne coate he would cut, and it distribute glad.

40

The fourth appointed by his office was,
Poore prisoners to relieue with gracious ayd,
And captiues to redeeme with price of brass,
From Turkes and Sarazins, which them had staid;
And though they faultie were, yet well he waid,
That God to vs forgiueth euery howre
Much more then that why they in bonds were layd,
And he that harrow'd hell with heauy stowre, (bowre.
The faulty soules from thence brought to his heauenly
The

Figure 4. Jonson's Copy of 1617 Spenser Folio (*FQ*), sig. D6ᵛ.

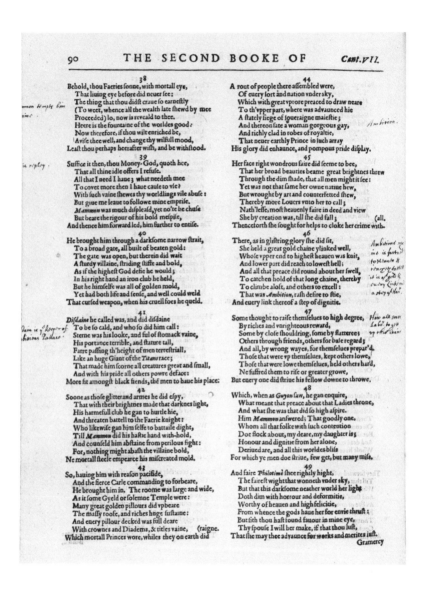

Figure 5. Jonson's Copy of 1617 Spenser Folio (*FQ*), sig. H4ᵛ

4   M. VITRVVII POLL.

vt etiam in aquarum ductionibus.In curfibus enim & circuitioni-
bus, & librata planicie expreffionibus, fpiritus naturales aliter at-
que aliter fiunt, quorum offenfionibus mederi nemo poterit, nifi
qui ex Philofophia principia rerū naturæ nouerit. Item quicunq;
Ctefibij aut Archimedis libros, & cæterorum qui eiufmodi gene-
ris præcepta confcripferunt,leget, cum ijs fentire non poterit,ni-
fi his rebus à Philofophis fuerit inftitutus. Muficen autem fciat
oportet , vti canonicam rationem , & Mathematicam notam habeat : præterea baliftarum,catapultarum, fcorpionū temperaturas
poffit recte facere.In capitulis enim dextra ac finiftra,funt forami-
na homotonorum, per quæ tenduntur ergatis aut fuculis & vecti-
bus è neruo torti funes,qui non percluduntur nec præligantur,ni-
fi fonitus ad artificis aures certos & æquales fecerint.Brachia enim
quæ in eas tenfiones includūtur, cùm extendūtur æqualiter & pa-
riter vtraq; plagā emittere debent. Quod fi nō homotona fuerint,
impedient directā telorū miffionē. Item in theatris vafa ærea, quæ
in cellis fub gradibus Mathematica ratione collocantur,& fonitū
difcrimina , quæ Græci ηχεια vocant, ad fymphonias muficas fiue
cōcentus cōponuntur , diuifa in circinatione diateffarō & diapen-
te & diapafon, vti vox fcenici fonitus conueniens in difpofitioni-
bus,tactu cùm offenderit,aucta cum incremento,clarior & fuauior
ad fpectatorum perueniat aures. Hydraulicas quoque machinas,
& cætera quæ funt fimilia his organis, fine muficis rationibus effi-
cere nemo poterit. Difciplinam verò medicinæ nouiffe oportet,
propter Inclinationes cæli, quæ Græci κλιμαζα dicunt,& aëres lo-
corum, qui funt falubres aut peftilentes,aquarumq; vfus.Sine his
enim rationibus nulla falubris habitatio fieri poteft.Iura quoque
nota habeat oportet ea,quæ neceffaria funt ædificijs communibus
parietum, ad ambitum ftillicidiorum & cloacarum & luminum.
Item aquarum ductiones,& cætera quæ eiufmodi funt,nota oportet fint Architectis, vti ante caueant, quàm inftituant ædificia: ne
controuerfiæ , factis operibus , patribusfamiliarum relinquantur,
& vt legibus fcribendis prudentia caueri poffit & locatori & cōdu-
ctori. Nanq; fi lex perite fuerit fcripta, erit vt fine captione vterq;
ab vtroq; liberetur.Ex Aftrologia autem cognofcitur Oriens,Oc-
cidens, Meridies,Septentrio, & cæli ratio, æquinoctiū, folftitium,
aftrorum curfus: quorum notitiā fi quis non habuerit, horologio-
rum rationem omnino fcire non poterit.Cùm ergo tanta hæc di-
fciplina fit condecorata,& abundans eruditionibus varijs ac pluri-
                                                            bus,

Figure 6. Vitruvius, *De architectura* (1586), sig. A2ᵛ.

The Teares of the Mufes.

And all her Sifters with compassion like,
Did more increafe the fharpnes of her fhowre.
So ended fhe : and then the next in rew,
Began her plaint, as doth herein enfew.

VRANIA.

VVHat wrath of Gods, or wicked influence
Of Starres confpiring wretched men t'afflict,
Hath pourd on earth this noyous peftilence,
That mortall minds doth inwardly infect
With loue of blindnes and of ignorance,
To dwell in darknes without fouerance ?

What difference twixt man and beaft is left,
When th'heauenly light of knowledge is put out,
And th'ornaments of wifdome are bereft?
Then wandreth he in error and in doubt,
Vnweeting of the danger he is in,
Through flefhes frailtie, and deceit of fin.

In this wide world in which they wretches ftray,
It is the onely comfort which they haue,
It is their light, their loadftarre, and their day ;
But hell and darknes, and the griflie graue
Is ignorance, the enemy of grace,
That minds of men borne heauenly doth debace.

Through knowledge, we behould the worlds creation,
How in his cradle firft he foftred was :
And iudge of Natures cunning operation,
How things fhe formed of a formlefle mas:
(By knowledge we doe learne our felues to knowe,
And what to man, and what to God we owe.

From hence, we mount aloft vnto the skie,
And looke into the cryftall firmament :
There we behold the heauens great Hierarchie,
The Starres pure light, the Spheres fwift mouement,
The Spirits and Intelligences faire,
And Angels waiting on th'Almighties chaire.

And there,with humble mind and high infight,
Th'eternall Makers maieftie wee view,
His loue, his truth, his glorie, and his might ,
And mercie more then mortall men can view.
O foueraigne Lord, ô foueraigne happinefle,
To fee thee, and thy mercie meafurelefle !

Such happinefs haue they, that doe embrace
The precepts of my heauenlie difcipline ;
But fhame and forrow and accurfed cafe
Haue they,that fcorne the fchoole of Arts diuine,
And banifh me, which doe profeffe the skill
To make men heauenly wife, through humbled will.

How-euer yet they me defpife and fpight,
I feed on fweet contentment of my thought,
And pleafe my felfe with mine owne felfe-delight,
In contemplation of things heauenlie wrought:

So, loathing earth, I looke vp to the sky,
And beeing driuen hence, I thither flie.

Thence I behold the miferie of men,
Which want the blifs that wifedom would them breed,
And like brute beafts doe lie in loathfome den
Of ghoftly darknes, and of gaftly dreed :
For whom I mourne and for my felfe complaine,
And for my Sifters eake whom they difdaine.

With that, fhee wept and waild fo pitioufly,
As if her eyes had beene two fpringing wells :
And all the reft,her forrow to fupplie,
Did throw forth fhrikes and cries and dreery yells.
So ended fhee, and then the next in rew,
Began her mournfull plaint as doth enfew.

POLYHYMNIA.

A Dolefull cafe defires a dolefull fong,
Without vaine art or curious complements:
And fqualid Fortune into bafenes flong,
Doth fcorne the pride of wonted ornaments.
Then fitteft are thefe ragged rimes for me,
To tell my forrowes that exceeding be.

For the fweet numbers and melodious meafures,
With which I wont the winged words to ty,
And make a tunefull Diapafe of pleafures ;
Now beeing let to runne at libertie
By thofe which haue no skill to rule them right,
Haue now quite loft their naturall delight.

Heapes of huge words vphoorded hideoufly,
With horrid found though hauing little fence,
They thinke to be chiefe praife of Poëtry ;
And thereby wanting due intelligence,
Haue mard the face of goodly Poëfie,
And made a monfter of their fantafie.

Whilome in ages paft none might profeffe
But Princes and high Priefts that fecret skill.
The facred lawes therein they wont expreffe,
And with deepe Oracles their verfes fill :
Then was fhe held in foueraigne dignitie,
And made the nourfling of Nobilitie.

But now nor Prince nor Prieft doth her maintaine,
But fuffer her profaned for to be
Of the bafe vulgar, that with hands vncleane,
Dares to pollute her hidden myfterie ;
And treadeth vnder foote her holy things,
Which was the care of Kefars and of Kings.

One onely liues, her ages ornament,
And mirror of her Makers maieftie,
That with rich bountie and deare cherifhment,
Supports the praife of noble Poëfie :
Ne onely fauours them which it profeffe,
But is her felfe a peerelefs Poëtefle.

Moft

Figure 7. Jonson's Copy of 1617 Spenser Folio
("Teares of the Muses"), sig. I2ᵛ.

The Teares of the Muses.

Most peereleſſe Prince, moſt peereleſſe Poëtreſſe,
The true P A N D O R A of all heauenly graces,
Diuine E L I Z A, ſacred Empereſſe,
Liue ſhe for euer, and her royall P'laces
Be fild with praiſes of diuineſt wits,
Tharher eternize with their heauenly writs.

Some few, beſide, this ſacred skill eſteme,
Admirers of her glorious excellence;
Which beeing lightned with her beauties beme,
Are thereby fild with happy influence,
And lifted vp aboue the worldes gaze,
To ſing with Angels her immortall praize.

But all the reſt as borne of ſaluage brood,
And hauing beene with Acornes alwaies fed,
Can no whit ſauour this celeſtiall food;
But with baſe thoughts are into blindneſſe led,
And kept from looking on the lightſome day :
For whom I waile and weepe all that I may.

Eftſoones ſuch ſtore of teares ſhe forth did powre,
As if ſhe all to water would haue gone;
And all her ſiſters ſeeing her ſad ſtowre,
Did weep and waile, and made exceeding mone,
And all their learned inſtruments did breake.
The reſt, vntold, no liuing tongue can ſpeake.

F I N I S.

I₃   VIR-

Figure 8. Jonson's Copy of 1617 Spenser Folio
("Teares of the Muses"), sig. I3.

The Teares of the Muses.

And launce your hearts with lamentable wounds.
Of secret sorrow and sad languishment,
Before your Loues did take you vnto grace;
Those now renew, as fitter for this place.

For I that rule, in measure moderate,
The tempest of that stormie passion,
And vse to paint in rimes the troublous state
Of louers life in likest fashion,
Am put from practise of my kindlie skill,
Banisht by those that Loue with leawdnes fill.

Loue wont to be schoole-master of my skill,
And the deuicefull matter of my song;
Sweet Loue deuoyd of villanie or ill,
But pure and spotlesse, as at first he sprong
Out of th'Almighties bosome where he nests;
From thence infused into mortall brests.

Such high conceit of that celestiall fire,
The base-borne brood of blindnes cannot ghesse,
Ne euer dare their dunghill thoughts aspire
Vnto so loftie pitch of perfectnesse,
But rime at riot. and doe rage in loue;
Yet little wote what doth thereto behoue.

Faire CYTHEREE, the Mother of delight,
And Queene of beautie, now thou maist goe pack:
For lo. thy Kingdome is defaced quight,
Thy scepter rent, and power put to wrack,
And thy gay Sonne, the winged God of Loue,
May now goe prune his plumes like ruffed Doue.

And yee three Twins to light by VENVS brought,
The sweet companions of the Muses late,
From whom what euer thing is goodly thought,
Doth borrow grace, the fancie to aggrate;
Go beg with vs, and be companions still,
As heretofore of good, so now of ill.

For neither you nor we shall any more,
Find entertainment, or in Court or Schoole:
For that which was accounted heretofore
The learneds meede, is now lent to the foole:
He sings of loue, and maketh louing layes;
And they him heare, and they him highly praise.

With that she poured forth a brackish flood
Of bitter teares, and made exceeding mones;
And all her Sisters seeing her sad mood,
With lowd laments her answered all at one.
So ended she: and then the next in rew,
Began her grieuous plaint, as doth ensew.

CALLIOPE.

TO whom shall I my euill case complaine,
Or tell the anguish of my inward smart,
Sith none is left to remedie my paine,
Or deignes to pittie a perplexed hart?

But rather seekes my sorrow to augment
With foule reproach, and cruell banishment.

For they to whome I vsed to apply
The faithfull seruice of my learned skill,
The goodly of-spring of I OVES progenie,
That wont the world with famous acts to fill;
Whose liuing praises in heroïck stile,
It is my chiefe profession to compile;

They all corrupted through the rust of time,
That doth all fairest things on earth deface,
Or through vnnoble sloth, or sinfull crime,
That doth degenerate the noble race:
Haue both desire of worthy deeds forlorne,
And name of learning vtterly doe scorne.

Ne doe they care to haue the auncestrie
Of th'old Heroes memorizde anew:
Ne doe they care that late posteritie
Should know their names, or speak their praises dew:
But die forgot from whence at first they sprong,
As they themselues shalbe forgot ere long.

What bootes it then to come from glorious
Forefathers, or to haue beene nobly bred?
What oddes twixt IRVS and old INACHVS,
Twixt best and worst, when both alike are dead;
If none of neither mention should make,
Nor out of dust their memories awake?

Or who would euer care to doe braue deed,
Or striue in vertue others to excell;
If none should yeeld him his deserued meed,
Due praise, that is the spur of dooing well;
For if good were not praised more than ill,
None would chuse goodnes of his owne free-will.

Therefore the nurse of vertue I am hight,
And golden Trumpet of eternitie,
That lowly thoughts lift vp to heauens hight,
And mortall men haue powre to deifie:
BACCHVS and HERCVLES I raisd to heauen,
And CHARLEMAINE, amongst the Starris seauen.

But now I will my golden Clarion rend,
And will henceforth immortalize no more:
Sith I no more find worthy to commend
For prize of value, or for learned lore:
For noble Peeres whom I was wont to raise,
Now onely seeke for pleasure, nought for praise.

Their great reuenues all in sumptuous pride
They spend, that nought to learning they may spare;
And the rich fee which Poets wont diuide,
Now Parasites and Sycophants doe share:
Therefore I mourne and endlesse sorrow make,
Both for my selfe, and for my Sisters sake.

With that she lowdly gan to waile and shrike,
And from her eyes a sea of teares did powre,

I 2   And

Figure 9. Jonson's Copy of 1617 Spencer Folio ("Teares of the Muses"), sig. I2.

14   MOTHER HVBBERDS TALE.

But it diſſembled, and vpon his head
The Crowne, and on his back the skin he did,
And the falſe Foxe him helped to array.
Then when he was all dight, he tooke his way
Into the forreſt, that he might be ſeene
Of the wilde beaſts in his new glory ſheene.
There the two firſt, whom he encountred, were
The Sheepe and th'Aſſe, who ſtriken both with feare
At ſight of him, gan faſt away to flye,
But vnto them the Foxe aloud did cry,
And in the Kings name bad them both to ſtay,
Vpon the paine that thereof follow may.
Hardly nath'leſſe were they reſtrained ſo,
Till that the Foxe forth toward them did go,
And there diſſwaded them from needleſſe feare,
For that the King did fauour to them beare;
And therefore dreadleſſe bad them come to Corte:
For no wilde beaſts ſhould doe them any torte
There or abroad, ne would his maieſtie
Vſe them but well, with gracious clemencie,
As whom he knew to him both faſt and true;
So he perſwaded them with homage due
Themſelues to humble to the Ape proſtrate,
VVho gently to them bowing in his gate,
Receiued them with chearfull entertaine.
     Thence, forth proceeding with his princely traine,
He ſhortly met the Tygre, and the Bore,
Which with the ſimple Camell raged ſore
In bitter words, ſeeking to take occaſion,
Vpon his fleſhy corps to make inuaſion :
But ſoone as they this mock-King did eſpy,
Their troublous ſtrife they ſtinted by and by,
Thinking indeed that it the Lion was.
He then to proue whether his power would paſs
As currant, ſent the Foxe to them ſtraight way,
Commaunding them their cauſe of ſtrife bewray;
And if that wrong on either ſide there were,
That he ſhould warne the wronger to appeare
The morrow next at Court, it to defend;
In the meane time vpon the King t'attend.
     The ſubtile Foxe ſo well his meſſage ſaid,
That the proud beaſts him readily obayd :
Whereby the Ape in wondrous ſtomack woxe,
Strongly encourag'd by the crafty Foxe;
That King indeed himſelfe he ſhortly thought,
And all the beaſts him feared as they ought :
And followed vnto his Palace hie,
Where taking Conge, each one by and by
Departed to his home in dreadfull awe,
Full of the feared ſight which late they ſawe.
     The Ape thus ſeized of the Regall throne,
Eftſoones by counſell of the Foxe alone,
Gan to prouide for all things in aſſurance,
That ſo his rule might lenger haue endurance.
Firſt, to his Gate he pointed a ſtrong gard,
That none might enter but with iſſue hard :
Then for the ſafegard of his perſonage,
He did appoint a warlike equipage
Of forraine beaſts, not in the forreſt bred,
But part by land, and part by water fed;

For tyrannie is with ſtrange ayde ſupported.
Then vnto him all monſtrous beaſts reſorted
Bred of two kindes, as Griffons, Minotaures,
Crocodiles, Dragons, Beauers, and Centaures :
With thoſe himſelfe he ſtrengthned mightilie,
That feare he need no force of enemy.
Then gan he rule and tyrannize at will,
Like as the Foxe did guide his graceleſſe skill,
And all wilde beaſts made vaſſals of his pleaſures,
And with their ſpoyles enlarg'd his priuate treaſures.
No care of iuſtice, nor no rule of reaſon,
No temperance, nor no regard of ſeaſon
Did thenceforth euer enter in his minde,
But crueltie, the ſigne of curriſh kinde,
And ſdeignfull pride, and wilfull arrogance;
Such followes thoſe whom fortune doth aduance.
     But the falſe Fox moſt kindly plaid his part :
For, whatſoeuer mother wit, or arte
Could worke, he put in prooſe : no practiſe ſlie,
No counterpoint of cunning policie,
No reach, no breach, that might him profit bring,
But he the ſame did to his purpoſe wring.
Nought ſuffered he the Ape to giue or graunt,
But through his hand muſt paſſe the Fiaunt.
All offices, all Leaſes by him lept,
And of them all what-ſo helikte, he kept.
Iuſtice he ſolde iniuſtice for to buy,
And for to purchaſe for his progeny.
Ill might it proſper, that ill gotten was :
But ſo he got it, little did he paſs,
He fed his cubs with fat of all the ſoyle,
And with the ſweet of others ſweating toyle,
He crammed them with crums of Benefices,
And fild their mouthes with meeds of malefices,
He cloathed them with all colours ſaue white,
And loaded them with Lordſhips and with might,
So much as they were able well to beare,
That with the weight their backs nigh broken were;
He chaffied Chayres in which Churchmen were ſet,
And breach of lawes to priuie ferme did let.
No ſtatute ſo eſtabliſhed might be,
Nor ordinaunce ſo needfull, but that he
VVould violate, though not with violence,
Yet vnder colour of the confidence
The which the Ape repoſ'd in him alone,
And reckned him the kingdoms corner-ſtone.
And euer when he ought would bring to paſs,
His long experience the platforme was :
And when he ought not pleaſing would put by,
The cloke was care of thrift, and husbandry,
For to encreaſe the common treaſures ſtore;
But his owne treaſure he encreaſed more,
And lifted vp his lofty towres therby,
That they began to threat the neighbour sky;
The whiles the Princes Palaces fell ruſh
To ruine : (for what thing can euer laſt?)
And whil'ſt the other Peeres for pouertie
VVere forc't their auncient houſes to let lie,
And their old Caſtles to the ground to fall,
VVhich their forefathers (famous ouer all)

                                    Had

Figure 10. Jonson's Copy of 1617 Spenser Folio
("Mother Hubberds Tale"), sig. A6ᵛ.

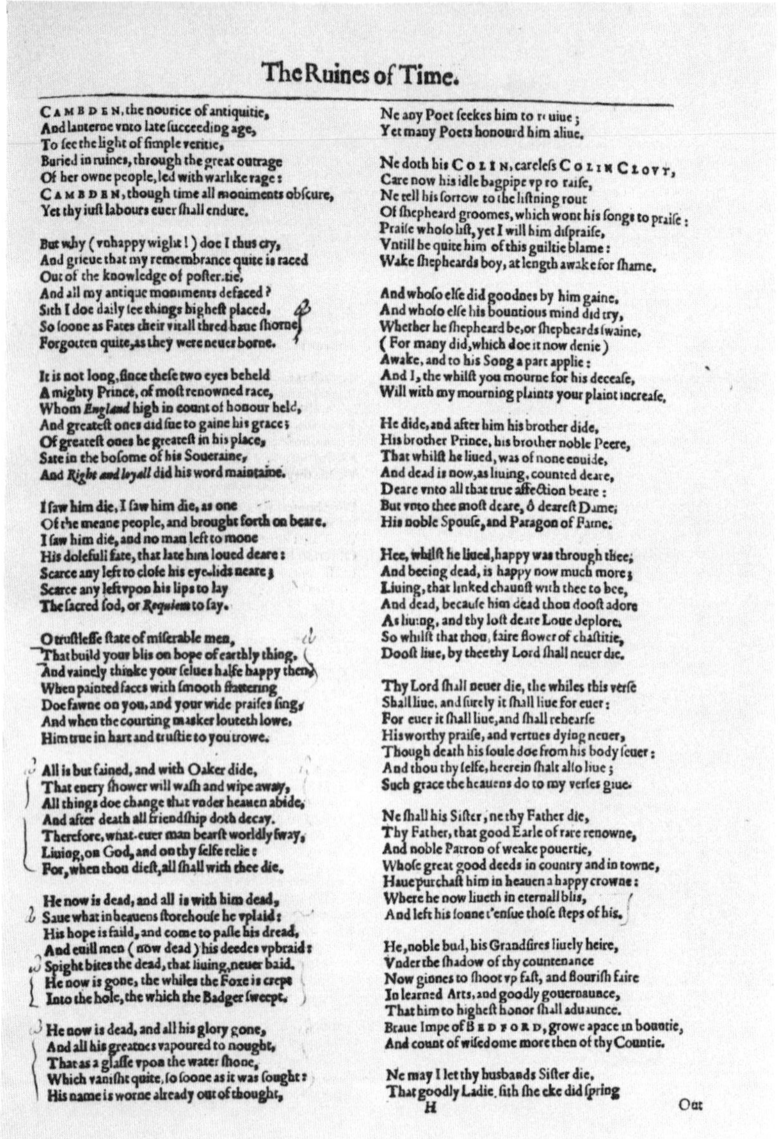

The Ruines of Time.

CAMBDEN, the nourice of antiquitie,
And lanterne vnto late ſucceeding age,
To ſee the light of ſimple veritie,
Buried in ruines, through the great outrage
Of her owne people, led with warlike rage:
CAMBDEN, though time all moniments obſcure,
Yet thy iuſt labours euer ſhall endure.

But why (vnhappy wight!) doe I thus cry,
And grieue that my remembrance quite is raced
Out of the knowledge of poſteritie,
And all my antique moniments defaced?
Sith I doe daily ſee things higheſt placed,
So ſoone as Fates their vitall thred haue ſhorne,
Forgotten quite, as they were neuer borne.

It is not long, ſince theſe two eyes beheld
A mighty Prince, of moſt renowned race,
Whom *England* high in count of honour held,
And greateſt ones did ſue to gaine his grace;
Of greateſt ones he greateſt in his place,
Sate in the boſome of his Soueraine,
And *Right and loyall* did his word maintaine.

I ſaw him die, I ſaw him die, as one
Of the meane people, and brought forth on beare.
I ſaw him die, and no man left to mone
His dolefull fate, that late him loued deare:
Scarce any left to cloſe his eye-lids neare;
Scarce any left vpon his lips to lay
The ſacred ſod, or *Requiem* to ſay.

O truſtleſſe ſtate of miſerable men,
That build your blis on hope of earthly thing,
And vainely thinke your ſelues halfe happy then,
When painted faces with ſmooth flattering
Doe fawne on you, and your wide praiſes ſing,
And when the courting masker louteth lowe,
Him true in hart and truſtie to you trowe.

All is but fained, and with Oaker dide,
That euery ſhower will waſh and wipe away,
All things doe change that vnder heauen abide,
And after death all friendſhip doth decay.
Therefore, what-euer man bearſt worldly ſway,
Liuing, on God, and on thy ſelfe relie:
For, when thou dieſt, all ſhall with thee die.

He now is dead, and all is with him dead,
Saue what in heauens ſtorehouſe he vplaid:
His hope is faild, and come to paſſe his dread,
And euill men (now dead) his deedes vpbraid:
Spight bites the dead, that liuing, neuer baid.
He now is gone, the whiles the Foxe is crept
Into the hole, the which the Badger ſwept.

He now is dead, and all his glory gone,
And all his greatnes vapoured to nought,
That as a glaſſe vpon the water ſhone,
Which vaniſht quite, ſo ſoone as it was ſought:
His name is worne already out of thought,
Ne any Poet ſeekes him to reuiue;
Yet many Poets honourd him aliue.

Ne doth his COLIN, careleſs COLIN CLOVT,
Care now his idle bagpipe vp to raiſe,
Ne tell his ſorrow to the liſtning rout
Of ſhepheard groomes, which wont his ſongs to praiſe:
Praiſe whoſo liſt, yet I will him diſpraiſe,
Vntill he quite him of this guiltie blame:
Wake ſhepheards boy, at length awake for ſhame.

And whoſo elſe did goodnes by him gaine,
And whoſo elſe his bountious mind did try,
Whether he ſhepheard be, or ſhepheards ſwaine,
(For many did, which doe it now denie)
Awake, and to his Song a part applie:
And I, the whilſt you mourne for his deceaſe,
Will with my mourning plaints your plaint increaſe.

He dide, and after him his brother dide,
His brother Prince, his brother noble Peere,
That whilſt he liued, was of none enuide,
And dead is now, as liuing, counted deare,
Deare vnto all that true affection beare:
But vnto thee moſt deare, ô deareſt Dame;
His noble Spouſe, and Paragon of Fame.

Hee, whilſt he liued, happy was through thee;
And beeing dead, is happy now much more;
Liuing, that linked chaunſt with thee to bee,
And dead, becauſe him dead thou dooſt adore
As liuing, and thy loſt deare Loue deplore.
So whilſt that thou, faire flower of chaſtitie,
Dooſt liue, by thee thy Lord ſhall neuer die.

Thy Lord ſhall neuer die, the whiles this verſe
Shall liue, and ſurely it ſhall liue for euer:
For euer it ſhall liue, and ſhall rehearſe
His worthy praiſe, and vertues dying neuer,
Though death his ſoule doe from his body ſeuer:
And thou thy ſelfe, heerein ſhalt alſo liue;
Such grace the heauens do to my verſes giue.

Ne ſhall his Siſter, ne thy Father die,
Thy Father, that good Earle of rare renowne,
And noble Patron of weake pouertie,
Whoſe great good deeds in country and in towne,
Haue purchaſt him in heauen a happy crowne:
Where he now liueth in eternall blis,
And left his ſonne t'enſue thoſe ſteps of his.

He, noble bud, his Grandſires liuely heire,
Vnder the ſhadow of thy countenance
Now ginnes to ſhoot vp faſt, and flouriſh faire
In learned Arts, and goodly gouernaunce,
That him to higheſt honor ſhall aduaunce.
Braue Impe of BEDFORD, growe apace in bountie,
And count of wiſedome more then of thy Countie.

Ne may I let thy husbands Siſter die,
That goodly Ladie, ſith ſhe eke did ſpring

H Out

Figure 11. Jonson's Copy of 1617 Spencer Folio ("Ruines of Time"), sig. H1.

The Ruines of Time.

All happinesse in HERBES siluer bowre,
Chosen to be her dearest Paramoure,

So raisde they eke faire LEDAES warlike twinnes,
And interchanged life vnto them lent,
That when th'one dies, the other then beginnes
To shew in heauen his brightnes orient;
And they for pitty of the sad wayment,
Which ORPHEVS for EVRIDICE did make,
Her back againe to life sent for his sake.

So happy are they, and so fortunate,
Whom the PIERIAN sacred Sisters loue,
That freed from bands of impacable fate,
And powre of death, they liue for aye aboue,
Where mortall wreakes their blis may not remoue:
But with the Gods, for former vertues meede,
On Nectar and Ambrosia doe feede.

For deeds doe die, how euer noblie doonne,
And thoughts of men doe in themselues decay:
But wise words taught in numbers for to runne,
Recorded by the Muses, liue for aye;
Ne may with storming showers be washt away,
Ne bitter breathing winds with harmfull blast,
Nor age, nor enuie shall them euer wast.

In vaine doe earthly Princes then, in vaine
Seeke with Pyramides, to heauen aspired;
Or huge Colosses, built with costly paine;
Or brasen Pillours, neuer to be fired,
Or Shrines, made of the metall most desired;
To make their memories for euer liue:
For how can mortall immortalitie giue?

Such one MAVSOLVS made, the worlds great wonder,
But now no remnant doth thereof remaine:
Such one MARCELLVS, but was torne with thunder:
Such one LISIPPVS, but is worne with raine:
Such one King EDMOND, but was rent for gaine,
All such vaine monuments of earthlie masse,
Deuour'd of Time, in time to nought doe passe.

But Fame with golden wings aloft doth flie,
Aboue the reach of ruinous decay,
And with braue plumes doth beat the azure skie,
Admir'd of base-borne men from farre away:
Then whoso will with vertuous deeds assay
To mount to heauen, on PEGASVS must ride,
And with sweet Poets verse be glorifide.

For not to haue been dipt in LETHE lake,
Could saue the sonne of THETIS from to die;
But that blind Bard did him immortall make,
With verses, dipt in deaw of CASTALIE:
Which made the Easterne Conqueror to crie,
O fortunate young man, whose vertue found
So braue a Trompe, thy noble acts to sound.

Therefore in this, halfe happie I doe read
Good MELIBAE, that hath a Poet got,

To sing his liuing praises beeing dead,
Deseruing neuer here to be forgot,
In spight of enuie, that his deeds would spot:
Since whose decease, learning lies vnregarded,
And men of Armes doe wander vnrewarded.

These two be those two great calamities,
That long agoe did grieue the noble spright
Of SALOMON, with great indignities;
Who whilome was aliue the wisest wight.
But now his wisedome is disproued quight;
For, such as now haue most the World at will,
Scorne th'one and th'other in their deeper skill.

O griefe of griefes! ô gall of all good harts!
To see that vertue should despised bee
Of such as first were raisd for vertuous parts,
And now broad spreading, like an aged tree,
Let none shoote vp that nigh them planted bee:
O! let not those, of whom the Muse is scorned,
Aliue nor dead, be of the Muse adorned.

O vile worlds trust, that with such vaine illusion,
Hath so wise men bewitcht, and ouerkeft,
That they see not the way of their confusion:
O vainenesse to be added to the rest,
That doth my soule with inward griefe infest:
Let them behold the pitious fall of mee,
And in my case their owne ensample see.

And whoso else that sits in highest seat
Of this worlds glorie, worshipped of all,
Ne feareth change of time, nor fortunes threat,
Let him behold the horror of my fall,
And his owne end vnto remembrance call;
That of like ruine he may warned bee,
And in him selfe be moou'd to pittie mee.

Thus hauing ended all her pitious plaint,
With dolefull shrikes she vanished away,
That I through inward sorrowe wexen faint,
And all astonished with deepe dismay,
For her departure, had no word to say:
But sate long time in senselesse sad affright,
Looking still, if I might of her haue sight.

Which when I missed, hauing looked long,
My thought returned grieued, home againe,
Renuing her complaint with passion strong,
For ruth of that same womans pitious paine;
Whose words recording in my troubled braine,
I felt such anguish wound my feeble hart,
That frozen horror ran through euery part.

So inly grieuing in my groning breast,
And deepely muzing at her doubtfull speach,
Whose meaning, much I laboured forth to wrest,
Beeing aboue my slender reasons reach:
At length, by demonstration me to teach,
Before mine eyes strange sights presented were,
Like tragicke Pageants seeming to appeare.

H 2   I saw

Figure 12. Jonson's Copy of 1617 Spenser Folio
("Ruines of Time"), sig. H2.

The Ruines of Time.

Out of this stocke, and famous familie,
Whose praises I to future age do sing,
And forth out of her happy wombe did bring
The sacred brood of learning and all honour;
In whom the heauens pourd all their gifts vpon her.

Most gentle spirit breathed from aboue,
Out of the bosome of the makers blis,
In whom all bountie and all vertuous loue
Appeared in their natiue properties,
And did enrich that noble breast of his,
With treasure passing all this worldes worth,
Worthy of heauen it selfe, which brought it forth.

His blessed spirit, full of power diuine,
And influence of all celestiall grace,
Loathing this sinfull earth and earthly slime,
Fled backe too soone vnto his natiue place;
Too soone for all that did his loue embrace,
Too soone for all this wretched world, whom he
Robd of all right and true nobilitie.

Yet ere his happy soule to heauen went
Out of this fleshly gaole, he did deuise
Vnto his heauenly Maker to present
His body, as a spotlesse sacrifice;
And chose, that guiltie hands of enemies
Should poure forth th'offring of his guiltlesse blood:
So life exchanging for his countries good.

O noble spirit, liue there euer blessed,
The worlds late wonder, & the heauens new ioy,
Liue euer there, and leaue me here distressed
With mortall cares, and cumbrous worlds anoy.
But where thou doost thir happines enioy,
Bid me, O bid me quickly come to thee,
That happy there I may thee alwaies see.

Yet whilst the Fates affoord me vitall breath,
I will it spend in speaking of thy praise,
And sing to thee, vntill that timely death
By heauens doome doe end my earthly daies:
Thereto doe thou my humble spirit raise,
And into me that sacred breath inspire,
Which thou there breathest, perfect and entire.

Then will I sing: but who can better sing,
Then thine owne Sister, peerelesse Lady bright,
Which to thee sings with deepe harts sorrowing,
Sorrowing tempered with deare delight,
That her to heare, I feele my feeble spright
Robbed of sense, and rauished with ioy,
(O sad ioy!) made of mourning and anoy.

Yet will I sing: but who can better sing,
Then thou thy selfe, thine owne selfes valiance,
That whilst thou liuedst, mad'st the forrests ring,
And fields resownd, and flocks to leape and daunce,
And Shepheards leaue their lambes vnto mischaunce,
To runne thy shrill *Arcadian* Pipe to heare:
O happy were those dayes, thrice happy were.

But now more happy thou, and wretched wee,
Which want the wonted sweetnes of thy voice,
Whiles thou now in *Elysian* fields so free,
With Orpheus, with Linus, and the choice
Of all that euer did in rimes reioice,
Conuersest, and doost heare their heauenly layes,
And they heare thine, and thine doe better praise.

So there thou liuest, singing euermore,
And here thou liuest, beeing euer long
Of vs, which liuing, loued thee afore,
And now thee worship, mongst that blessed throng
Of heauenly Poets, and Heroës strong.
So thou both here and there immortall art,
And euerie where through extellent desart.

But such as neither of themselues can sing,
Nor yet are sung of others for reward,
Die in obscure obliuion, as the thing
Which neuer was: ne euer with regard
Their names shall of the later age be heard,
But shall in rustie darknes euer lie,
Vnlesse they mentiond be with infamie.

What booteth it to haue beene rich aliue?
What to be great? what to be gracious?
When after death no token doth suruiue
Of former beeing in this mortall hous,
But sleepes in dust dead and inglorious,
Like beast, whose breath but in his nostrils is,
And hath no hope of happinesse or blis.

How many great ones may remembred be,
Which in their daies most famously did florish
Of whom no word we heare, nor signe now see,
But as things wipt out with a spunge do perish,
Because they liuing, cared not to cherish
No gentle wits, through pride or couetize,
Which might their names for euer memorize.

Prouide therefore (ye Princes) whilst ye liue,
That of the Muses ye may friended bee,
Which vnto men eternitie doe giue:
For they be daughters of Dame Memorie,
And Ioue, the Father of eternitie,
And doe those men in golden thrones repose,
Whose merits they to glorifie doe chose.

The seauen-fould yron gates of grisly Hell,
And horrid house of sad Proserpina,
They able are with power of mightie spell
To breake, and thence the soules to bring away
Out of drad darknes, to eternall day,
And them immortall make, which else would die
In foule forgetfulnesse, and namelesse lie.

So whilome raised they the puissant brood
Of golden-girt Alcmena, for great merit,
Out of the dust, to which the Obtaean wood
Had him consum'd, and spent his vitall spirit;
To highest heauen, where now he doth inherit

All

Figure 13. Jonson's Copy of 1617 Spenser Folio
("Ruines of Time"), sig. H1ᵛ.

9
Diuerse discourses in their way they spent,
Mongst which Cymochles of her questioned,
Both what she was, and what that viage ment,
Which in her cot she daily practised.
Vaine man, said she, that would'st be reckoned
A stranger in thy home, and ignorant
Of Phaedria (for so my name is red)
Of Phaedria, thine owne fellow seruant;
For, thou to serue Acrasia thy selfe doost vaunt.

10
In this wide Inland sea, that hight by name
The Idle lake, my wandring ship I rowe,
That knowes her Port, and thither sailes by ayme,
Ne care, ne feare I, how the wind doe blowe,
Or whether swift I wend, or whether slowe:
Both slowe and swift alike doe serue my tourne,
Ne swelling Neptune, ne loud thundring Ioue
Can change my cheare, or make me euer mourne;
My little boat can safely passe this perilous bourne.

11
Whiles thus she talked, and whiles thus she toyd,
They were farre past the passage which he spake,
And come vnto an Iland waste and voyd,
That floted in the midst of that great lake:
There her small Gondelay her Port did make,
And that gay paire issuing on the shore
Disburdned her. Their way they forward take
Into the Land that lay them faire before,
Whose pleasaunce she him shew'd, & plentiful great store.

12
It was a chosen plot of fertile land,
Emongst wide waues set like a little nest,
As if it had by Natures cunning hand,
Beene choicely picked out from all the rest,
And layd forth for ensample of the best:
No daintie flowre or herbe that growes on ground,
No arboret with painted blossoms drest,
And smelling sweet, but there it might be found
To bud out faire, & her sweet smels throwe all around.

13
No tree, whose branches did not brauely spring;
No branch, whereon a fine bird did not sit:
No bird, but did her shrill notes sweetly sing;
No song but did containe a louely dit:
Trees, branches, birds, & songs were framed fit
For to allure fraile men to carelesse ease.
Carelesse the man soone wox, and his weake wit
Was ouercome of thing, that did him pleafe;
So pleased, did his wrathfull purpose faire appeafe.

14
Thus when she had his eyes and senses fed
With false delights, and fild with pleasures vaine,
Into a shady dale she soft him led,
And laid him downe vpon a grassie PLaine;
And her sweet selfe, without dread or disdaine
She set beside, laying his head disarm'd
In her loose lap, it softly to sustaine,
Where soone he slumbred, fearing not be harm'd.
The whiles with a loud lay she thus him sweetly charm'd.

15
Behold, ô man, that toyle-some paines doost take,
The flowres, the fields, and all that pleasant growes,
How they themselues doe thine ensample make,
Whiles nothing envious Nature them forth throwes
Out of her fruitfull lap; how, no man knowes,
They spring, they bud, they blossome fresh & faire,
And deck the world with their rich pompous showes;
Yet no man for them taketh paines or care,
Yet no man to them can his carefull paines compare.

16
The Lilly, Lady of the flowring field,
The Flowre-delice, her louely Paramoure,
Bid thee to them thy fruitlesse labours yield,
And soone leaue off this toylesome weary stoure;
Lo, lo, how braue she decks her bountious boure,
With silken curtens and gold couerlets,
Therein to shrowd her sumptuous Belamoure,
Yet neither spines nor cardes, ne cares nor frets,
But to her mother Nature all her care she lets.

17
Why then doost thou, ô man, that of them all
Art Lord, and eke of nature Soueraigne,
Wilfully make thy selfe a wretched thrall,
And waste thy ioyous houres in needlesse paine,
Seeking for danger and adventures vaine?
What bootes it all to haue, and nothing vse?
Who shall him rew, that swimming in the maine,
Will die for thirst, and water doth refuse?
Refuse such fruitlesse toyle, and present pleasures chuse.

18
By this, she had him lulled fast asleepe,
That of no worldly thing he care did take;
Then she with liquors strong his eyes did steepe,
That nothing should him hastily awake:
So she him left, and did herselfe betake
Vnto her boat againe, with which she cleft
The slothfull waues of that great griesly lake;
Soone shee that Iland farre behind her left,
And now is come to that same place, where first she weft.

19
By this time was the worthy Guyon brought
Vnto the other side of that wide strond,
Where she was rowing, and for passage sought:
Him needed not long call, she soone to hond
Her ferry brought, where him she byding fond,
With his sad guide; himselfe shee tooke aboord,
But the Black Palmer suffred still to stond,
Ne would for price, or prayers once affoord,
To ferry that old man ouer that perlous foord.

20
Guyon was loath to leaue his guide behind,
Yet beeing entred, might not backe retire;
For, the flit barke, obaying to her mind,
Forth launched quickly, as she did desire,
Ne gaue him leaue to bid that aged Sire
Adieu, but nimbly ran her wonted course
Through the dull billowes thick as troubled mire,
Whom neither wind out of their seat could force,
Nor timely tides did driue out of their sluggish sourse.

H   And

Figure 14. Jonson's Copy of 1617 Spenser Folio (FQ), sig. H1.

Figure 15. William Austin, *Haec Homo* (1637), sig. E2ᵛ.

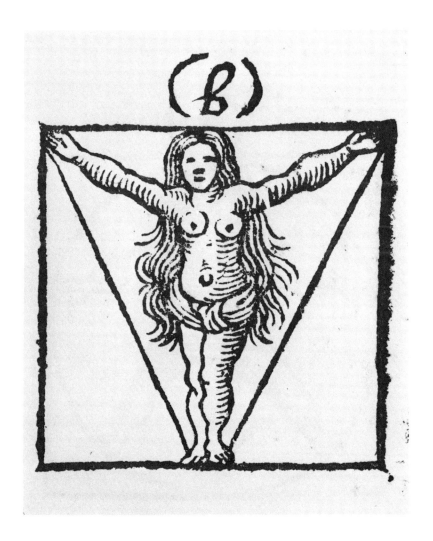

Figure 16. William Austin, *Haec Homo* (1637), E3.

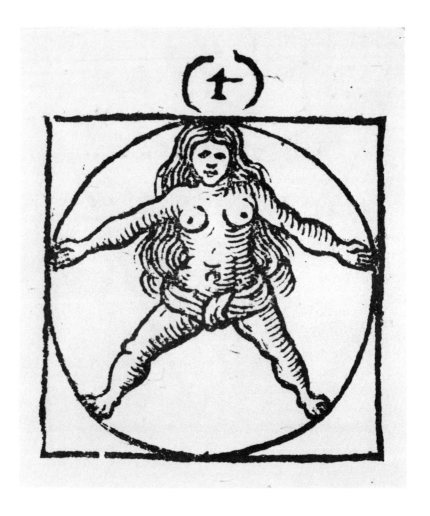

Figure 17. William Austin, *Haec Homo* (1637), sig. E3ᵛ.

Figure 18. William Austin, *Haec Homo* (1637), sig. E4.

Figure 19. Vitruvius, *De architectura* (1660), p. 47.

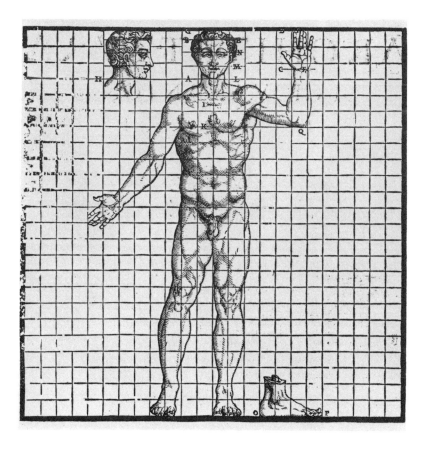

Figure 20. Vitruvius, *De architectura* (1660), p. 46.

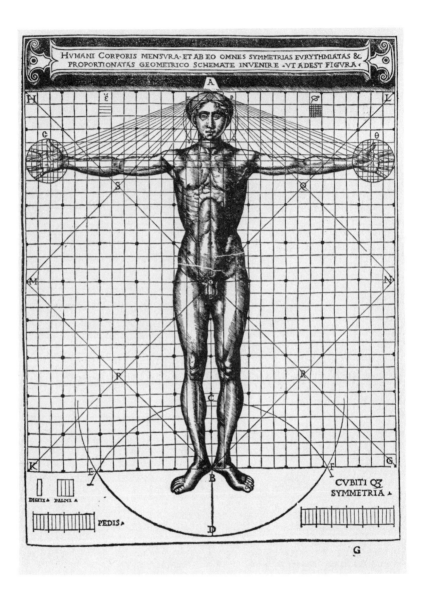

Figure 21. Vitruvius, *De architectura* (1521), sig. G1.

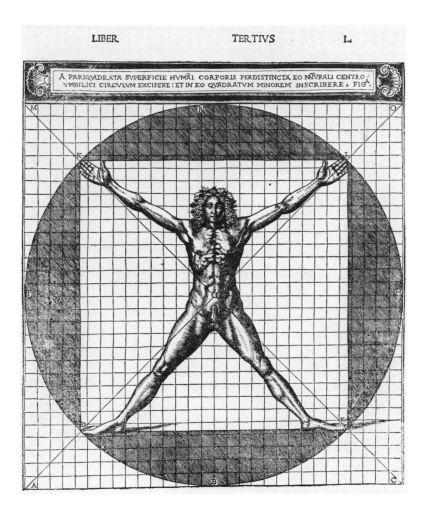

Figure 22. Vitruvius, *De architectura* (1521), sig. G2.

Jonson's Annotations and Representative Marks to the 1617 Spenser Folio

In the following pages we cite both page numbers and signatures, if both are present. For some works, there are no page numbers in the Folio; signature numbers follow the respective gatherings. Underlinings in the right-hand column indicate Jonson's underlinings, not italics. Matter enclosed within pointed brackets represent our conjectures about text that has been lost, almost always because of cropping of pages when the book was rebound, probably in the eighteenth century.

[Inside cover:]

"Important Literary Discovery"

"suggested meanings of words or illusions [sic] in
the poem, and other notes and marks, which
indicate the most careful and word-by-word study of
the author."

Title page[1]

[top right]   <tanquam Explorator>[2]

[At the bottom, right]   Sum Ben: Jonsonij

---

[1] See figure 1, p. 138.
[2] See introduction.

Page	Sig.	Stanza	Line	Annotation

THE FAERIE QUEENE
BOOK 1

Canto 1

Page	Sig.	Stanza	Line	Annotation
2	A2ᵛ	1	(above) 1	St George!
		3	9	The Divel.
		4	1	Religion.
3	A3	14	6	Errour.
4	A3ᵛ	29		Hypocrisy.
5	A4	43		* [before "*Archimago*"] * Hypocresy.

Canto 2

Page	Sig.	Stanza	Line	Annotation
7	A5			[hand pointer]
8[10]¹	A5ᵛ	16	1	Simile.
9	A6	22	7	The Pope.
		31	1–3	[hand pointer]

¹ There is a pagination error in 1609 and 1611 Folios.

Page	Sig.	Stanza	Line	Annotation
Canto 3				
12	B1ᵛ	16–17	(above) 1	<u>Sacrilege</u>.
		18	4	<u>Blind devotion</u>.
13	B2	31	1	<u>Simile</u>.
Canto 4				
16	B3ᵛ	12	1	<u>Pride</u>.
		18	6	<u>Sloth</u>.
17	B4	21	1	<u>Glutto</u>ny.
		24	1	<u>Lust.</u>
		27	1	<u>Covetise</u>.
		30	1	<u>Envie</u>.
18	B4ᵛ	33	1	<u>Wrath</u>.
		36	2	<u>Sathan</u>.
Canto 5				
		2	1–3	[hand pointer]
20	B5ᵛ	8	1	<u>Simile</u>.
21	B6	19	1	[hand pointer]
22	B6ᵛ	28		[hand pointer]
24	C1ᵛ	48		<u>Alex. Maj</u>
Canto 10				
43	D5	4	3	<u>Holines</u>.
			6	Fayth. Hope
			7	Charity.

Page	Sig.	Stanza	Line	Annotation
44	D5ᵛ	5	8	<u>Humility</u>.
		6	6	<u>Zeale</u>.
		7	6	<u>Reverence</u>.
		8	6	True <u>Religion</u>.
45	D6	17	9	<u>obsequious</u>
		20	3	The
			4–5	Powers
			6	of
			7	True <u>Fayth</u>
		23	9	Patience, the
			below 9	<u>Physitian</u>.
		27	1	<u>Penance</u>.
			3	<u>Remorse</u>.
			5	<u>Repentance</u>.
46	D6ᵛ	34	4	<u>Mercy</u>.
		36	4	7 <u>Workes</u>
			7	of
			8	<u>Charity</u>
		37	4	<u>Lodging</u>.
			5	giving
			6	<u>Harbrough</u>.
		38	3	giving
			4	<u>Almes</u>.
			6	feeding
			ʔ	the
			9	<u>hungry</u>

Page	Sig.	Stanza	Line	Annotation
		39	5	clothe the
			6	<u>naked</u>.
		40	2–3	redeeme
			4	<u>prisoners</u>.
47	E1	41	4	Visit the
			6	<u>sick</u>.

Canto 11

50	E2ᵛ	5		[hand pointer]
52	E3ᵛ	29	3	<u>Baptisme</u>.
53	E4	48	1	<u>The Euch\<arist\></u>

Book 2

Canto 2

67	F5	24	2–3	Simile

Canto 3

69	F6	1	4–	Descrip.
				of the morninge
70	F6ᵛ	4	3	\<Desc\>r of a base and
			4	\<vai\>ne glorious man
71	G1	22	5–6	An excelent D\<escr.\>
			7	of a butifull La\<dy\>
72	G1ᵛ	36	1	An excell.
			2	Simile to
			3	expresse [word crossed out]
			4	cowardnesse.

Page	Sig.	Stanza	Line	Annotation

Canto 4

Page	Sig.	Stanza	Line	Annotation
74	G2ᵛ	4	3	Furor.
			4	Occasion
		7	2	The dainger of
			3	Fury that it
			6	woundes it selfe
			8	Simile
	G3	11	2	The way to over
			3	come Fury is
			4	to restrayne
			5	Occasion
76	G3ᵛ	23	3	\<Jea\>losy
77	G4	34	3	Affections unre=
			4	strained, are
			5	the rates¹ of all
			6	afflictions.
		42		*[after *"Atin"*]
				< TIS?>² *Contention

Canto 5

Page	Sig.	Stanza	Line	Annotation
78	G4ᵛ	2	5	Simile
79	G5	10	3	An excellent simile
			4	Of a furious
			4–5	man.
		13	8	Hast breads repen\<tance\>

¹ "The rates," i.e., the payment, recompence, or wages (as of sin), honce, consequences.
² These four characters appear to be hand printed capitals.

Page	Sig.	Stanza	Line	Annotation
		16	2	Wise men should avoyde <the>
			3	cause of contention which <is, grows?>
			4	within themselves.
80	G5ᵛ	20	2–3	<Py>rrhocles having released
			3–4	<Fu>ry and Occasion is by
			4–5	<Fu>ry challenged and by
			5	<b>oth of them abused
		27	4	excesse of pleasur
			5	enervats the body
			6	and exanimates¹
			7	the strongest.
81	G6	32	2	An excellen Des=
			3–4	of a man drownd
			4–5	in pleasures.
		35		*[before *Atin*]
			2	*Contention prompt<s Cymochles>
			3	to Revenge his b<rother>
			4–5	Pyrrhochles.

Canto 6

Page	Sig.	Stanza	Line	Annotation
82	G6ᵛ	3	1	<Vain>e delight
			4	<L>ady ministers
			5	<ma>tter of mirth to
			6	<he>r selfe.

---

¹ "Exanimates," a cognate of Donne's "interinanimates," means "to deprive of life" (*OED*).

Page	Sig.	Stanza	Line	Annotation
		6	1	Chymochles [word crossed out] is
			2	led by vaine delight
			3	to forgett his vowed
			4	revenge and carried by her
			5	throughe the Idle Lake
			6	into the Iland of pleasure
		8	7	Delight extinguishes
			8	our godliest and best reso=
			9	lutions.
83	H1	12	1–2	An Exce. Descr.
			2–3	of a pleasant
			4	Iland.
		15	1	Vaine delight cha<nges>
			2	the senses of frail<e>
			3	man into a sec<ure>
			5	carlessenesse.
		17		Reminiscé[1] [Between stanzas in margin}
		19	4	Sr Guyon carried by
			5	the Lady Vaine deligh<t>
			6	into the Iland of plesu<re>
84	H1ᵛ	25	2	<Vain>e delight endevors
			3	<to> drawe Sr Guyon from
			4	<his> vowed course.
		27	1	Chymochles awakes

[1] Reminiscé is between **stanzas** 16 and 17, in margin.

Page	Sig.	Stanza	Line	Annotation
			2	and collectes himselfe
			3	out of those charmes
			4	of Vaine delight.
		28	1	He meets and fights
			2	With Sir Gyon in the Iland
			3	of pleasure.
		32	1	Pheadria or
			2	vaine delight
			3	by her intercession
			4	parts the combat.
85	H2	38	1	Sir Guyon is by
			2	Phaedria feried
			3	from the Iland of plea=
			4	sure as not being
			5	fitt for her purpose=
		43	8	Pyrrhochles after his
			9	contention with Furo<r> is soe enraged that to[1]
		44	2	quench those burning
			3	flames he leps into
			4	the Idle Lake
86	H2ᵛ	46	1–2	<Ati>n leaps into the
			2–3	<Id>le Lake
			6–7	<N>ature of the Lake
		48	2–3	<H>ypocresy.

[1] Between stanzas 43 and 44.

Page	Sig.	Stanza	Line	Annotation

Canto 7

Page	Sig.	Stanza	Line	Annotation
87	H3	3	2–3	Descr. of a covitous
			3–4	man.[1]
		11	1[2]	the power of mony
		12	4–5	Riches the root of dis\<qui>
			6	etnesse.
88	H3ᵛ	15	4–5	\<Nat>ura paucis contenta.
		16	1	\<S>tate of
			2	\<Ma>ns innocency
			6	\<Hi>s declininge through
			7	Lust and pride intro=
			9	\<duc>ed the use of mony
			9[3]	\<tha>t brough in
				covituousnesse.
		18	3	\<M>ammons counsell to
			4	\<Si>r Gyon.
		19	1	\<H>is Aunswere
		21	1	The way to welthe
			2	described first to
			3–4	brode and Large
			4–5	and Leads to Hell
			5–6	by the side of which sitts
			7	infernall paine, and

---

[1] This is an instance of Jonsonian interpretation, i.e., of Spenser's description of Mammon in stanza 3, prior to Mammon's being named (except in the Argument) in the text.

[2] Above margin.

[3] Below line 9.

Page	Sig.	Stanza	Line	Annotation
			8	strife by her
		22	1	On the other side satt
			2	Revenge, Despight
			3	Treason. Hate, Jelosy
			4	satt by her selfe. feare
			5	went up and downe
			6	Sorrowe and shame
		23	1	Horrour flewe
			2	over thiere heades
		24	5	the door of Riches
			6	and the Gate of Hell [word crossed out]
			7	are within a stride
		25	1	At the door sat selfe
			2	consuminge care
			6	the gate of Hell is
			7	betwixt the gate
			8	of slepe and riches
89	H4	32	1–2	the keeping of all the
			2–3	wealth was committed
			4	to covituousnesse
		33	9	M.[1]
		35	2	Mammon shews Sir G<yon>
			3	the furnaces where
			4	they melt and coyn
			5	their gold.

[1] Presumably, like "Reminiscé," in that it marks a passage (lines 8 and 9 are underlined) that Jonson had selected for memorization.

Page	Sig.	Stanza	Line	Annotation
		36	1–2	The severall imploy\<ments>
			2–3	of the Fiends in melt\<ing>
			3–4	it.
90	H4ᵛ	38	3–4	\<Ma>mmon tempts him
			4–5	\<ag>aine.
		39	4–5	\<H>is repley.
		41	2	\<Dis>dain is the keeper of
			3	\<Am>bitions Pallace.
		44	6	Ambition.
		46	1–2	Ambitions cha=
			2–3	ine is fastned
			3–4	to Heaven and
			4–5	reacheth to Hell
			6	it is of gold and
			7	every Linkeroad
			8	a step of Honor.
		47	1	How all sorts
			2	Labor: to gett
			3	up this chaine
91	H5	52	2–3	The garden of the
			3–4	Queene of Hell
92	H5ᵛ	65	7–8	Slepe and food
			9	the uphouldrs
		below 9	of mans life[1]

[1] Uncharacteristically, this note is not in the margin, but in the center of the page, between columns, as are several other notes, thus identified, below.

Page	Sig.	Stanza	Line	Annotation
Canto 8				
		2	2–3	\<Th>e Heavenly Angells
			3–4	have chardge and take
			9[1]	care of us.
93	H6	10	2	Pyrrhochles and
			3	Cymochles the Sonn\<es>
			4	of Acrates which is
			5	Dispight.
				* [before *"Archimago"*]
			7	*Hypocresy.
		11		*[before *"Atin"*
			4	*contention.
		13	6	We must not vilify
			7	the dead.
95	I1	29	1	Guilty contin=
			2	ewes to the posterity
96	I1ᵛ	42	1	Excellent Simile.
		48	4–5	Simile*[2]
		50	3	M.[3]
Canto 9				
97	I2	1	2	Mans body the
			3	glorious creat
			4	ure. but being

---

[1] See 2.3.1; this notation seems to be below line 4 in a stanza which is broken so that it is printed with one portion in each stanza.

[2] In center, between columns.

[3] In center, between columns; again, like "Reminisce," an imperative which Jonson addresses to himself: Memorize.

Page	Sig.	Stanza	Line	Annotation
			5	by passion disordred,
			6	the mo[n]strousest
		3	1–2	If the picture be so glor<ious>
			2–3	what then is the person <?>
98	I2ᵛ		15	*[after "idle shades]
			3	*By these sorte
			4	I conceive to be
			5	ment Errors
			6	and vanities
			6–7	which beseidge
			7–8	Alma that is our
			9	reason.
99	I3	16	5	Simile
		18		*[before "<u>Alma</u>"]
			1	*Mans Reason
		21	1	* [after *Castle wall]
			2	*By this I conceiv
			3	he meanethe the
			4	skinne of the Body
			5	of man.
		22		*[before stanza; commentary begins upward of rule.] the circular signe represents th<e> Soule the Triangular the body <of>
			1	Man.

Page	Sig.	Stanza	Line	Annotation
			3	the Body is mortall and of it<selfe>
				*[before line 4]
			4	imperfecte without the Soule <which>
			4–5	is in lewe of a maker and actu<ator of>
			5	it.
				*[before "a quadrat"]
			5–6	By this Quadrat is meant <the>
			6–7	principall Humours in man<s>
			7	body.
			8	*[after "seaven"]
				*By seven and 9 are ment <the>
			9	Planetes and the Angells which ar<e>
			22–23	[Between stanzas] distributed into a Hierarc<hy> which governe the body.
		23	1	*[before "gates"] *Mouth and fundam.
			6	*[after "disparted"] *the upper and lower Jawe
		24	1	*[after "hewen"] the Jawe bones.
			5	*[after "twine"] *the beard of a man
			6	*[after "Porcullis"] *the Nose

Page	Sig.	Stanza	Line	Annotation
		25	1	*[after "sate"]
				*the Tounge
			9	*[before "Early"]
				He praide morning and
				eve\<ning\>
		26	2	*[before "Twice"]
				*the Teethe
		27	1	the Mouth.
100	I3ᵛ	29	1	\<th\>e Stomacke
		30	4	*[Before "An huge"]
				The Lunges
				*[after "Parlour"
		33	6	the Minde
		34	1	the Ladies were named
			2	praise desire and
			3	shamefastnesse.
		35	1	*[before "Diverse"]
				*the Passions of
			2	the minde.
		37	1	*[before "In"]
				Desire of praise
101	I4	40		*[before "Another"]
			2	Shamefastnesse
		45	1	the Heade
		46	2	*[after "Beacons"]
			2–3	*the Eyes.

Page	Sig.	Stanza	Line	Annotation
		47	7	*[after "three"]
			7–8	viz 1 Phantesy. 2
				Judg\<ment\>
			8–9	3 memory.
		48	4	*[After *"Phylian"*] Nestor
		49	2	Phantesey.
		51	1–2	the severall imaginati\<ons\>
			2–3	which flott in our phanse\<y\>
102	I4ᵛ	53	2	\<Ju\>dgment or discre=
			3	\<t\>ion.
		55	3–4	\<M\>emory.

Canto 10

Page	Sig.	Stanza	Line	Annotation
103	I5	6		*[after *"Albion"*]
			6	England was first n\<amed\>
			7	Albion ab Alpis Rup\<ertis\>
			8	from the white rocks on \<the\>
			9	Southerne coast.
		7	1	It was inhabited by
			2–3	Gyants.
104	I5ᵛ	12	2	\<Cor\>ineus had the west
			3	\<cou\>ntry assigned him
			4	\<by\> Brutus. and from him
			5	\<it\> was called Cornew=
			6	\<all\>. Debons share
			7	\<was\> Devonsheire and
			8	⸢Br⸣utus had Canutium
			9	\<no\>w called Kent

Page	Sig.	Stanza	Line	Annotation

Canto 11

Page	Sig.	Stanza	Line	Annotation
110	K2ᵛ	6	1	*[after "Captaine"]
				*Evell Actions
			6	that is the Doer of
			7	our Reason
		7	2	*[after "great"]
				*our five senses
		8	2	Unlawfull
			3	Lusts beseidge
			4	the sight.
111	K3	10	2	Backbitings
			3	and flatteries
			4	beseidge the
			5	sense of Hearing
		11	3	Delights for
			4	the sense of
			5	smellinge
		12	2–3	Gluttanous
			3–4	desires besidge
			5	the Taste
		13	2–3	Carnell Lusts
			3–4	beseidge feling
		19	4–5	Simile
112	K3ᵛ	22	3	<?>er. of Maleger.
		32	4	Simile[1]

---

[1] In center, between columns.

Page	Sig.	Stanza	Line	Annotation
113	K4	36	6–9	Simile[1]

Canto 12

Page	Sig.	Stanza	Line	Annotation
114	K4ᵛ	3	1	Guyon in his Expe=
			2	dition of the Pallace
			3	of sensuall delightes
			4	passe by first the
			5	Gulfe of gredinesse
			6	and then the Rocke
			7	of dispaire
115	K51	4	2	Eschewing the
			3	gulfe of gredinesse[2][
			4	men fall upon the
			5	Rocke of prodi=
			6	gallity.
		7	1–2	the misery of
			2–3	prodigality
			6–7	Memento[3]
		10	2	An excellent Des<cr.>
			2–3	of Rowinge
116	K5ᵛ	18	1	Unthriftinesse 1
			2	<of> suncke estate.
		23	7	the Descrp: of
			8–9	certaine mon=

[1] In center, between columns.
[2] There appears to be some overwriting on the "in" of "gredinesse."
[3] Stanzas 7, 8 and 9 are bracketed with a line in the margin.

Page	Sig.	Stanza	Line	Annotation
		23–24 [Between stanzas]		sterous fishes.
117	K6	32	2–3	the Song of the
			3–4	Mermaides to
			4–5	Sir Guyon
		36	5–6	the Desr. of the ill bod<ing>
			7–8	Birds.
		39		*[after "beasts"]
			1–2	*By these Beasts are ment
			2–3	Men transformed by Pleasures
			4	into the nature of Beasts.[1]
118	K6ᵛ	41	3	<the> vertues of the
			4–5	<P>almers staffe
		42	5	Despr. of the bouer of
			5–6	Blisse.
		46		*[before "sate"]
			3	Mans evell
			4–5	genius.
		47	1	the Despr: of mans
			2–3	good genius.
119	L1	54	2–3	A excellent Depr:
			4	of a vine.
		55	5–6	Excesse.[2]

---

[1] Jonson crosses out "shapes" before "of beasts."

[2] It appears that Jonson crossed out the lower word and spilled ink, which marks the opposite pages as well as this one. It appears that the crossing out followed Jonson's botching of a medial "e" and a smeared capital "E."

Page	Sig.	Stanza	Line	Annotation
		58	5	An excellen D<esrp.>
			6	of a most pleasant <place>
120	L1ᵛ	71	2–3	Admirable Desr.
			4	of a melodious
			5	sound.
		74	1	A song shewing the
			2–3	the shortnesse of plea=
			3–4	sures and the Life of
			4–5	man, and therefore
			5–6	enviting to the enjoy
			6–7	inge of it.
121	L2	78	1–2	the Desr. of a f[a]ire
			3	woman.

BOOK 3

Canto 1

Page	Sig.	Stanza	Line	Annotation
124	L3ᵛ	4	2	<I>t was a Damsell
			3	called Britomart

Canto 2

Page	Sig.	Stanza	Line	Annotation
130	L6ᵛ	1	6	<W>omen in former
			7	<a>ges have excelld in
			8	<b>old deeds of armes.
			9	<S>ee. Sands Ovid.
131	M1	19	1	Merlins magicke
			3	glasse descrid.
		20	3	Ptolomes inchaun
			5	ted Tower.

Page	Sig.	Stanza	Line	Annotation
133	M2	44	6	Narcissus

Canto 3

Page	Sig.	Stanza	Line	Annotation
135	M3	8	1	the Cave of Merlin
			3	in Cayr-marden
			4	described.

Canto 4

Page	Sig.	Stanza	Line	Annotation
142	M6ᵛ	17	4	\<An ex>cellent Simile
145	N2	56	6	An excellent De\<scr.>
			8	of Night, the con\<sort>
			9	of Evell Action

Canto 5

Page	Sig.	Stanza	Line	Annotation
147	N3	12	4–5	Timias.

Canto 12

Page	Sig.	Stanza	Line	Annotation
182	Q2ᵛ	7	3–4	\<G>aynimede

Book 4

Canto 1

Page	Sig.	Stanza	Line	Annotation
191	R3	20	1	The Description of the
			2–3	dwelling of Ate
192	R3ᵛ	27	1	The Desrp:
			2–3	of Ate \<or>
			3–4	strife.

Canto 8

Page	Sig.	Stanza	Line	Annotation
222	T6ᵛ	1	1–2	\<D>ispleasure of the

Page	Sig.	Stanza	Line	Annotation
			2–3	\<mig>hty is fatall.
224	V1ᵛ	24	1–2	the Descr: of
			2–3	slaunder.
225	V2	30	1	the Innocency
			2	of the old time

Canto 10

Page	Sig.	Stanza	Line	Annotation
233	V6	12	1–2	Doubte
			2–3	described
		16	1	the Descr: of the gate of go\<od>
			2	deserte.

Canto 11

Page	Sig.	Stanza	Line	Annotation
239	X3	28		*[after "Troynovant"]
			8	London

BOOK 5

Canto 1

Page	Sig.	Stanza	Line	Annotation
249	Y2	12	6	That is Like for Li\<ke>

Canto 6

Page	Sig.	Stanza	Line	Annotation
271	2A1	19	3–4	Named Dolon which is
			4–5	Describd

Canto 8

Page	Sig.	Stanza	Line	Annotation
278	2A4	2		*[after "swaine"]

Page	Sig.	Stanza	Line	Annotation
			1	\<S\>ampson.
				*[after "Knight"]
			4	Hercules

Canto 10

| 288 | 2B3ᵛ | 7 | 1 | \<C\>ountry of Belgia |
| | | | 3–4 | \<?\> Provinces |

Book 6

Canto 9

| 337 | 2F4 | 19 | 2 | the hapinesse of a mea\<n\> |
| | | | 3 | estate. |

Book 7

Canto 7

| 360 | 2H3ᵛ | 17 | 1–2 | \<All\> things subject= |
| | | | 3–4 | \<e\>d to Mutability |

Page	Sig.	Stanza	Line	Annotation

PROSOPOPOIA. OR MOTHER HUBBERDS TALE

Line numbers for "Mother Hubberds Tale" and "The Ruines of Time" are from *YSP*.

A3			4	Astraea
			6	or
			7–8	Justice
A4ᵛ			386	\<Th>e Cuntry
			387–88	\<P>arsons
			392	abusing
			393	of the papists
Sig. A5			477	the beautie
			479	of the thing
Sig. A6			723–24	the worthy
			725	man
Sig. A6ᵛ			841	Sutors
Sig. A7ᵛ			1148	Lord Treserors

Page	Sig.	Stanza	Line	Annotation

THE RUINES OF TIME

	G6		46	the vanity of this Wor<ld>[1]
	H1ᵛ		338	the immorta=
			339	lity of
			340	vertue
			348	oblivion is
			349	the rewarde
			350	of the vitious
			360	the eternity
			367–68	of the Muses
	H2		403	verses eter=
			404–05	nise the ver
			405–06	tuous.
			428–29	Achilles
			429–30	eternised by
			431	Homer: and for
			432	that envied by
			433	Alexander
			444–45	Salomon was greived w<ith>
			445–46	this consideration
			458	the Inconstancy of this
			459	worlds Felicity

[1] The top of the flourish of "d" is visible.

Jonson's Markings in *The Shepheardes Calender*

These consist of markings in the margins and the under-lining of words (whole or in part). Unless otherwise noted, the markings are in pen. Line numbers refer to *YSP*; spelling and typography are those of the 1617 Folio. Markings in margins are to the left of lines, unless otherwise noted.

Epistle

line

1	*Uncouth, unkist*
2	*Chaucer*
4–5	the Loadstarre of our language
7	Roman *Tytirus Virgil*
44–45	sure I thinke, . . . thinke I thinke not
102	whose first shame . . . are not ashamed

175	for that they
177	*Shepheards Kalender*

GENERALL ARGUMENT

55–56	*a custome of counting*
59	*Redeemer the Lord Christ*
66	*in elder times, when as yet* [pencil]
67–68	*afterward it was by* Julius Cæsar [pencil]
71	*Moneth* Abib, . . . *wee call March* [pencil]
78–80	*the odde wandring . . . Greekes were called Hyperbaainontes, of the Romanes Intercalares* [pencil]
85–86	Numa Pompilius, . . . Romane Ceremonies, and Religion [pencil]
90–92	beginne the yeare at Januarie, . . . so called tanquam Janua anni, . . . gate and entrance of the yeere [pencil]
97	[in margin, next to line] —)
97–98	Egyptians beginne [pencil]
98	September
100–01	God made the World in that Moneth, that is called . . . them Tisri [pencil]

"JANUARIE"

54	[in margin, next to line] —)

Glosse

[60]   Ovid shadoweth . . . Julia

"APRIL"

Glosse

[42]   [in margin, next to lines] ⟩

"MAY"

57   [in margin, next to line] —
58   [in margin, next to line] —
303   [in margin, next to line] —)

"JUNE"

Glosse

[10]   Paradise . . . is thought . . . Mesopotamia

"JULY"

146   [in margin, next to line] —)
Glosse
[34]   [in margin, next to line] —

"SEPTEMBER"

18   [in margin, next to line] —)
28   [in margin, next to line] —

29   [in margin, next to line] —

141   [in margin, next to line] —

153   [in margin, next to line] —

168   [in margin, next to line] —

261   [in margin, next to line] —)

Glosse

[153]   <u>for that the most part. . .</u>

[155]   <u>no part of Christendome</u>

[211]   [in margin, next to line] —)

"OCTOBER"

(In the "Argument," the words "Poetrie" and "a divine
         gift" are underlined)

20   [in margin, next to line] —

Glosse

[65]   [after the verses from Petrarch, the entire para-
         graph, beginning with "And that such account"
         seems to be set off]

[67]   [in margin, next to line] —

[96]   [in right margin, next to line] —)

NOTES

Notes to Introduction

1. "Retrieving Jonson's Petrarch," *SQ* 45 (1994), 89–92. Martin points out that the Petrarch was sold in 1915 at Hodgson's and sold again, later in the same year, at Anderson Galleries in New York, where "acting on Henry Clay Folger's behalf, the New York dealer George D. Smith purchased the volume for $62. It remained in Folger's private collection until becoming part of the Library holdings at the institution's opening in 1932, where it has rested, overlooked but in otherwise unruffled condition, ever since" (90).

2. D. D. C. Chambers, ed., "General Introduction," *Thomas Traherne, Commentaries of Heaven: The Poems*, Salzburg Studies in English Literature: Elizabethan & Renaissance Studies, Gen. Ed., Dr. James Hogg (Salzburg: Institüt für Anglistik und Amerikanistik, 1989), ii.

3. Jeanne Shami's book on the subject, *John Donne's 1622 Gunpowder Plot Sermon*, is forthcoming from Duquesne Univ. Press.

4. *The Spenser Encyclopedia*, ed. A. C. Hamilton, Donald Cheney, W. F. Blissett, David A. Richardson, and William W. Barker (Toronto: Univ. of Toronto Press, 1990), 411.

5. David McPherson, *Ben Jonson's Library and Marginalia: An Annotated Catalogue, Studies in Philology, Texts and Studies* 71.5 (Dec. 1974): 91.

6. A. N. L. Munby, *The Libraries of English Men of Letters* (London: Library Association, 1965), 6.

7. W. C. Hazlitt, *Contributions towards a Dictionary of English Book-Collections* (1898).

8. This was James Crossley, barrister, of Manchcster, S. M. Ellis's "great bibliographer," who, according to Ellis, "accumulated a vast and wonderful library, and specialized in ancient learning, his knowledge of seventeenth century literature being especially marked" (*Wilkie Collins, Le Fanu, and Others* [London: Constable, 1931; rept. 1951], 223). He was born at Halifax on 31 March 1800 and died at Manchester, 1 August 1883. He was at one time president of the Spenser Society, and he formed over his lifetime a library estimated to contain 100,000 volumes, which was dispersed in auctions in Manchester in May 1884 and in London at Sotheby's in 1884 and 1885 (Ellis, 223–65, *passim*). Early in his career Crossley had written, among other pieces for *Blackwell's Magazine*, "Notices of Old English Comedies. No 1 *Eastward Hoe*—Jonson, Chapman, and Marston" (10 [1821]); see C. G. Petter, ed., *Eastward Ho!*, The New Mermaids (London: Benn, 1973, xiii, and R. W. Van Fossen, ed., *Eastward Ho*, The Revels Plays (Manchester: Manchester Univ. Press and Baltimore: Johns Hopkins Univ. Press, 1979), 7.

9. Shelfmark S.—C. P. 100 (6).

10. A. N. L. Munby, *The Formation of the Phillipps Library from 1841 to 1872*. Phillipps Studies no. 4 (Cambridge: Cambridge Univ. Press, 1956).

11. Baltimore: Johns Hopkins Press (1933), 33–48.

12. An observation about the various parts in the New STC could be misleading: "The parts bound with this [1617 tp and *FQ*] should ideally be: 23086.7 [Letter to Raleigh, 1617], 23094 [*SC*], 23077.7 [*Colin Clouts*, 1617], 23087 [*Mother Hubberds*, 1612–13]. Instead of the last, a few copies have 23087.5 [*Mother Hubberds*, 1628]." If the dates of the various parts could constitute an "ideal" collection (which is not certain), the implied order suggests a coherence that may have held little or no interest for the men who issued the volume. The STC "ideal" collections of parts for 23083.3, 23083.7, 23084, and 23085 (the 1611 and 1617 folios) correspond to Johnson's Groups 1 through 4.

13. There is some chronological significance in this detail. Johnson notes that the second printing of *Mother Hubberds Tale* "cannot have been issued earlier than January 31, 1620 [n. s.]," and that the "most likely" date for it "is 1627 or 1628" (42).

14. R. B. McKerrow and F. S. Ferguson, *Title-page Borders used in England & Scotland, 1485–1640* (London: The Bibliographical Society, 1932), #212. For a full description of the border, see Margery Corbett and Ronald Lightbown, *The Comely*

Frontispiece: The Emblematic Title-page in England, 1550–1660 (London, Henley, Boston: Routledge & Kegan Paul, 1979), 59–65; see also, Jean Robertson, ed., *Sir Philip Sidney, The Countess of Pembroke's Arcadia* (Oxford: The Clarendon Press, 1973), xlviii–xlix.

15. "The *Arcadia* (1593) Title-page Border," *The Library*, 5th Series, 4 (June 1949), 71.

16. W. W. Greg, et al., eds., *English Literary Autographs* (Oxford: Oxford Univ. Press, 1932), 23, 24. P. J. Croft, *Autograph Poetry in the English Language*, 2 vols. (New York: McGraw Hill, 1973), 1:27.

17. Croft makes much the same point (though not, of course, with our concern in mind) when he discusses "the Secretary formation which Jonson employs with the most stylish effect, . . . the *a* that starts high above the line of writing with a long diagonal downstroke, normally producing a pronounced 'spur' to the left. . . . The horizontal tendency [of the letter] may arise spontaneously when the hand is writing freely."

18. McPherson, no. 40. British Library shelfmark C. 45. f. 15, 16. They appear frequently, although not at the beginnings of lines of verse, where Jonson spells out "Et."

19. See chapter 2, n. 9.

20. See chapter 2, n. 9.

21. In light of that argument, we feel safe in saying that, for a time at least, Jonson's copy of Spenser was in Digby's possession, as, no doubt, were other of Jonson's books. For instance, Sir John Denham reported seeing a copy of Mancinus that had been owned by both Jonson and Digby (McPherson, no. 112).

Notes to Chapter 1

1. John Dryden, *Essay of Dramatic Poesy*, in *Essays of John Dryden*, ed by W. P. Ker, 2 vols. (Oxford: Clarendon Press, 1926), 1:82.

2. Dryden, "A Discourse Concerning the Original and Progress of Satire," *Essays* 2:18.

3. For an extensive discussion of why they suggest that this may be the case, see H&S 11:231–33.

4. David Norbrook, *Poetry and Politics in the English Renaissance* (London: Routledge & Kegan Paul, 1984), 318n.

5. Norbrook, 177.

6. David Riggs, *Ben Jonson: A Life* (Cambridge, Mass.: Harvard Univ. Press, 1989), 97–98.

7. Stephen Orgel describes the entertainment as "brief

but exemplary" (*The Jonsonian Masque* [Cambridge, Mass.: Harvard Univ. Press, 1965], 37).

8. William Macneile Dixon, *English Epic and Heroic Poetry* (London, New York: J. M. Dent, E. P. Dutton & Co., 1912), 148; we are not suggesting that this remark is typical, but only that it is far from unique.

9. Dixon, 150.

10. *Ben Jonson: His Life and Work* (London: Routledge & Kegan Paul, 1986), 29.

11. R. F. Patterson, *Ben Jonson's Conversations with William Drummond of Hawthornden* (London: Blackie and Son, 1923), vii; hereafter cited in text.

12. Sir Kenelm Digby, Jonson's literary executor, thought Jonson was, in fact, the major poetic heir of Spenser: "And herein Spencer hath bin very happy, that he hath had one immediatly succeeding him of partes and power to make what he planted take deepe rootes, and to build up that worke whose foundations he so fairely layed: for it is beyond the compasse and reach of our short life and narrow power to have the same man begin and perfect any great thing: No Empire was ever settled to long continuance, but in the first beginninges of it there was an uninterrupted succession of heroyke and brave men to extend and confirme it; A like necessity is in languages; and in ours we may promise our selves a long and florishing age, when divine Spencers sunne was no sooner sett, but in Johnson a new one rose with as much glory and brightnesse as ever any shone withall; who being himselfe most excellent and admirable in the judicious compositions that in several kindes he hath made, thinketh no man more excellent and more admirable then this his late praedecessor in the laurell crowne." "Concerning Spencer that I wrote att Mr. May His Desire" (B. L. Add. MSS. 41,846), in E. W. Bligh, *Sir Kenelm Digby and His Venetia* (London: Sampson Low, Marston & Co., 1932), 278–79.

13. *The Bookman*, August 1923, rept. in George Saintsbury, *A Last Vintage: Essays and Papers* (London: Methuen, 1950), 193–94.

14. Edmund Kemper Broadus, *The Story of English Literature* (New York: Macmillan, 1931), 175.

15. For clarification of the political implications of the taste for pastoral in Renaissance England, see Annabel Patterson, *Pastoral and Ideology: Virgil to Valéry* (Berkeley: Univ. of California Press, 1987), esp. chaps. 2 and 3.

16. *Poetry and Politics*, 206.

17. P. 177. John S. Mebane also talks of the "mockery" of *The Faerie Queene* in *The Alchemist* in "Renaissance Magic

and the Return of the Golden Age: Utopianism and Religious Enthusiasm in *The Alchemist*," *Renaisance Drama*, n. s. 10 (1979), 117–39.

18. "On Jonson's distaste for Elizabethan Symbolism see Frances Yates's (rather too solemn) discussion" (316, n. 4).

19. *Shakespeare's Last Plays: A New Approach* (Routledge & Kegan Paul: London, 1975), 115. As Norbrook supposes that Jonson's failure to produce an elegy on the death of Prince Henry has political significance, so Yates supposes Jonson did not write a masque for the marriage of Princess Elizabeth because "he disapproved of it, like the Spanish ambassador who refused to attend. And he must have disapproved of the whole movement of Elizabethan revival around Prince Henry and Princess Elizabeth" (117). Herford and Simpson could have enlightened both Yates and Norbrook: "[Jonson] produced no play between *Catiline* (1611) and *Bartholomew Fair* (1614), and no masque between *Love Restored*, Twelfth Night, 1612, and *A Challenge at Tilt*, December, 1613. During a great part of the interval Jonson himself was absent from the country, and thus took no part either in the obsequies of Prince Henry (who died on November 6, 1612) or in the wedding festivities of the Princess Elizabeth, celebrated with extraordinary splendour in February, 1613" (1:64).

In one respect their concern with the "Elizabeth cult" leads Yates and Norbrook to opposite conclusions. Yates sees poets as being independent enough that one like Jonson could "disapprove" of a movement centered on Prince Henry and Princess Elizabeth; Norbrook, on the other hand, sees poets as mouthpieces for their patrons.

20. *The Triple Thinkers* (London: John Lehmann, 1952), 217.

21. See J. A. Riddell, "Ben Jonson and '*Marlowes* mighty line,'" in *A Poet and a filthy Play-maker: New Essays on Christopher Marlowe*, ed. Kenneth Friedenreich, Roma Gill, and Constance Kuriyama (New York: AMS Press, 1988), 37–40.

22. R. F. Patterson, 17n.

23. Rosalind Miles writes: "years later Jonson had to explain some of Spenser's highly wrought and clouded meanings to Sir Walter Raleigh, who found it [sic] beyond him" (*Ben Jonson*, 29).

24. See *Conversations* (H&S 1:138) and H&S 1:162, where they cite C. H. Firth, *Sir Walter Raleigh's History of the World* (*Proceedings of the British Academy*, vol. 8). "The Mind of the Frontispiece to a Book" (*Und* 24, somewhat altered from the original) was Jonson's commendatory poem for *The History of the World* (1614).

25. Willard M. Wallace, *Sir Walter Raleigh* (Princeton:

Princeton Univ. Press, 1959), 68–71.

26. See Richard Helgerson, *Self-Crowned Laureates: Spenser, Jonson, Milton, and the Literary System* (Berkeley: Univ. of California Press, 1983), esp. chap. 3 on Jonson's learning.

27. Just how imperfect the Heroologia was at the time of the fire that destroyed much of Jonson's library in 1623, we cannot say. As David Riggs (258) points out, Jonson makes no specific mention of the work in "An Execration upon Vulcan." But that does not mean that the poem was not part of the "So many [his] Yeares-labours" destroyed in the fire. Like Jonson's copy of the 1617 Folio of Spenser's Fae*rie Queene*, it may yet show up.

28. For a more extensive discussion of the various kinds of Jonson marks and annotations in the 1617 Folio, see chapter 3.

29. For convenience, when referring to passages in Spenser's minor poems marked by Jonson in the 1617 Folio, we will cite line numbers in *YSP*, while following the text that Jonson was actually reading. Our reasons for proceeding in this way should be clear as the argument unfolds, but we are aware of the revisions made for later editions of, say, "The Ruines of Time." See chap. 2.

30. Adelheid Gaertner notices the influence of Catullus as well as of Spenser (*Die englische Epithalamienliteratur im siebzehnten Jahrhundert und ihre Vorbilder* [Coberg: A. Rossteutscher, 1936], 9, 11).

31. Virginia Tufte, *The Poetry of Marriage: The Epithalamium in Europe and its Development in England*, University of Southern California Studies in Comparative Literature (Los Angeles: Tinnon-Brown, 1970), 217.

32. For an illuminating discussion of Spenser and avian imagery, see Patrick Cheney, *Spenser's Famous Flight: A Renaissance Idea of a Literary Career* (Toronto: Univ. of Toronto Press, 1993), chap. 4, esp. 189–209.

33. "To Penshurst" was written some 20 years earlier, by November 1612; see H&S 11:33.

34. J. B. Bamborough, *Ben Jonson* (London: Hutchinson Univ. Library, 1970), 157.

35. Richard A. McCabe, *The Pillars of Eternity: Time and Providence in* The Faerie Queene (Dublin: Irish Academic Press, 1989), 16.

36. *Mercurie Vindicated* and *Golden Age Restored* end with, respectively, "Chorus" and "Quire." But do both terms mean that the recitation of each is in song? This seems to be the case for "Chorus," since the parts to which it responds are described in the stage directions as songs. As for "Quire," there

is little point in calling it by that name unless the lines are sung. The three masques that do not end in song are *The Speeches at Prince Henries Barriers, The Challenge at a Tilt, at a Marriage* and *Hymenaei*. The first two have no songs in them; the third ends with a long speech by "Truth."

37. During the print run a piece of type that was broken during the machining of 4Q1^v–4, after the speeches had been rearranged to Astraea/Pallas, a comma, its face somewhat broken, went adrift. Since, in the ordinary scheme of things in the Renaissance print shop, commas do not repair themselves, the order of the closing speeches that Jonson intended must have been Astraea/Pallas. See J. A. Riddell, "The Concluding Pages of the Jonson Folio of 1616," *SB* 47 (1994), 147–54.

38. Riggs, 216–18.

39. G. Gregory Smith, *Ben Jonson*, English Men of Letters (London: Macmillan, 1919), 41n.

Notes to Chapter 2

1. Jewel Wurstsbaugh, *Two Centuries of Spenser Scholarship (1609–1805)* (Baltimore: The Johns Hopkins Univ. Press, 1936; rept. New York: AMS Press, 1970), 15.

2. William R. Mueller, *Spenser's Critics: Changing Currents in Literary Taste* (Syracuse: Syracuse Univ. Press, 1959), 1.

3. Jonson's reference in the *MofQ* bears upon an argument we make about his knowledge of a change in "The Ruines of Time"—see below, n. 14.

4. Sir Kenelm Digby, *Observations on the 22. Stanza in the 9th. Canto of the 2d. Book of Spencers Faery Queen* (1643).

5. Transcribed by Graham Hough, with Foreward by the Earl of Bessborough (Stansted: privately printed, 1964; rept. Folcroft, Pa.: Folcroft Press, 1969).

6. W. W. Greg, "The Riddle of Jonson's Chronology," *The Library*, 4th Ser., 6 (1925–26), 345.

7. For a discussion of Jonson and the sonnet, see J. A. Riddell, "Cunning Pieces Wrought Perspective: Ben Jonson's Sonnets," *JEGP* 87 (1988): 193–212.

8. Edwin Greenlaw, *Studies in Spenser's Historical Allegory* (Baltimore: The Johns Hopkins Press; London: Humphrey Milford, 1932), 117.

9. One must be cautious here. There are several instances in the poem where Jonson underlines beginnings or ends of lines and makes additional markings in the margins, as in the stanza immediately above the one under discussion. Since the ink and

pencil markings—the former apparently superimposed upon the latter—almost certainly signify that Jonson read some poems at least twice, we are tempted to argue that some underlinings signify yet a "third," but this cannot be demonstrated. Color and consistency seem to be about the same in all ink markings. Jonson used pencil markings elsewhere; see, for instance, the flowers and lines in his copy of the 1623 Stobaeus, *Dicta Poetarum* (one of at least three copies of Stobaeus that Jonson owned) now in the Huntington Library (shelfmark 57326), sigs. 2G3^v–2H2^v, and in his copy of Vitruvius, *De architectura*, now in the Ogden Collection of University College, London, (shelfmark A 293), sig. A1^v.

10. John Jortin, *Remarks on Spenser's Poems* (London, 1734). Jortin's dual interests in source citation and in such matters as "inaccuracy of expression" (35) appear throughout, but see esp. 165–67, for his observations on "The Ruines of Time."

11. "Possible Recollection of Spenser in Jonson's 'Immortal Memory' Ode," *N&Q*, n.s. 32 (1985): 487.

12. S. K. Heninger, Jr., *Sidney and Spenser: The Poet as Maker* (University Park: The Pennsylvania State Univ. Press, 1988), 14–15.

13. It should be noted that the variant in the first line of the couplet is recorded in *YSP*, but the variant in the second line is not. Unlike *Var*, *YSP* does not undertake a full listing of variants (see *YSP*, 788; *Var* 7:690).

14. Jonson knew the 1591 edition of *Complaints*, as he quoted a passage from "The Ruines of Time" in his *MofQ* (see above, n. 3), which antedates the first folio collection of Spenser's works by two years.

15. *Harvard Studies and Notes in Philology and Literature* 20 (1938): 29–42.

16. Kurt Weber, *Lucius Cary, Second Viscount Falkland* (New York: Columbia Univ. Press, 1940), 283.

17. *Imitation and Praise in the Poems of Ben Jonson* (New Haven: Yale Univ. Press, 1981), 207. For a probing analysis of Jonson's attitude toward suicide, see William Kerrigan, "Ben Jonson Full of Shame and Scorn," *SLI* 6 (1973): 199–217.

18. The Cary/Morison ode has been assessed in ways that have led to some confusion, much of it the result of insufficient attention to detail and to the context in which the ode was written. We can scarcely fault those who have not been aware of the context to which we have recently been granted access, Jonson's notes on "The Ruines of Time." In light of those notes, the reservations Peterson has about the significance of the Infant's life—which are, in one manner or another,

shared by other modern observers (e.g., Arthur F. Marotti, "All About Ben Jonson's Poetry," *ELH* 39 [1972]: 226n; Paul H. Fry, *The Poet's Calling in the English Ode* [New Haven: Yale Univ. Press, 1980], 18–19)—need to be reassessed.

It is, perhaps, want of context that has led to attempts to locate Jonson within the ode; and, of course, the sensible place to locate him is where he locates himself, between the third Counter-turne and its Stand. Jonson's bold naming of himself and even more bold splitting of his name, half in one stanza, half in the next, was bound to draw attention. In a much-cited essay, Mary I. Oates sees in Jonson's naming of himself a close connection between this poem and Jonson's epigram "On my First Sonne," where Jonson's name also appears in the text. (Oates credits E. W. Tayler with calling her attention to "the possibility that Jonson meant to associate the two poems" ["Jonson's 'Ode Pindarick' and the Doctrine of Imitation," PLL 11 (1975): 129n; see also David Riggs, *Ben Jonson: A Life,* 315].) However, she vests the connection with greater meaning than is warranted, as she contends that Jonson:

> had used his own name in almost as bold a manner [as in the Cary/Morison ode] just once before: . . . "Rest in soft peace and, asked, say here doth lie/ *BEN. Jonson,* his best piece of poetrie" (EP[igrams] 70). Here it is the phrase after the last comma that reveals the doubleness of Jonson's meaning: at first "Ben Jonson" seems to name the dead child; then, by using the archaic genitive, Jonson refers to himself. (134)

Apart from some casual and trifling errors (it is BEN. JONSON, not BEN. *Jonson* [This is the most striking, but not the only, alteration of Jonson's typography, faithfully reproduced by H&S. The full couplet should read: "Rest in soft peace, and, ask'd, say here doth lye / BEN. JONSON his best piece of *poetrie.*"] and it is *Epig* 45, not 70), there are two significant ones. The term "archaic genitive" suggests that Jonson is calling particular attention to a construction to invite us to ponder its implications. But the construction could hardly seem "archaic" to a man who presented to the world such title pages as *Sejanus his Fall* (1605) or *Catiline his Conspiracy* (1611) or, even more to the point, *B. Jon: his part of King James his Royall and Magnificent Entertainment . . .* (1604). Beyond this, in the second line of the couplet the comma on which so much hinges is itself an issue. It is not in the Folio of 1616, where the poem first appears, or in H&S, which is cited as the source of all Oates's quotations from Jonson. We did find the comma in The *Oxford Anthology of English Poetry* (Frank Kermode, John Hollander, et al., eds. [London: Oxford Univ. Press, 1973], 1:1082) and, although we did not find another instance of it, we suppose that such may exist. However, the point is that the pointing is false, and that details meant to support Oates's argument fail to do so. (By obliterating chronology, Fry claims more for Oates's argument than she does, saying that she "has noted the close relation between the ode and Jonson's epitaph 'on my First Sonne,' written in the same year" [284n].) There is a kind of general association between the two poems, both concerned with lives too soon ended, but we do not think that Jonson uses his name in the two poems to the same—or even similar—end. As the succeeding paragraphs will show, we see the Cary/Morison ode not as being an expression of personal grief that one finds in *Epig* 45 (cf. Ian Donaldson, "Jonson's Ode to Sir Lucius Cary and Sir H. Morison," *SLI*, 6 [1973]: 142, 145) but, rather, as being Jonson's rigorous exploration of the kind of formalized grief that one finds in "The Ruines of Time" (and, for that matter, in *Lycidas*).

19. We are aware that our remarks here may not go unchallenged. Thomas O. Calhoun suggests that Jonson's Sir Henry Morison was a poet, if not a very accomplished one. The two poems that Calhoun seems to have in mind appear in a miscellaneous collection—prose and verse in various hands, on a large variety of paper. Of four poems in the collection that appear together (same hand, same paper), the first and last have full titles, in which the author is identified as Sir William Harrington, and must have been written by 1613, the year of his death (at which time the Morison of Jonson's poem was about three years old). He was the brother of Lady Elizabeth Morison, the mother of Henry Morison and Lettice, the sister who was wed by Cary shortly after Morison's death. The second poem of the four has the heading "Ha. Morrison," the third "Mr. Morrison to Lady Morrison." The latter title is impossible as an address to Sir Henry Morison's sister because Lettice Morison was never Lady Morison. Indeed, before marriage, she was of modest place in the world, which was why Cary's father was so opposed to the connection with her. In the text of both of the "Morrison" poems, the subject is identified as the sister of the poet, and her name, by way of an apparently clumsy (and inappropriate?) anagram, "Armor Sion," is shown to be "Morrison." There are a number of ways to account for the inconsistencies. We suggest that most likely the ascription to "Ha. Morrison" is the error of someone trying to account for a sister who was Lady Morison. We believe that Sir William Harrington is probably the author of all four poems. In any case, even if a Sir Henry Morison (or Mr. Morison) did write the verses that

we have examined, it does not follow that Jonson knew them. And even if he knew them, he might have held the texts as evidence that Morison had not yet begun to write poetry.

20. Peterson, 200; Maddison, *Apollo and the Nine: A History of the Ode* (Baltimore: The Johns Hopkins Univ. Press, 1960), 149.

21. *Ben Jonson: Poems* (London: Oxford Univ. Press, 1975), 233n.

22. Shelfmark G. 11548; this copy has been reproduced in facsimile by The Scolar Press (Menston, 1968). For a recent discussion of Jonson's markings in another volume, his 1602 edition of Chaucer, see Robert C. Evans, "Ben Jonson's Chaucer," *ELR* 20 (1990): 325–45.

23. For our reservations about this matter, see our discussion in the Introduction of Jonson's hand in "Mother Hubberds Tale."

24. Thomas Watson, *An Eclogue Upon the death of the Right Honorable Sir* Francis Walsingham, Watson's translation of his *Meliboeus* (1590), sig. C2ᵛ.

25. We use the term "poetry" in the broad Renaissance sense discussed at length in Heninger, chaps. 2–3, esp. pp. 77–80, 110–13, 142–43; drawing on Plato's *Phaedrus*, Renaissance critics often emphasized the divine, creative function of poetry as a verbal art.

26. Harold Stein writes: "Even a superficial examination reveals the fact that *The Ruines of Time* is not a finished and workmanlike job, that it is uneven in quality, that its transitions are awkward, and that it consists of four loosely articulated sections" (*Studies in Spenser's Complaints* [New York: Oxford Univ. Press, 1934], 35); again, "*The Ruines of Time* . . . is a most disjointed poem" (38).

27. Richard Helgerson, *Self-Crowned Laureates: Spenser, Jonson, Milton, and the Literary System*, esp. chaps. 2 and 3.

Notes to Chapter 3

1. Camille Paglia, *Sexual Personae: Art and Decadence from Nefertiti to Emily Dickinson* (New Haven: Yale Univ. Press, 1990), 170; unless otherwise indicated, hereafter cited in text.

2. John Milton, *Areopagitica* (1644), ed. Ernest Sirluck, in *The Complete Prose Works of John Milton*, gen. ed., Don M. Wolfe, 8 vols. (New Haven: Yale Univ. Press, 1953–82), 2:516.

3. Ronald Arthur Horton, *The Unity of the Faerie Queene* (Athens: Univ. of Georgia Press, 1978), 187; although Horton

argues this thesis throughout, see esp. introduction and §10.

4. Claude J. Summers and Ted-Larry Pebworth, eds., "Introduction," *Renaissance Discourses of Desire* (Columbia: Univ. of Missouri Press, 1993), 1. More than 30 years ago Wesley Trimpi discussed what he called "a genuine misunderstanding of Jonson's love poetry," arising from failure to come to grips with "the basic qualities of Jonson's style," which is in fact "the most personal style" (*Ben Jonson's Poems: A Study of the Plain Style* [Stanford: Stanford Univ. Press, 1962], 234).

5. See Appendix A.

6. Occurring at: 1.2.16, lines 1–6; 1.3.31, lines 1–9; 1.5.8, lines 2–9; 2.2.24, lines 1–9; 2.3.36, lines 1–8 ("excellent"); 2.4.7, lines 8–9; 2.5.2, lines 4–5; 2.5.10, lines 1–9 ("excellent"); 2.8.42, lines 1–7 ("excellent"); 2.8.48, lines 1–3; 2.9.16, lines 1–9; 2.11.19, lines 4–5; 2.11.36, lines 6–9; 3.4.17, lines 1–8 ("excellent").

7. Occurring at: 2.3.1, lines 1–4; 2.3.4, lines 2–5; 2.3.22–25 ("excellent"); 2.5.32–34 ("excellent"); 2.6.3 lines 1–9; 2.6.12–13 ("excellent"); 2.12.10, lines 1–4 ("excellent"); 2.12.36, lines 4–9; 2.12.42–45; 2.12.47, lines 1–8; 2.12.54, lines 1–9 ("excellent"); 2.12.58–59 ("excellent"); 3.4.56–60 ("excellent"); 4.1.20, lines 4–9 and following four stanzas; 4.1.27, through first four lines of 29; 4.8.24–26.

8. See William E. Slights, "The Edifying Margins of Renaissance English Books," *RQ* 42 (Winter 1989): 682–716. Although his article is concerned exclusively with printed marginalia, Slights's comment on "the oft-repeated phrase, 'Here an excellent simile,'" refers to marginalia in general. Slights goes on to speculate about "the marginalist's apparent obsession with simply flagging . . . [a great number of] similes," and concludes that it is the result of the "similitude or metaphoric likeness [which] lies at the heart not only of poetry but also of Renaissance poetics" (690).

9. The exception is at 2.12.10, where four lines are indicated. Jonson's comment is: "An excellent Des<cr.> of Rowinge."

10. In his *Britain*, trans. Philémon Holland (1610), Camden offers a number of possibilities for the derivation of *Albion*, one of which has to do with "*the white Ile*" (sigs. B6–B6ᵛ); he suggests a couple of possible derivations for Cornwall, allowing one of them to be from *Cornius*, "I know not what companion of Brutus" (sig. P6ᵛ); *Devonshire*, or *Denshire*, is *Devonis*, derived from the "Cornish-Britans['] *Devinan*" (sig. R2); *Kent* is *Cantium* (sig. 2D4).

11 John Dixon, *The first commentary of the Faierie Queene, being an analysis of the annotations in Lord*

Bessborough's copy of the first edition of the Faerie queene, transcribed by Graham Hough, Foreword by the Earl of Bessborough 8, hereafter cited in text.

12. John Erskine Hankins, *Source and Meaning in Spenser's Allegory: a Study of* The Faerie Queene (Oxford: Clarendon Press, 1971), 118–19; cited by A. C. Hamilton in his Longman's edition of *The Faerie Queene.*

13. David McPherson, *Ben Jonson's Library and Marginalia: An Annotated Catalogue,* no. 136.

14. An excellent edition of this work, "with limited modifications" (xv), ed. by Karl K. Halley and Stanley T. Vandersall, makes it easily accessible (Lincoln: Univ. of Nebraska Press, 1970).

15. The auction was the second day of a Sotheby's sale, on 21 July 1936, which included 23 lots, "The Property of Mrs. Aylmer Digby, King's Ford, Colchester." The Jonson/Digby Sandys was number 258.

16. *Ovid's Metamorphosis,* trans. George Sandys (Oxford, 1632), sig.2N1; hereafter cited in text. For convenience, when discussing Sandys's translation, we follow his spelling of the poem's title.

17. The extensiveness of Jonson's activity at this stage of his life has been variously assessed. David Riggs holds that in the early 1630s Jonson "was now a crippled invalid who had no commerce with the outside world, who spent much of his time in solitude, and was approaching the end of his days" (331). Herford and Simpson, on the other hand, observe that "there are various indications that his philological interests were particularly active in 1633–34," and that this and other occupations "did not prevent Jonson's life from being, at least until the last two years before his death, an eminently social one" (1:105). We agree with the latter point of view. See also in introduction, "Jonson's hand in the volume."

18. See Paglia, esp. chap. 2, and Philippa Berry, *Of Chastity and Power: Elizabethan Literature and the Unmarried Queen* (London: Routledge, 1989), esp. chap. 6.

19. Riggs, 307.

20. We concede, too, that other copies of Spenser might appear with comparable Jonson annotations.

21. Riggs, 288.

22. Mary J. Carruthers, *The Book of Memory: A Study of Memory in Medieval Culture* (Cambridge: Cambridge Univ. Press, 1990), esp. 174–85.

23. *Daniel Heinsius and Stuart England* (Leiden: Lciden Univ. Press; London: Oxford Univ. Press, 1968).

24. This statement, placed rather near the beginning of the collection, is reminiscent of a similar "explanatory" statement that Jonson provides in the ninth poem in his collection of *Epigrammes*:

> TO ALL, TO WHOM I WRITE.
> May none, whose scatter'd names honor ,my booke,
>   For strict degrees of ranke, or title looke:
> 'Tis 'gainst the manners of an *Epigram*:
>   And, I a *Poet* here, no *Herald* am.

25. That is, *Timber: or, Discoveries*. An epigraph, we suggest, must be authorial; it is not the sort of thing a printer (or even an "editor") would have reason to append.

26. Trans. G. G. Ramsay, Loeb Edition (London: Heinemann; New York: Putnam's, 1918).

27. It may be, for instance, that the flowers and other markings were simply reminders that Jonson set down for himself to use as lecture notes when he was teaching at Gresham College, as C. J. Sisson suggested he may have been, "at a time when foreigners in considerable numbers came to London to learn English and to further their general education" ("Ben Jonson of Gresham College," *TLS*, Friday, 21 September 1951, p. 604).

28. Petrarch had devised three dialogues with St. Augustine; this passage, given to Augustine, is in Dialogue Two. Quoted by Carruthers, who also discusses Petrarch as an authority on memory (163).

29. There were numerous early printings, the first being *Natalis Comitis Mythologiae, sive Explicationum Fabularum, Libri X* (Venice, 1551).

30. Douglas Bush, *Mythology and the Renaissance Tradition*, 1932, rev. ed. (New York: W. W. Norton, 1963), 29.

31. See C. W. Lemmi, "The Symbolism of the Classical Episodes in *The Faerie Queene*," *PQ* 8 (1929): 270–87, and H. G. Lotspeich, *Classical Mythology in the Poetry of Edmund Spenser* (Princeton: Princeton Univ. Press, 1932), 18–23; at the time of this writing, John Mulryan is preparing an English translation of Conti's *Mythologiae* for publication.

32. Cf. the last two stanzas with Peni-boy Senior's description of Pecunia as he addresses her in *The Staple of News* (1626):

> You are a noble, young, free, gracious *Lady*,
> And would be every bodies, in your bounty,
> But you must not be so. They are few
> That know your merit, *Lady*, and can valew't.
> Your selfe scarce understands your proper powers.

They are *all-mighty*, and that wee, your servants,
That have the honour here to stand so neere you,
Know; and can use too. All this *Nether-world*
Is yours, you command it, and doe sway it,
The honour of it, and the honesty,
The reputation, I, and the religion,
(I was about to say, and had not err'd)
Is Queene *Pecunia's*. For that stile is yours,
If mortals knew your *Grace*, or their owne good.

(2.1.31–44)

33. *Commentary on the Dream of Scipio*, trans. W. H. Stahl (New York: Columbia Univ. Press, 1952), 145.

34. A. C. Hamilton, ed., assisted by R. J. Manning, *Edmund Spenser: The Faerie Queene* (London: Longman, 1977), 281n.

35. Lotspeich, 106.

36. For a discussion of Jonson's acquaintance with Conti, see H&S 10:421.

37. Under "Scylla" in his *Thesaurus*, Thomas Cooper uses similar language: "*Decidit Scyllam cupiens vitare Charybdim*, proverbially, to fall into one daunger, while he coveteth to eschewe an other."

38. Of course, allegorizing the classics was a common practice in the Renaissance. Anthony Grafton points out that even the most devoted practitioners of the "historical mode of exegesis" (he gives the example of Erasmus) "often allegorized in [the] treatment of ancient texts and myths" ("Renaissance Readers and Ancient Texts: Comments on Some Commentaries," *RQ* 38 [Winter 1985]: 637).

Notes to Chapter 4

1. Ray Heffner, Dorothy E. Mason and Frederick M. Padelford, *Spenser Allusions in the Sixteenth and Seventeenth Centuries*, ed. by William Wells, *SP* Texts and Studies Series (1971–72).

2. For example: Francis Webb, *Panharmonicon* (London, 1815), 36 (Webb assumes Digby's preeminence; he doesn't assert it); H&S 1: 110; *Var* 2:472; Wurtsbaugh, 15; R. T. Petersson, *Sir Kenelm Digby, The Ornament of England, 1603–1665* (London: Jonathan Cape, 1956), 91–92; Jerry Leath Mills, "Spenser, Lodowick Bryskett, and the Mortalist Controversy: *The Faerie Queene*, II.ix.22," *PQ* 52 (1973): 174; A. C. Hamilton, ed. *The Faerie Queene*, 251n.; Riggs, 338.

3. Sir Kenelm Digby, *Observations on the 22. Stanza in the*

9th. Canto of the 2d. Book of Spencers Faery Queen (1644), 2;
hereafter cited in text. The date of 1644 does not, we think, jus-
tify the New Wing designation of "Anr ed." Rather, the more
appropriate term would be that in the British Library Catalogue: "variant."

4. This point requires comment. The cropped letter cannot
be an "i." Note the "i" two lines above, where the dot is directly above the stem. Also, the wide stroke after "Act" continues forward, and with a noticeable upswing, much like the "u"
in "Soule" in the line immediately above. Hence the word,
which must be a noun to parallel "maker," cannot be "activa-
tor," and seems almost surely to be "actuator."

5. Petersson, 91.

6. Hereafter, as we discuss the remainder of the Castle of
Alma portion of *The Faerie Queene*, we shall indicate in the
quoted matter where Jonson places stars, in the text and in the
marginal notations.

It may be noted that aside from book 2, canto 9, Jonson uses
stars rarely, and then only in *The Faerie Queene*, in canto 10
(once), 11 (twice) of book 2; in book 4 (once); in book 5 (twice).

7. Petersson misconstrues this to mean "fifteen minutes,"
92.

8. E. W. Bligh, *Sir Kenelm Digby and his Venetia* (London:
Sampson Low, Marston & Co., 1932), 220.

9. Stradling, an early casualty of the Civil War, was "taken
prisoner at Edge Hill fight and sent to Warwick Castle"; he
died at Oxford in June 1641 (*Alumni Oxonienses*).

10. Digby's "autobiographical romance," ed. Vittorio Gabrielli, Teme e Testi (Rome: Edizioni di Storia e Letteratura,
1968), 171–74. As long ago as 1815 Francis Webb wondered
about Digby's "stumbling upon" the solution to the riddle of
the twenty-second stanza (*Panharmonicon*, 34).

11. Alaister Fowler is more generous, suggesting that: "as
Digby himself modestly explains, his treatise was hastily put
together; so that it contains many notions incompletely or ob-
scurely expressed, . . . [that] Digby's *Discourse* [sic] was made
without the aid of books, 'the first halfe quarter of an houre'
after he saw the stanza" (*Spenser and the Numbers of Time*
[New York: Barnes and Noble, 1964], 269, 271). Fowler's point
of view is not extraordinary. Jewel Wurtsbaugh, for instance,
takes all of Digby's claims about the circumstances of his composition of the *Observations* at face value, 14–15.

12. In *The Poem's Two Bodies: The Poetics of the 1590
Faerie Queene* (Princeton: Princeton Univ. Press, 1988).

13. It might be argued that in Jonson's remark "masculine

authority" is (to be redundant) "hierarchically privileged," because Jonson talks of the soul and body of "man." But clearly Jonson means *homo* rather than *vir.*

14. For a discussion of this point in the context of popular literature and the commoners' methods of registering protest, see Annabel Patterson, *Reading Between the Lines* (Madison: Univ. of Wisconsin Press, 1993), 117–59.

15. "The Architecture of Spenser's 'House of Alma,'" *MLN* 58 (1943): 262–65. Fowler cites Camden and offers a rather detailed discussion of Austin, for whom he feels a measure of contempt ("Austin was something of an ass," 261) that we do not share.

16. Joseph Hunter, "An Account of the Scheme for erecting a Royal Academy in England, in the Reign of King James the First," *Archaeologia* 32 (1847): 133, 139, 142.

17. *Epistolae Ho-Elianae*, Bk I, sect. 5, § xiii. Cited in *DNB* as a letter of 20 August 1628, slightly misidentified as §12. The letter is not dated in the first edition (1645), though it is so dated in the 1650 and subsequent editions.

18. William Austin, *Haec Homo, Wherein the Excellency of the Creation of Woman is described By way of an Essay* (1637), sig. E3; hereafter cited in text.

19. Austin offers no explanation for his feminizing emendation of Spenser's "convaid" to "conceiv'd."

20. "The Houses of Mortality in Book II of *The Faerie Queene*," *Spenser Studies* 2 (1981): 122–23.

21. Francis Webb, *Panharmonicon* (London, 1815), 39; hereafter cited in text. On the title page, Webb explains that his treatise is "designed as an illustration of an engraved plate, in which is attempted to be proved, that the principles of harmony more or less prevail throughout the whole system of nature; but more especially in the human frame."

22. Leonard Barkan, *Nature's Work of Art: The Human Body as Image of the World* (New Haven: Yale Univ. Press, 1975), esp. chaps. 3 and 4; James C. Nohrnberg, *The Analogy of* The Faerie Queene (Princeton: Princeton Univ. Press, 1976), passim; Nohrnberg employs such terms as analogy, correspondence, mythopoeia, homologous forms, but, as his opening epigraph from Tasso's *Discourse on the Heroic Poem* indicates (3), the idea is functionally the same.

23. S. K. Heninger, Jr., *Sidney and Spenser: The Poet as Maker*, 24.

24. A. C. Hamilton, ed., *Edmund Spenser: The Faerie Queene*, 251n. To the inattentive reader, Hamilton may seem to support the kind of literal interpretation of the stanza that

we have been faulting. However, Hamilton goes on to make clear that "the simplest physical explanation" is only that.

25. John Freccero, "Donne's 'Valediction: Forbidding Mourning,'" *ELH* 30 (1963): 335–76.

26. S. K. Heninger, Jr., *Touches of Sweet Harmony: Pythagorean Cosmology and Renaissance Poetics* (San Marino: The Huntington Library, 1974), 193; and Heninger, *The Cosmographical Glass: Renaissance Diagrams of the Universe* (San Marino: The Huntington Library, 1977), 69, 74; and Heninger, *Sidney and Spenser*, 71, 208, 520n.

27. Vitruvius, *On Architecture*, ed. and trans. Frank Granger, The Loeb Classical Library, 2 vols (London: William Heinemann, 1931), 3.1; unless otherwise indicated, all citations from Vitruvius in our text will be from this edition, hereafter cited in text.

28. David McPherson, *Ben Jonson's Library and Marginalia*, nos. 199 and 200. It should be noted, however, that neither of these particular editions has anatomical illustrations. Jonson could, of course, have had access to any number of editions that did.

29. André Chastel, *The Myth of the Renaissance: 1420–1520*, trans. Stuart Gilbert (Geneva: Albert Skira, 1969), 138; hereafter cited in text.

30. Selwyn Brinton, *Francesco di Giorgio Martini of Siena: Painter, Sculptor, Engineer, Civil and Military Architect (1439–1502)*, 2 vols. (London: Besant & Co., 1935), 1:94.

31. We are grateful to James Nohrnberg for pointing out the connection between Spenser and this interesting figure of the Italian Renaissance; for a discussion of *Codex Magliabechiano*, see Brinton, 1:93.

32. Lila Geller, "The Acedalian Vision: Spenser's Graces in Book VI of *The Faerie Queene, RES*, N.S. 23 (1972): 275.

33. The parts of the castle are the focus of E. W. Naylor, who has strictly a piece of architecture in mind (with lines of guards standing at attention outside of the portcullis). "Taking the passage as a definite description of an actual building," he says, "it is not impossible to imagine a castle, or rather a temple or a palace, in three stories, the ground floor square, with a triangular hall over it, and a circular dome for roof" (*The Poets and Music* [J. M. Dent: London, 1928; rprt. Da Capo Press: New York, 1980], 134). And he provides an illustration for what must be one of the most literal of interpretations, one which, however, does not manage to place the quadrate "twixt the part circular and the part triangular," in which respect he bumps up against the same problem as does David Lee Miller.

34. The absence of some stars from notes at the left hand of verso pages—e. g., next to stanzas 29, 30, 33—may simply be the result of cropping when the book was rebound. See introduction, "Jonson's Hand in the Volume."

35. "Ben Jonson and Father Thomas Wright," *ELH* 14 (1947): 274–82.

36. Ideas from Wright's book and even its language are echoed in the poem. See Riddell, "Cunning Pieces Wrought Perspective," 200–01.

37. Ian Donaldson, ed., *Ben Jonson* (Oxford: Oxford Univ. Press, 1985), 715.

38. *The Passions of the Minde in Generall* (1604), sig. F4ᵛ; hereafter cited in text.

39. David O. Frantz, *Festum Voluptatis: A Study of Renaissance Erotica* (Columbus: Ohio State Univ. Press, 1989), 160; see his figs. 3 and 4, and his discussion of erotica in Renaissance England, chaps. 5–8, esp. the discussion of Spenser, 245–52.

40. See Hamilton's note on this stanza.

41. For a discussion of the criteria of possibility and probability, see E. D. Hirsch, Jr., *Validity in Interpretation* (New Haven: Yale University Press, 1967), esp. chap. 5. For a discussion of some confusions regarding "objectivity" in "historicist" theory, see Stanley Stewart, "A Critique of Pure 'Situating,'" *NLH* 25 (1994): 1–19.

INDEX

Achilles, 50, 68, 69
Alberti, Leo Battista, 121
Albion ab Alpis Rupertis (as name for England), 78, 204
Alchemist, The, 16, 21
Alexander, 50, 51, 68
Allegory, 95, 100, 106, 207. *See also* House of Alma
Amazons, 83
Amoretti, 52
Annalia Dubrensia, 20
Anne, Queen, 16–17, 37–38
Antistrophe, 64
Aquinas, St. Thomas, 74
Arcadia. *See* Countess of Pembrokes Arcadia
Archimago, 100
Architecture, 137, 143, 156–59: and human form. *See also* House of Alma
Aristotle, 88, 117, 125
Arte of English Poesie, The, 64
Arthur, King, 19, 26, 27, 100
Astraea, 37, 39, 43, 79, 199
Atalanta, 83, 84, 85
Augustus, 14, 50
Austin, William, 110–15, 131, 137, 152–55

Bamborough, J. B., 33
Barbaro, Danielo, 119
Barkan, Leonard, 117
Barnes, Barnaby, 42
Bartholomew Fair, 21
Barton, Anne, 3
Beaumont, Sir Francis, 13, 44–45
Ben Jonson's Library and Marginalia, 3

Berry, Philippa, 85–86
Bessborough, Lord, 48
Bodleian Library, 2
Body. *See* House of Alma
Bolton, Edmund, 111
Book of Memory, The, 88–89
"Brave Infant of Sanguntum," 55, 56–57, 59, 61, 62–63
Brinsley, J., 82
Britannia's Pastorals, 20
British Library, 2, 6, 64
Broadus, E. K., 20
Brutus, 79
Burghley, Lord, 53, 58–59, 69, 70
Bush, Douglas, 92–93

Cadby, J. H. W., 6
Calcinaio, S. Maria del, 120
Calhoun, Thomas O., 202
Calidore, Sir, 122, 123
"Calliope," 52
Camden, Carroll, 110
Camden, William, 78
Campion, 25, 28
Canterbury Tales, The, 42. *See also* Chaucer, Geoffrey
Canticles, the. *See* Song of Songs.
Carmarthan, 62, 63
Carruthers, Mary, 88–89, 90–92
Cary, Lucius, 57, 59–61, 63, 72, 202–03: funeral elegy for Donne, 59–60; / Morison ode ("Seneca's consolatory 113th Epistle"), 51, 54–56, 58, 62, 64, 65, 69, 71–72, 200–02; on Morison as poet, 61
Castle, parts of, 123, 210

213

About the Authors

JAMES A. RIDDELL is professor of English at California State University, Dominguez Hills. Dr. Riddell is a member of the advisory board of the *Ben Jonson Journal* and the recipient of National Endowment for the Humanities and British Academy Exchange fellowships.

STANLEY STEWART, professor of English at the University of California, Riverside, is the author of *George Herbert* (1986), *The Expanded Voice: The Art of Thomas Traherne* (1970) and *The Enclosed Garden: The Tradition and the Image in 17th-Century Poetry* (1966). With Bernd Magnus and Jean-Pierre Mileur, he coauthored *Nietzsche's Case: Philosophy as / and Literature* (1993). Dr. Stewart is a former Guggenheim and Mellon Fellow, and is working on a full-length study of the language of Renaissance criticism.

PR 2642 .L5 R53 1995
Riddell, James A.
Jonson's Spenser